CW01560571

Contents

Wood Automata Fitness Center

This is a collection of wood automata action figures all based on normal Fitness Center activities. Each figure offers a different aspect of automata.

A number of general construction techniques are offered in the last section of this book. I strongly recommend that you read those before beginning construction.

All of the materials for each project are readily available in any home improvement center. Most of the wood can be found in a dumpster near a new home construction site.

Standard shop tools are required:

1. Bandsaw
2. Belt sander
3. Drill press

Optional nice to have additional tools:

1. Lathe
2. Table saw
3. Scroll saw
4. Planar

Construction tips

1.Many of the pieces in the projects are smaller than you may have been used to working with. Start with a larger than required piece of wood and make as many cuts as you can before you trim it down to size.

2. When you need to drill a hole close to an edge, drill the hole first and then cut the piece down to size.

3. These projects utilize many small pieces of wood dowel. Usually the dowel is inserted into a hole with a very tight fit. Do not glue it in place unless you have to. The need to temporary disassemble is just a normal way of life when creating automata.

4. If a dowel does not fight tight in the hole you can coat the end of the dowel with a light coat of glue. Then let it dry. That often makes a tight fit for the dowel.

5. I am left handed so all of the projects favor my left hand for the crank. All of these projects can be reversed to favor the right hand.

6.You can use a variety of types of wood to dress up your project.

7. Painting is always optional. Try to avoid painting surfaces that will be rubbing together.

Also be aware that a layer of paint can change the dimensions enough to make movement difficult or not allow it at all. You may find that wood stain will work as an alternative.

8. Wood dowels.

    A. They are not always round. I often find some with partial flat surfaces.

    B. They are not straight. The longer they are the more crooked they are.

    C. I have access to only Poplar or Oak dowels.

        1) Poplar – less expensive. Slightly smaller in diameter than Oak dowel. The ends will compress when inserted into a hole. When you remove a Poplar dowel it will not fit as tight the next time you insert it.

        2) Oak – More expensive. Stronger than Poplar. Slightly larger in diameter than Poplar which can be to your advantage if you need a tight fit. The ends will not compress.

9. Drilling – Make sure the bed on your drill press is completely clean of any chips or sawdust. In most cases it is very important to have the hole drilled at an exact 90° angle. When drilling a hole for an axle, we want the disc to be 90° to the mount.

10. When making the cuts for the head, draw all the dimensions first. Then make the cuts for the top and back of the head. Do NOT cut all the way through. Stop the cuts ~1/8" from the end.

Then make all the side cuts. Make these cuts all the way through. Then go back and finish the top and back cuts. Otherwise you will have to draw the dimensions on rounded surfaces which is difficult to do.

11. If you have the skills or know someone that does, you can make clothes for the action figures which make them look much more realistic.

12. All of the projects require a hand crank for the motion. The crank handle design is limited only by your imagination. Adding extra cosmetics here does add a lot to your project.

If you have any questions or comments on the construction of any of these projects please send me a message on facebook.

Please take a look at my other automata construction books. Go to Amazon.com and enter

"Ken Schweim"

Push-up Guy

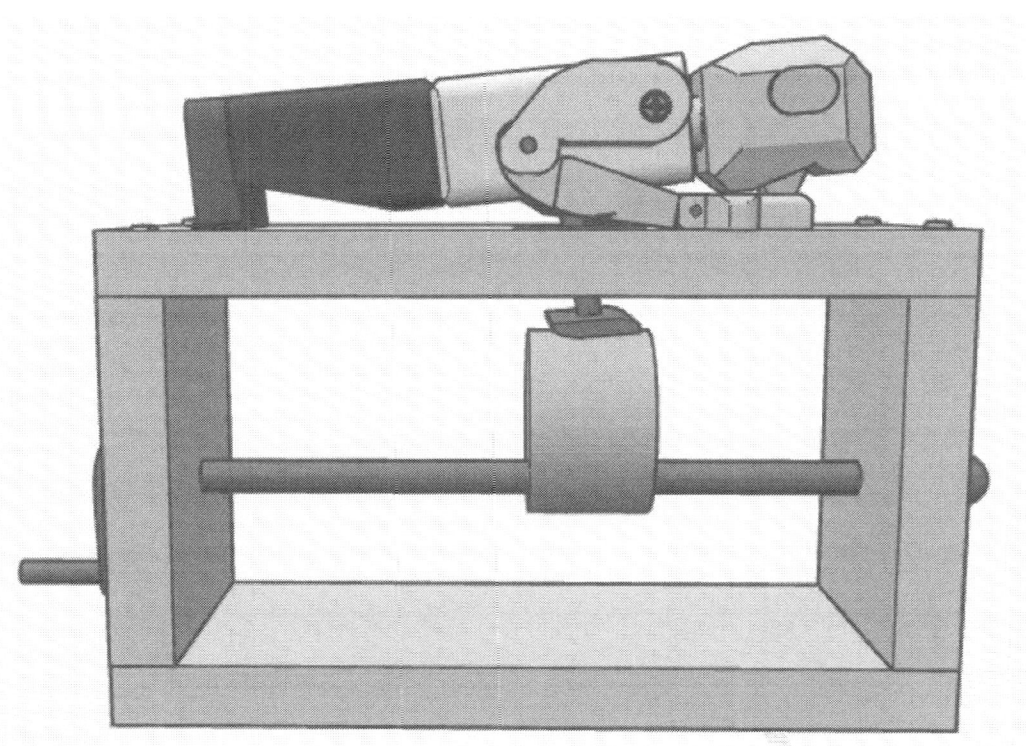

Main Frame

The main frame dimensions are shown below. All of the main frame pieces are 3/4" wood. Although I used 3/4" wood for the top and bottom pieces, 1/2" wood would work here also.

The top piece has a slot to allow the connecting linkage to pass through. Drill a 3/8" hole on each end of the slot as shown and then take out the wood between them.

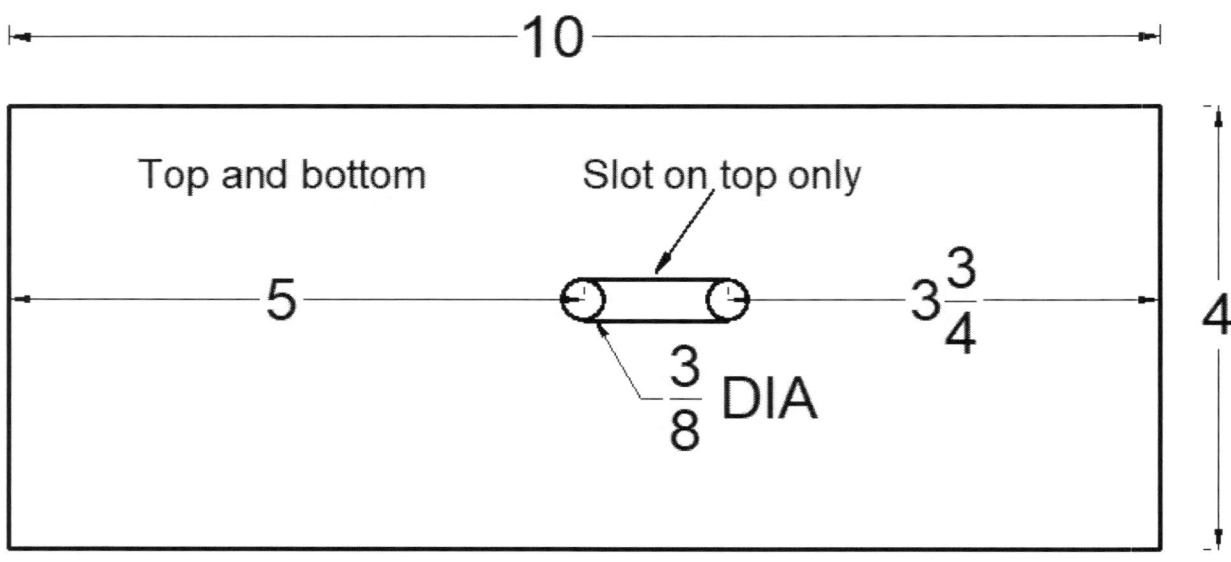

Top and bottom

Slot on top only

$\frac{3}{8}$ DIA

10

5

$3\frac{3}{4}$

4

The two end pieces are identical. I would strongly recommend you have the grain vertical on the end pieces. If not, they could split when attaching the tops and bottoms.

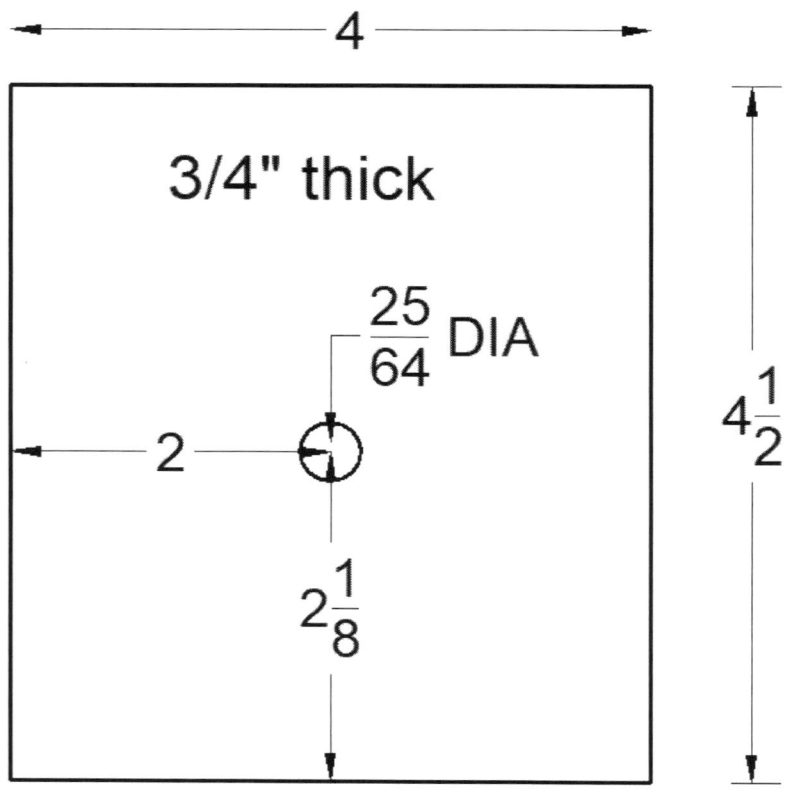

4

3/4" thick

$\frac{25}{64}$ DIA

2

$2\frac{1}{8}$

$4\frac{1}{2}$

Before you assemble the frame, pre-drill the holes to help prevent splitting. Attach the top and bottom pieces to the end pieces with 1 1/2" screws. Placement of the screws is your choice.

The type of screw is your choice. If you use a flathead screw, be sure to countersink before you insert the screw. Otherwise when you pull it tight the screw head may split the wood.

On my example I used a standard pan head screw. Countersink the holes on the bottom to provide a smooth surface to set the project on. You could also countersink the holes on the top and cover the screw head with a decorative wood bead found at most hobby stores and home improvement centers.

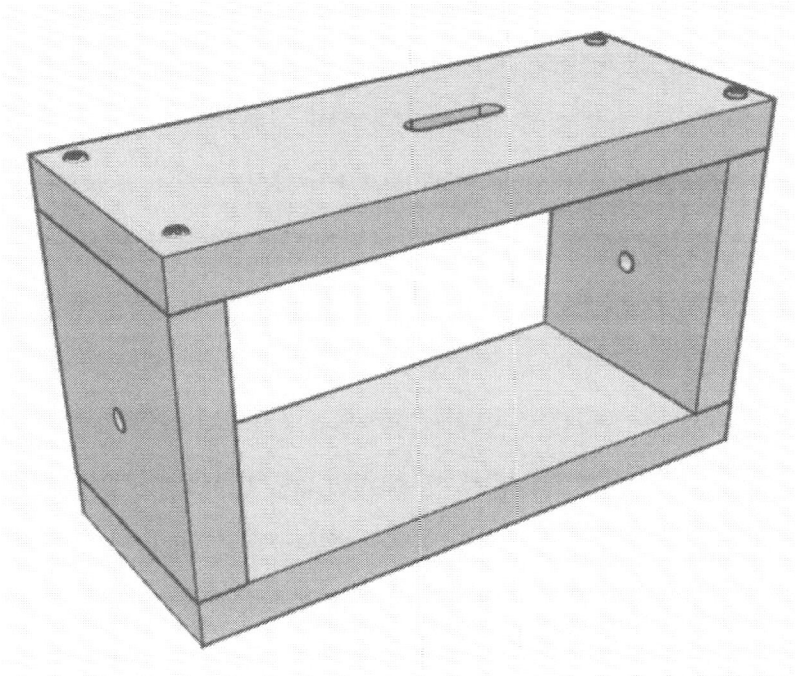

Insert a piece of 3/8" dowel through both sides. It should spin easily.

Using masking tape, make a mark across each corner joint. The operating frame may be disassembled and the marks will be used to re-assemble.

Even though you have carefully drilled each hole so they are identical on each side, if you don't re-assemble exactly as it was initially, it is possible you will have screw holes that will not line up and the edges will be offset.

Action figure

The action figure is made from a scrap piece of standard 2 x 4, 2 x 6, etc. which is normally 1 1/2" thick.

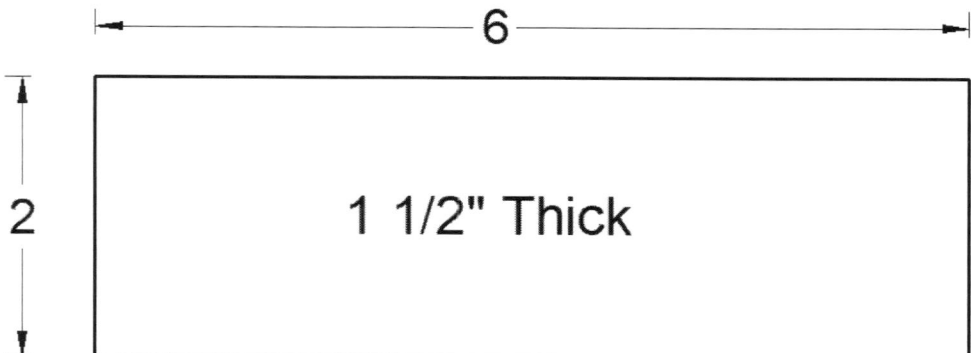

Next is the hole for the neck. That will allow us to create the head separately. That in turn will allow us to try a variety of heads and to turn the head as desired. Drill the neck hole on one end of the body block. The hole should be ~3/4" deep.

That is deeper than we need but it also allows you to set the length of the neck to whatever looks best for you. You can either measure for the hole or draw diagonal lines from the corners.

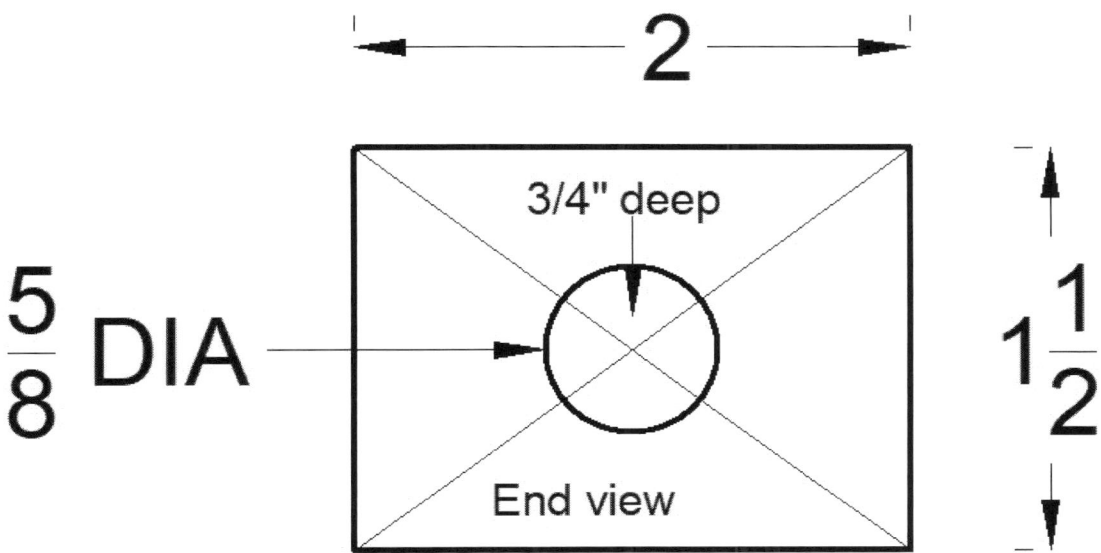

Shape up the body. The small diagonal cuts on each side are to show the beltline. The large diagonal cuts define the legs.

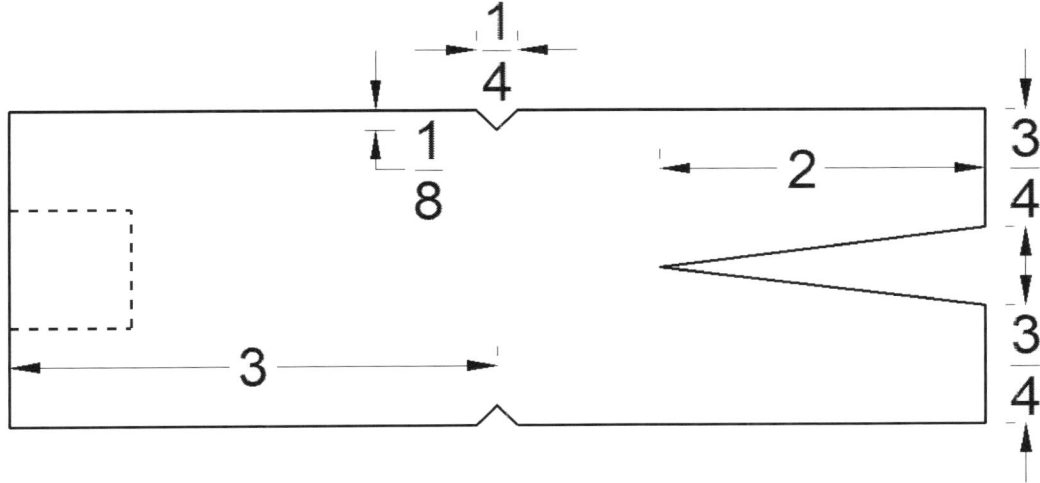

The next step is to trim the legs to make the shoes.

Tip: you may find it easier to make the shoes separately. Then you can make them slightly smaller and rounded to make it look like the pants are hanging over them. It will also be much easier to paint the shoes and the legs. If you choose that option, make the main block 5 ½" long rather than 6". Then cut two pieces ¾" wide, 1 1/2" long, and ½" thick for the shoes. Glue them to the bottom of the legs when complete.

The diagonal cuts on the front and back are to show the belt line and are at the same position as the side cuts.

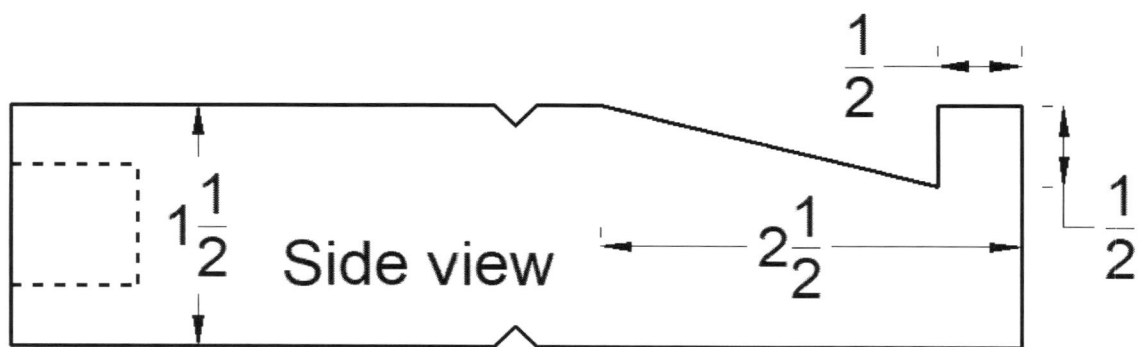

Drill a 1/4" hole, 3/8" deep for the push rod.

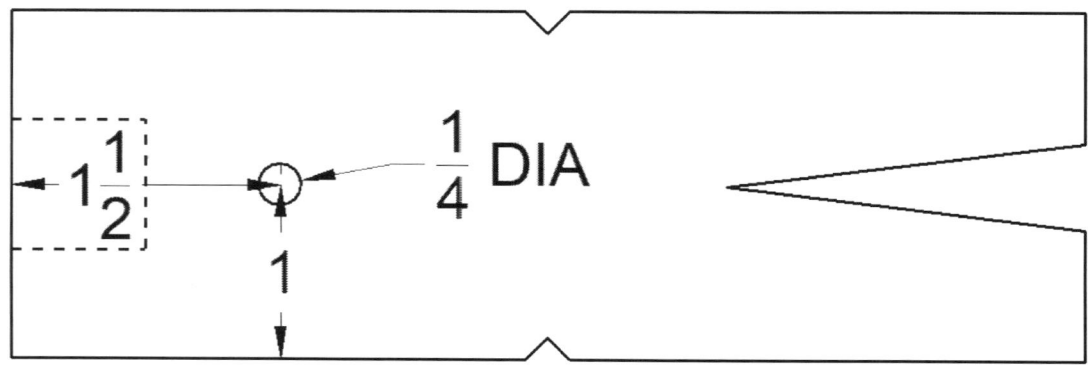

This is what the body should look like so far.

Round off all the corners except the top of the shoulders and the tips of the shoes to make the body more realistic. The tips of the shoes will be attached to the frame as pivot points.

The shoulder tops will be rounded after we attach the arms.

At this point you may want to consider painting on some clothes and shoes or whatever cosmetics you have the time, skill, or desire to add. Of course, if you have any wood carving skills you can add a lot to the figure.

The neck is made from standard 5/8" dowel rod. Start with a piece 1 ½" long.

The instructions for the head are on page 177.

Mount the head on the body with the neck piece. The length of the neck is your choice.

The arms are the "action" part of this figure. We'll start with the upper arm part. This part will be attached to the upper body as part of the shoulder. It will be attached with a screw for the arm to rotate on. The print below gives the rough block dimensions for the upper arm.

Although the instructions will only reference one piece, remember that there are two arms so make two of everything. Try to match the grain and color of this stock to the grain and color of the main body.

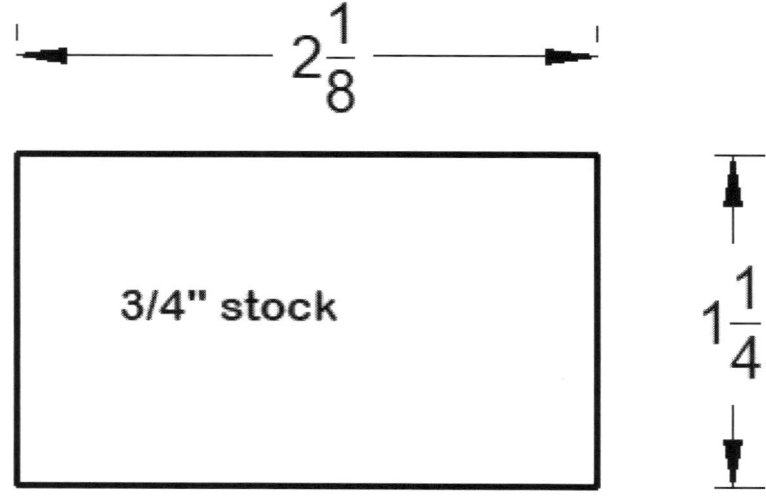

Drill a 3/16" hole for the mounting screw. Use a 3/8" drill to countersink the hole just enough to hide the head of the screw. Drill 3/16" hole to connect to the lower arm.

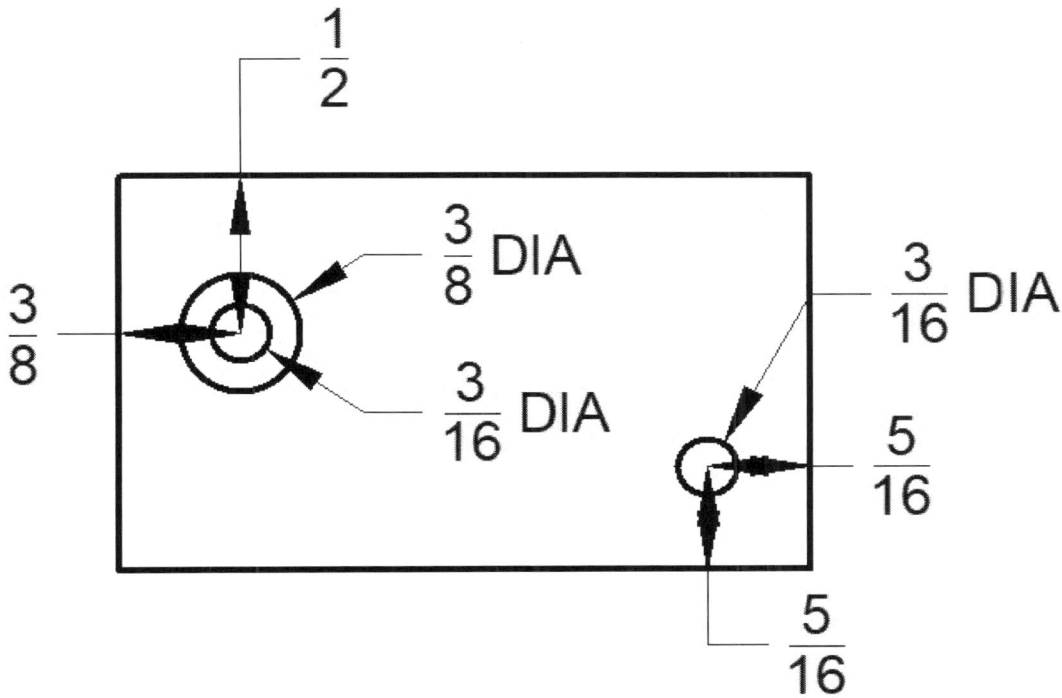

The arm is countersunk on opposite sides of both arms.

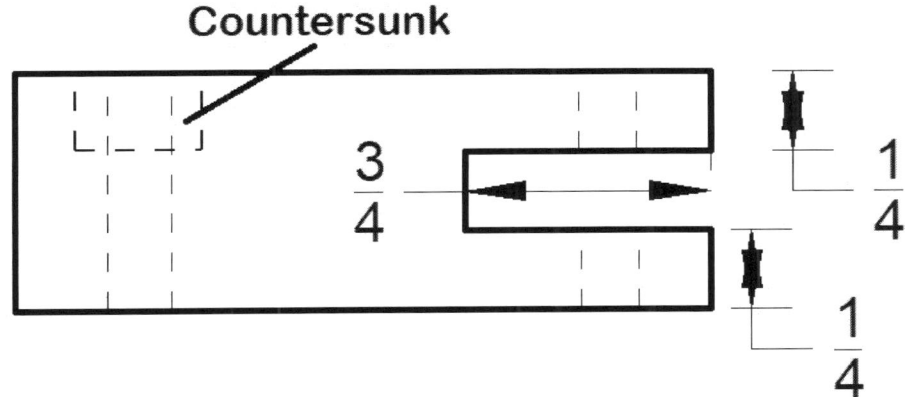

Stand the block on end and cut the slot.

The finish cuts for the upper arm are shown below.

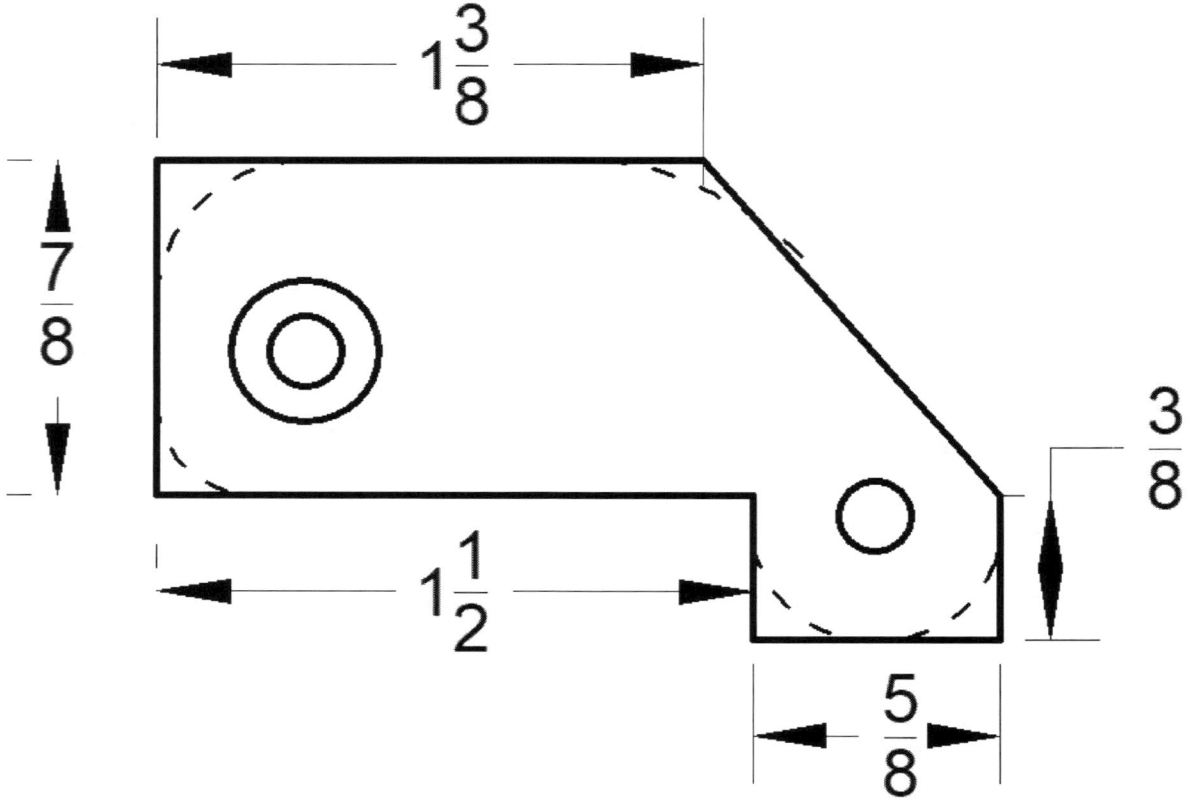

The dotted lines show suggested rounding for a more realistic look. After you attach the arm you will be able to see what surfaces need to be rounded off and how much for a more realistic looking arm.

Pay special attention to the countersunk holes on opposite sides for the attachment screws.

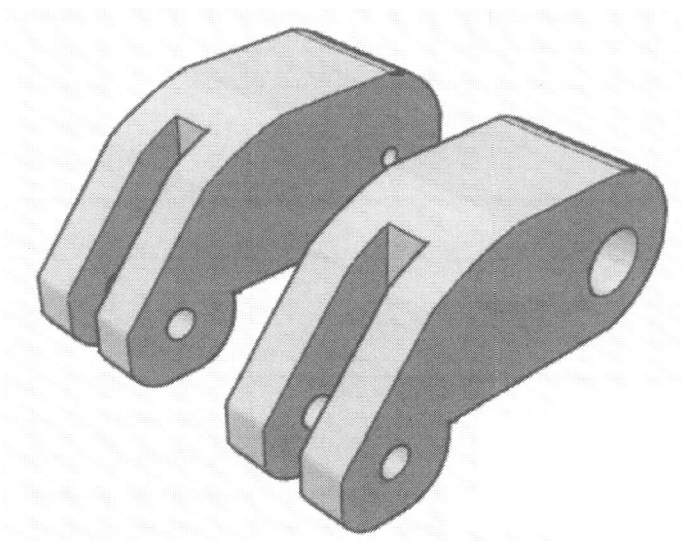

The forearm rough block dimensions are shown below.

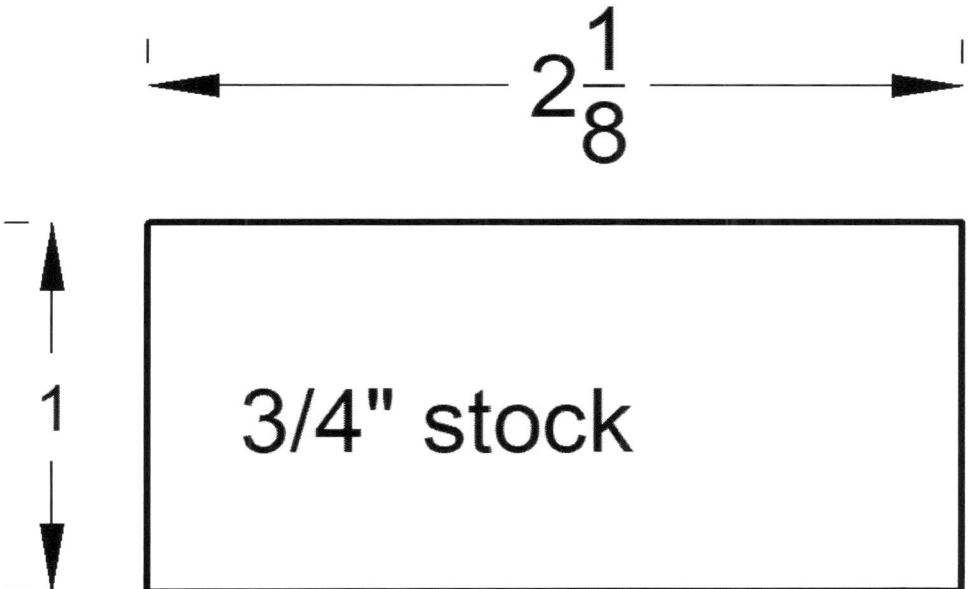

$2\frac{1}{8}$

1

3/4" stock

Note that the hole for the connecting pin is slightly larger than the corresponding hole in the upper arm. The connecting pin will pressure fit into the upper arm and the forearm will rotate on the pin.

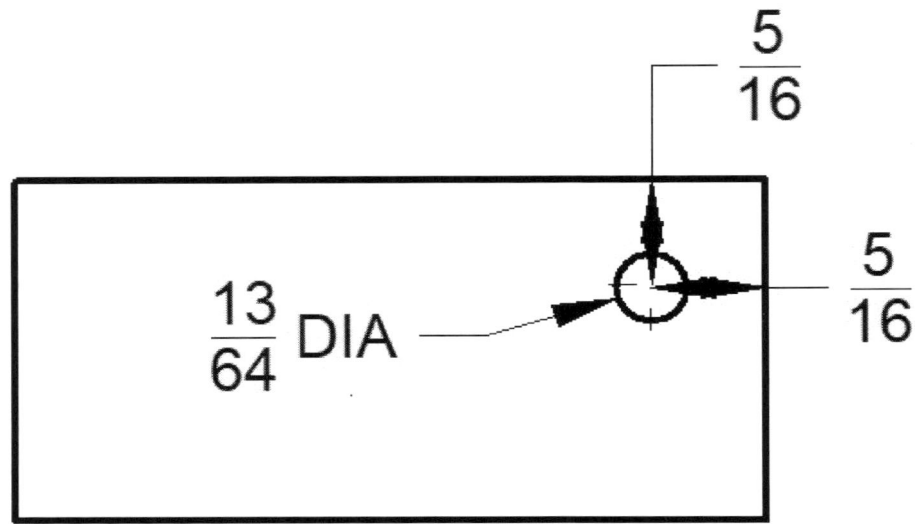

$\frac{5}{16}$

$\frac{5}{16}$

$\frac{13}{64}$ DIA

Trimming the forearm is the next step.

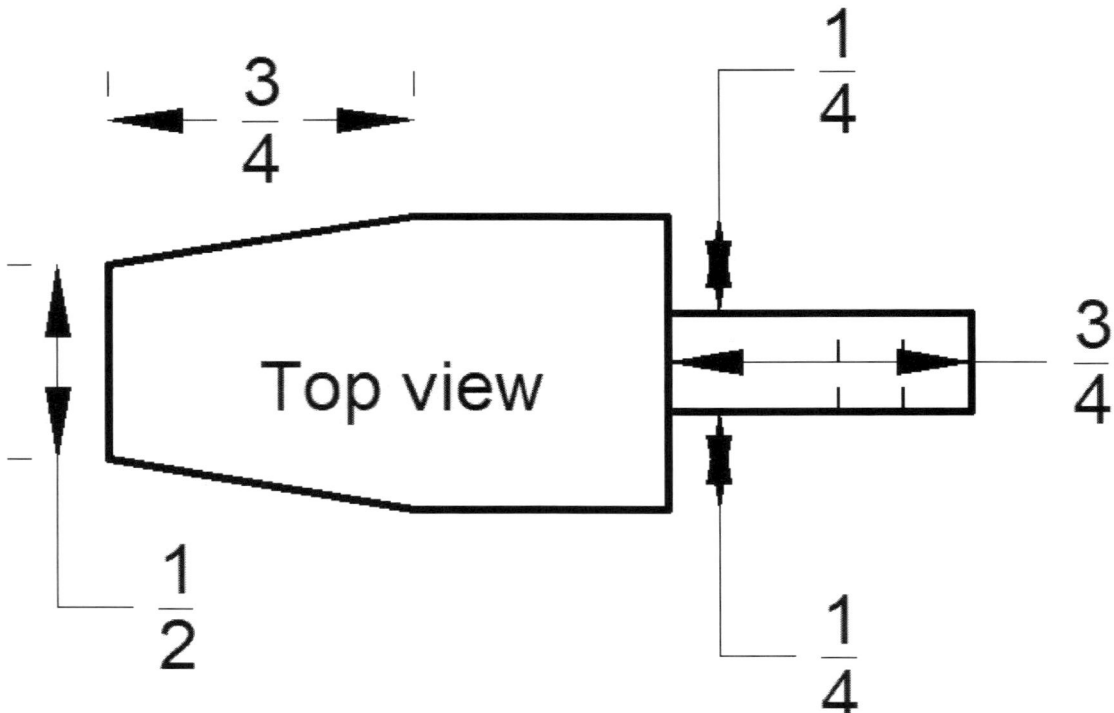

$\frac{3}{4}$

$\frac{1}{4}$

Top view

$\frac{3}{4}$

$\frac{1}{2}$

$\frac{1}{4}$

The end with the hole has to fit into the slot in the upper arm. After you make the cuts, insert the forearm into the upper arm. It should slide in and out easily.

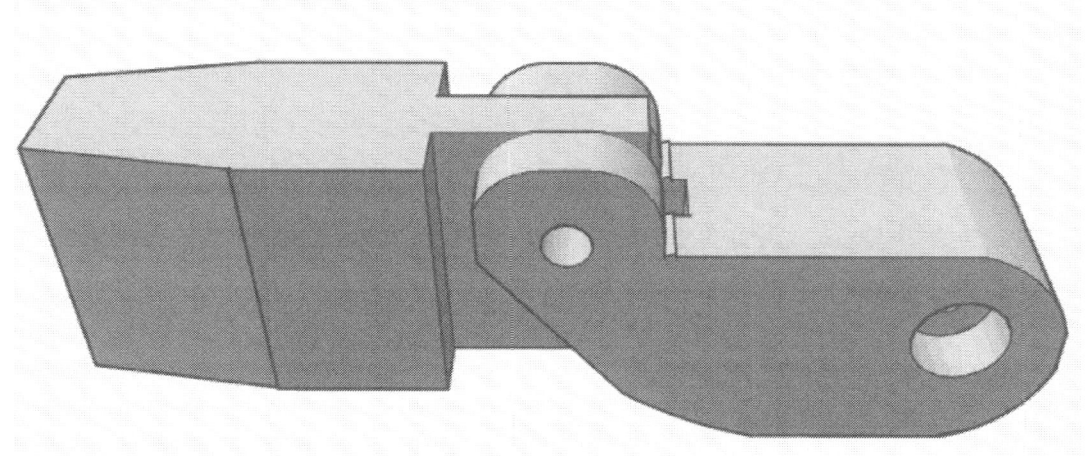

The bottom of the forearm will be trimmed down to form a wrist connected to the hand. The print below shows the finish cuts for the forearm. The area around the hole will have to be rounded to allow the forearm to pivot in the upper arm. Sand as needed.

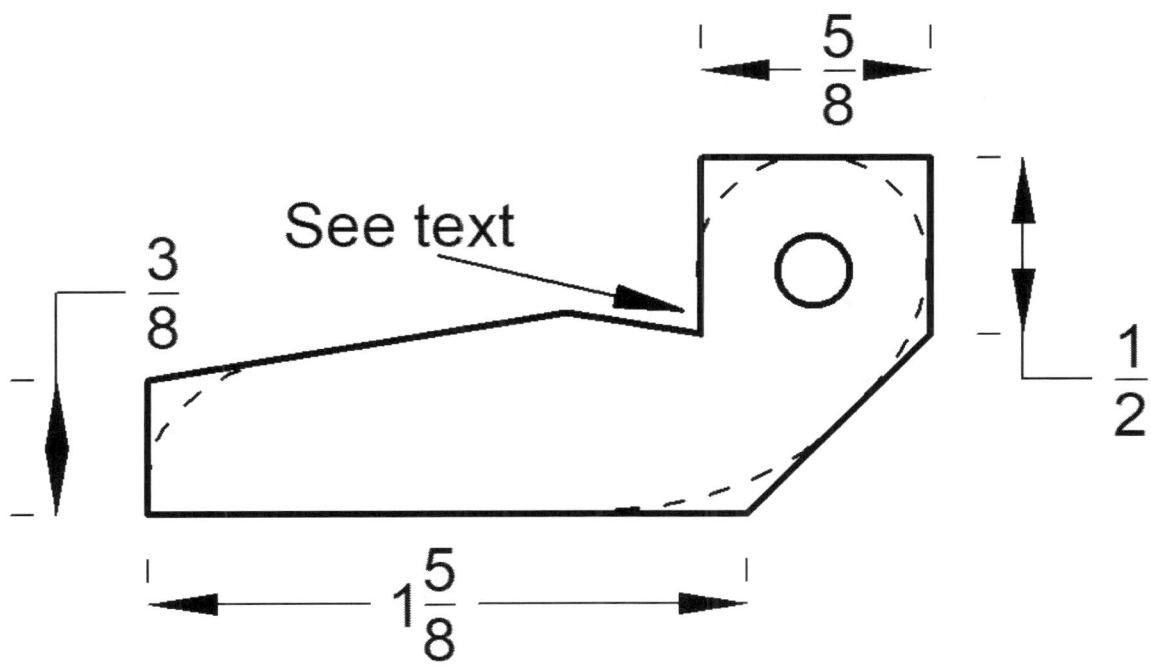

Again, the notch near the hole here will be determined by the amount of movement needed.

After you connect the upper arm and hand you will be able to round off the arm parts as desired.

Temporarily connect the forearm to the upper arm as shown with a piece of 3/16" dowel. Make sure the joint moves without restriction.

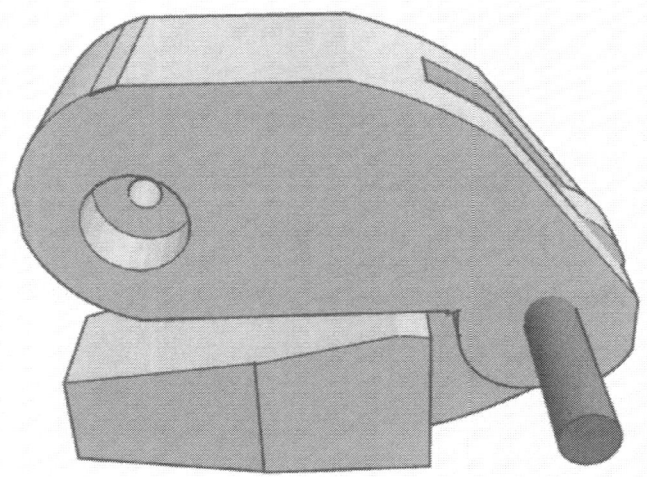

The dimensions for the hand are shown below. The hand is made from 3/8" stock. The hands may seem abnormally large but in automata we can change normal sizes to emphasize movement, draw attention to a particular element, or accommodate a special element of construction. In this case we need to have room for a slot and insert a connecting pin. Start with the block below.

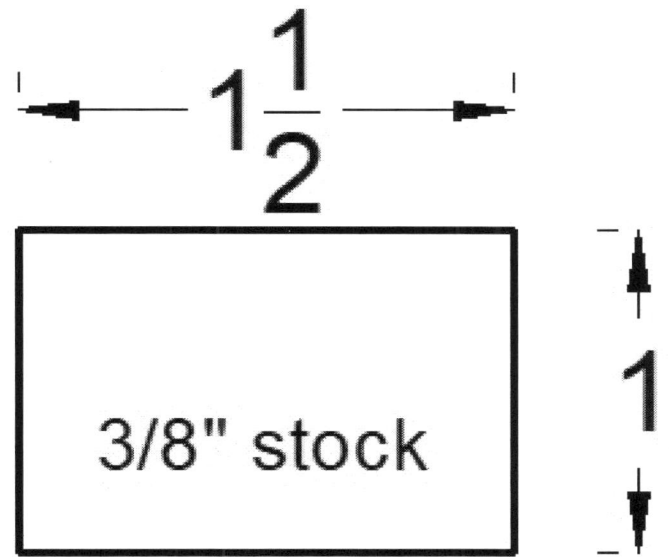

Shape the hand.

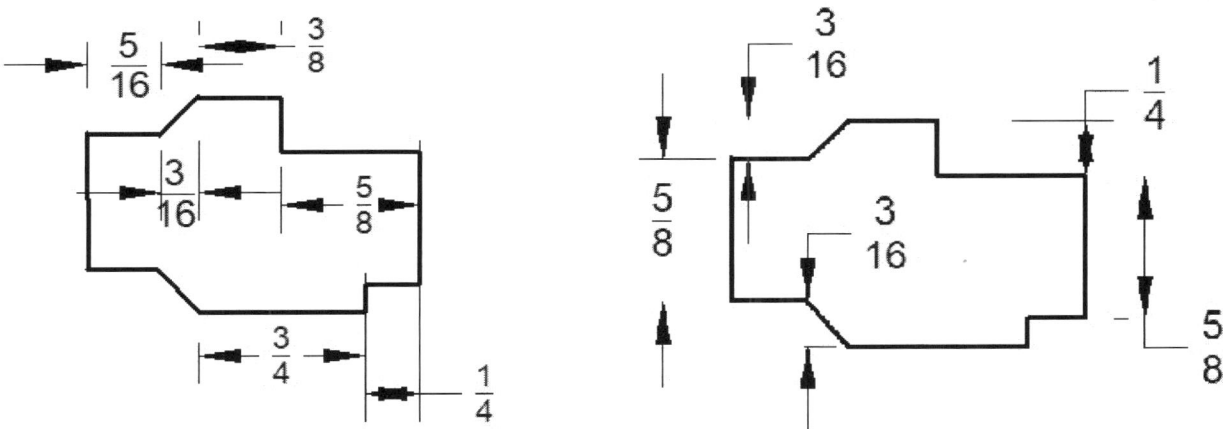

The last step for the hand is the slot to attach it to the forearm. Drill the hole before you cut the slot to prevent it from splitting out in the slot.

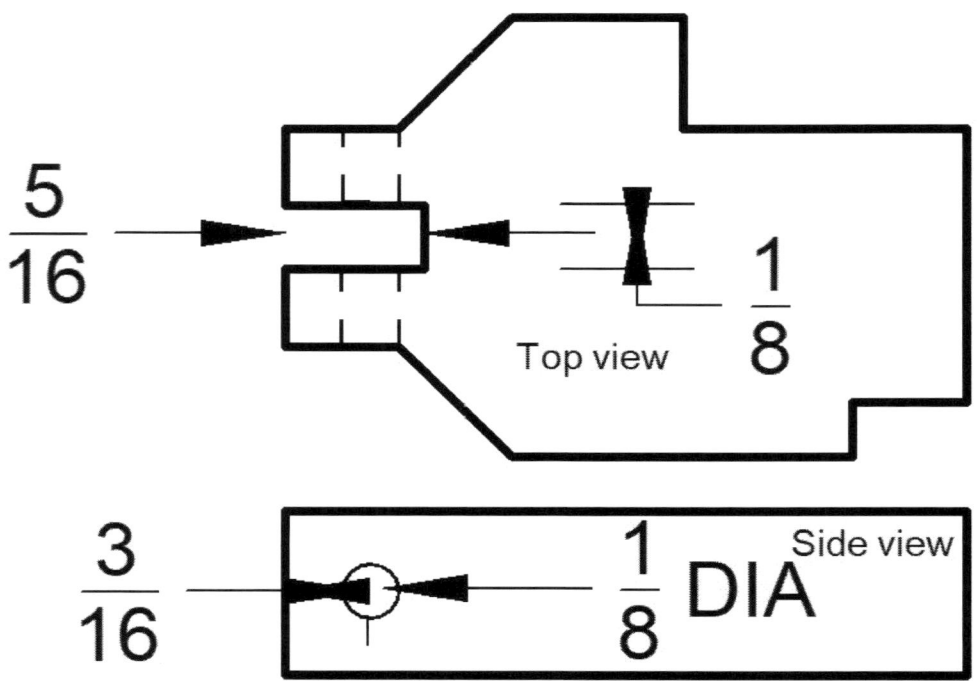

$\dfrac{5}{16}$

$\dfrac{1}{8}$

Top view

$\dfrac{3}{16}$

$\dfrac{1}{8}$ DIA

Side view

A screw eye will be attached to the center of the end of the forearm. The loop part will fit into the slot in the hand.

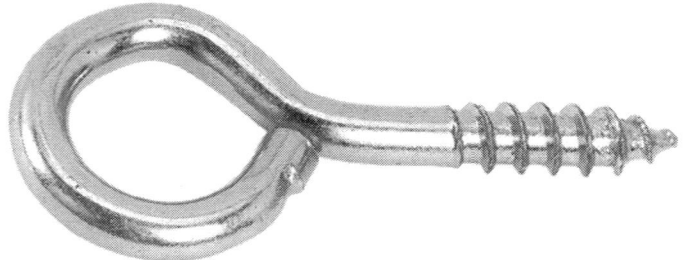

The size and depth of the slot in the hand will be determined by the size of your screw eye used. Get the smallest screw eye you can find that will still allow a 1/8" dowel to pass through it. You should now have all the parts required for a complete arm.

Temporarily assemble the entire arm. Do not attach the arm to the body yet until we fine tune the entire arm.

Test the complete arm for unrestricted movement. All of the arm parts are shown below.

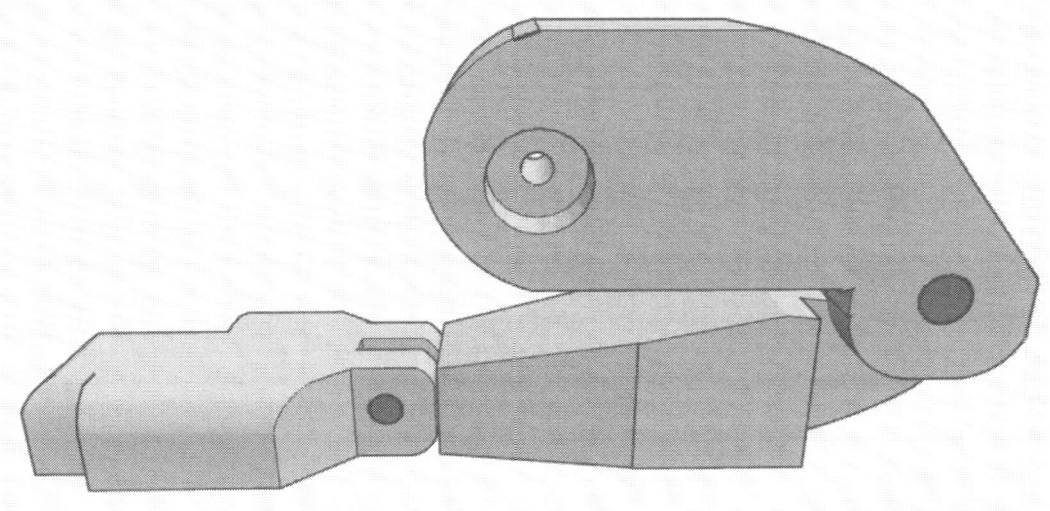

Now is the time to paint or stain as desired.

Set the pushup guy aside for now.

Drive Train

The final part of the project is the mechanical movements. The figure will receive motion from one standard cam.

The dimensions for the cam are shown below. The surface of the cam must be extremely smooth. The connecting rod "skid plate" will ride on this surface. Any imperfections here could make it somewhat difficult to turn the cam.

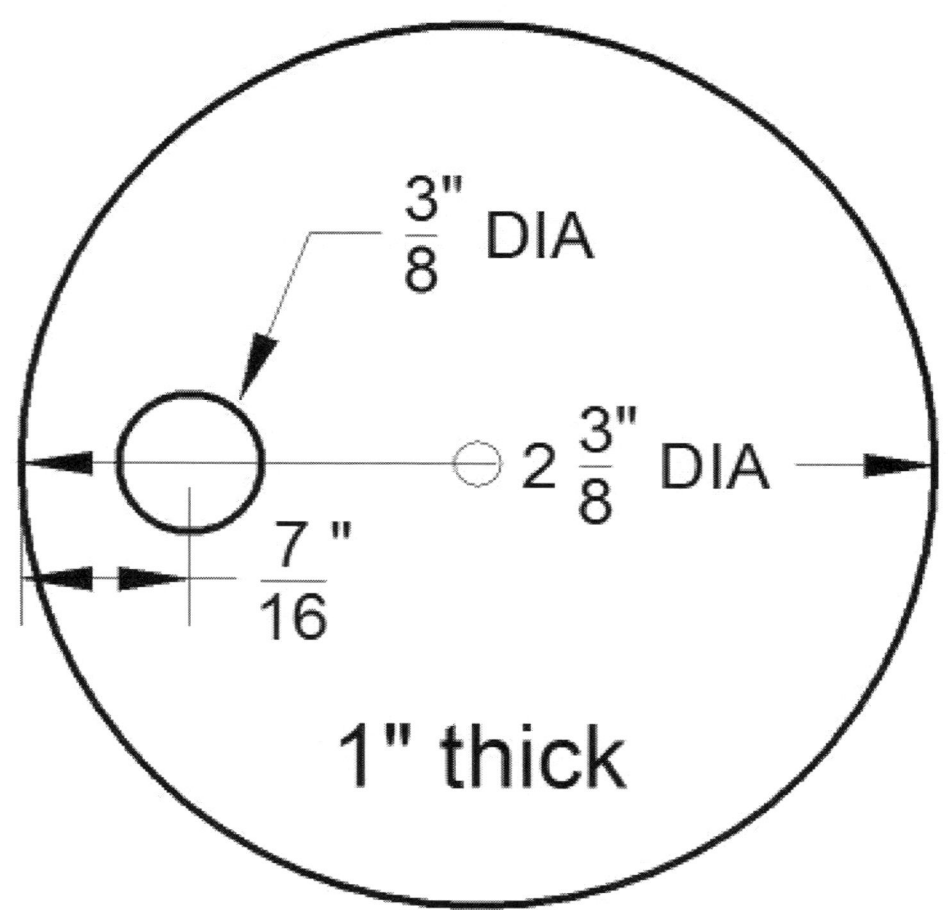

All the parts for the crankshaft are shown below.

The crank shaft is a piece of 3/8" dowel, which is initially 11" long. One end will extend out beyond the side and will have a cap installed. The other end of the shaft is attached to the crank.

The crank can be made out of any ¼" – ½" stock. The dimensions for the crank are shown below. Round the crank edges as shown in the dotted lines.

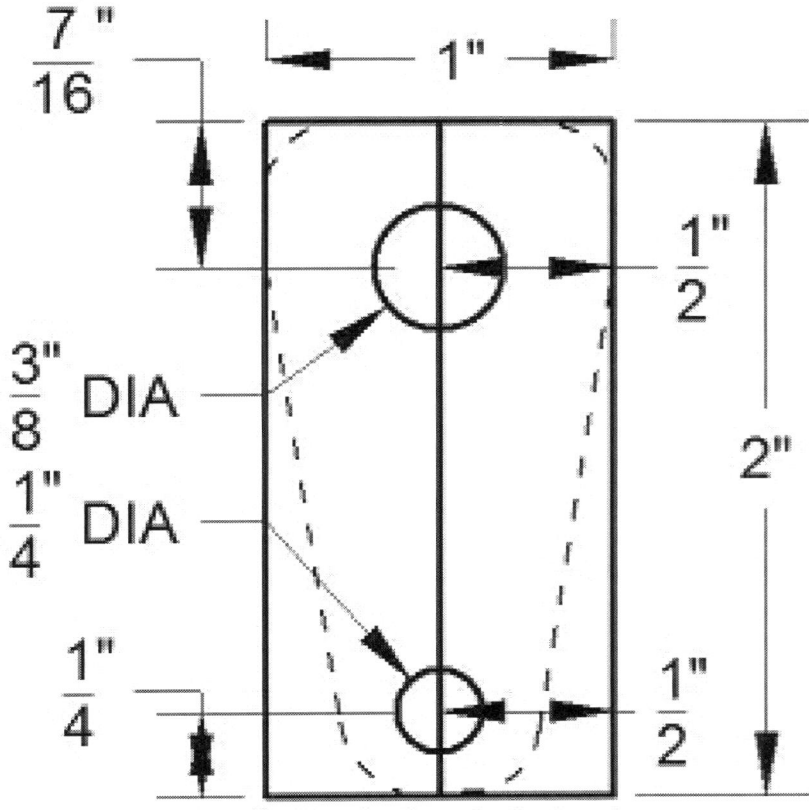

The crank handle is a piece of 1/4" dowel, ~2" long.

The last piece of the crank is the end cap. The endcap is a piece of 3/4" dowel. Drill a 3/8" hole, 3/8" deep and centered. Round the other end.

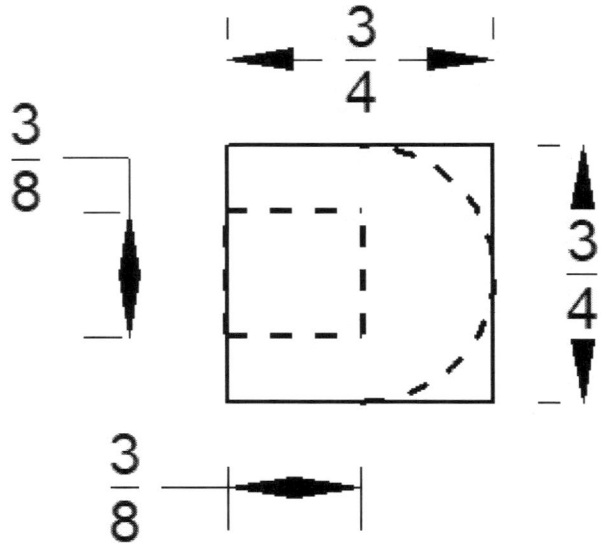

The last part to make for this project is the connecting rod and skid plate.

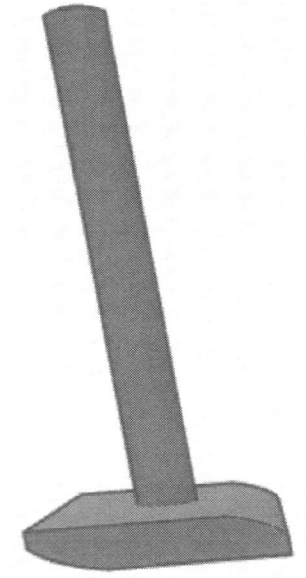

The connecting rod is an approximate 3 ½" piece of ¼" dowel. The length will be cut to an exact fit during assembly.

The connecting rod will have a "skid plate" attached to the bottom to ride on the cam. The skid plate is a ¼" piece of wood,1" x 1 ½".

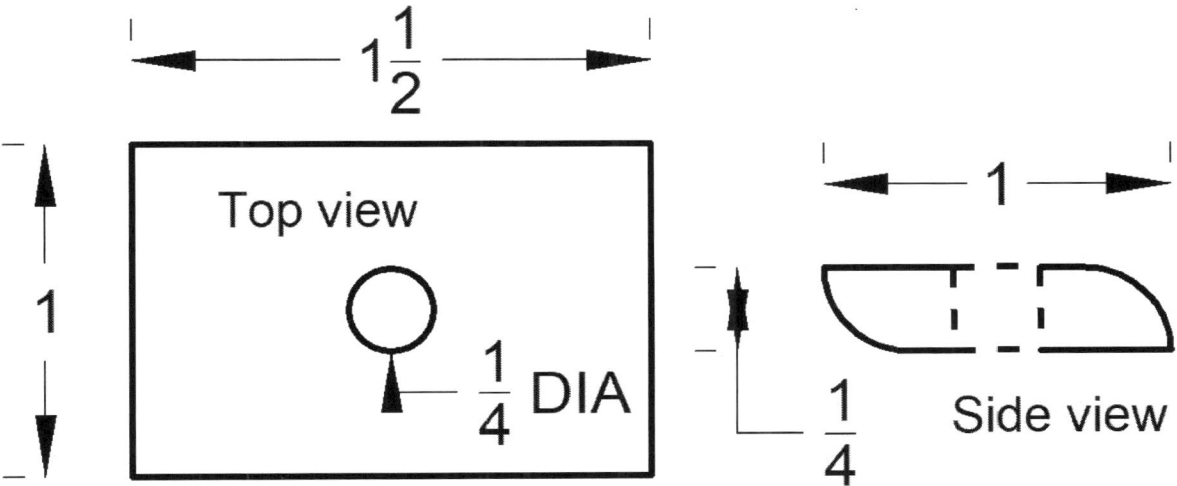

Drill a ¼" hole in the center of the skid plate to insert the connecting rod. Round the bottom edge of the skid plate. The skid plate will tilt as the push up guy is raised.

The upper edge is rounded to make a little more room between the skid plate and the frame top.

Insert and glue the connecting rod into the skid plate. Sand the bottom of the skid plate to make the connecting rod flush with the plate.

The connecting rod with the skid plate attached is shown below on the completed project.

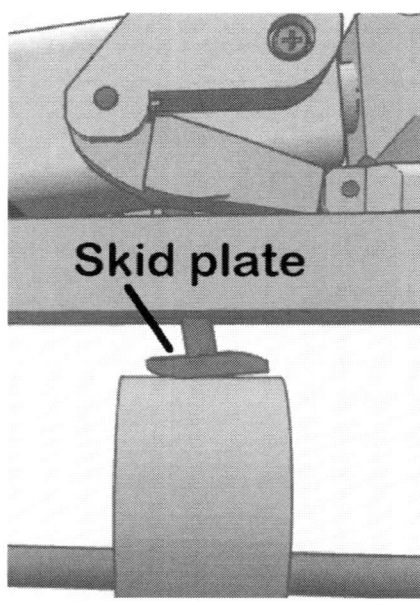

Skid plate

Final Assembly

We are now ready to assemble the project.

Slide the cam onto the crankshaft. The approximate position is shown below. The cam should end up directly under the slot in the top frame piece. Glue the cam in place.

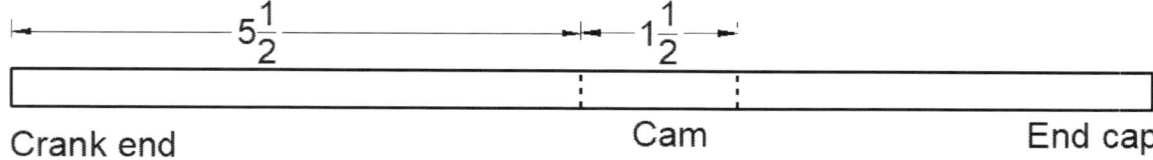

$5\frac{1}{2}$ $1\frac{1}{2}$

Crank end   Cam   End cap

Remove the endcap side of the frame. Insert the crank end of the crankshaft into the crank side. Temporarily set the endcap side in place. Turn the crankshaft to make sure the cam does not hit the bottom frame.

Insert and glue the handle into the crank.

Glue the crank onto the crankshaft.

Now is the time to trim the exact length of the crankshaft. Temporarily install the crankshaft endcap. You should have about 1/16" clearance between the crank and the frame and between the endcap and the frame.

When you have the crankshaft trimmed to the required length, permanently install the endcap frame side. Glue the endcap in place.

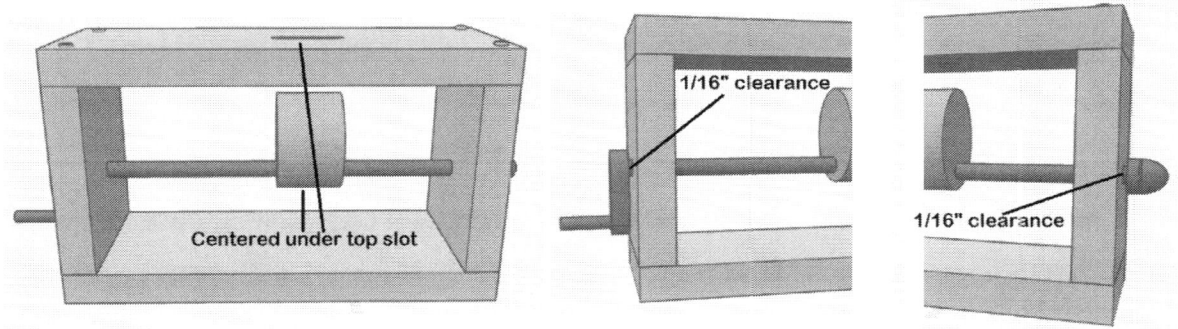

Hinges will be installed on the tips of the shoes to help hold the figure in place. I used small hinges available at my local home improvement center. Attach the hinges to the tip of the shoes.

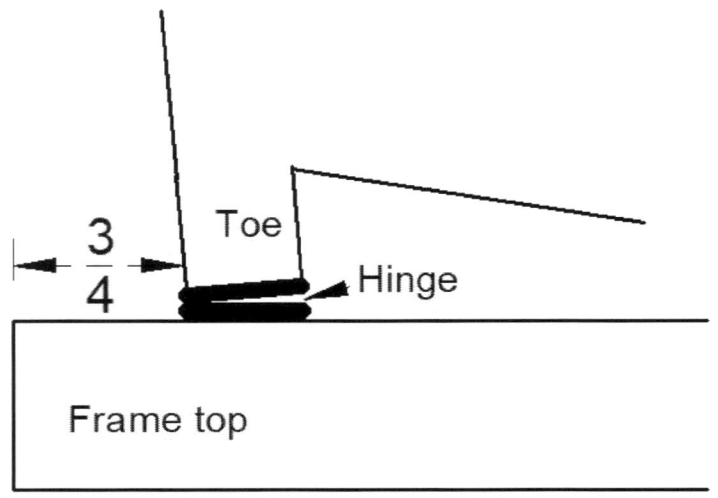

Position the cam at its lowest point. Set the figure into position as shown below. The bottom of the shoes of the figure should be 3/4" from the edge.

The nose of the figure should be ~1/8" from the operating frame. If not, adjust the length of the connecting rod until the nose is ~1/8" from the frame.

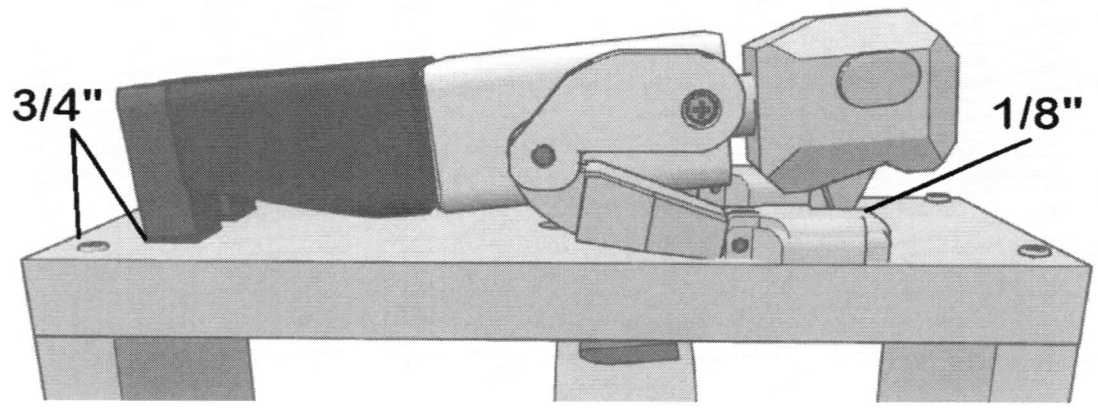

Lightly hold the figure near the toes while you turn the crank. The figure should easily ride up and down on the cam.

If it does not ride easily, make sure the surface of the cam and skid plate are as smooth as possible

Now attach both arms. The top of the shoulders should be centered and flush with the top of the chest.

Use masking tape to mark ¾" from the edge of the frame. Stand the push up guy on the frame with the back of the hinge on the ¾" mark. Attach the bottom of the hinges to the frame top. Be sure to center the push up guy so the connecting rod is centered in the frame slot.

Lay the push up guy in position. Turn the crank for one more check to make sure everything is working smooth.

You will need to experiment to find the position where both hands are flat on the top frame piece while still allowing full up and down movement of the body. Glue both hands to the top frame piece.

Your Push-up guy is now complete!

Pull up Guy
*****

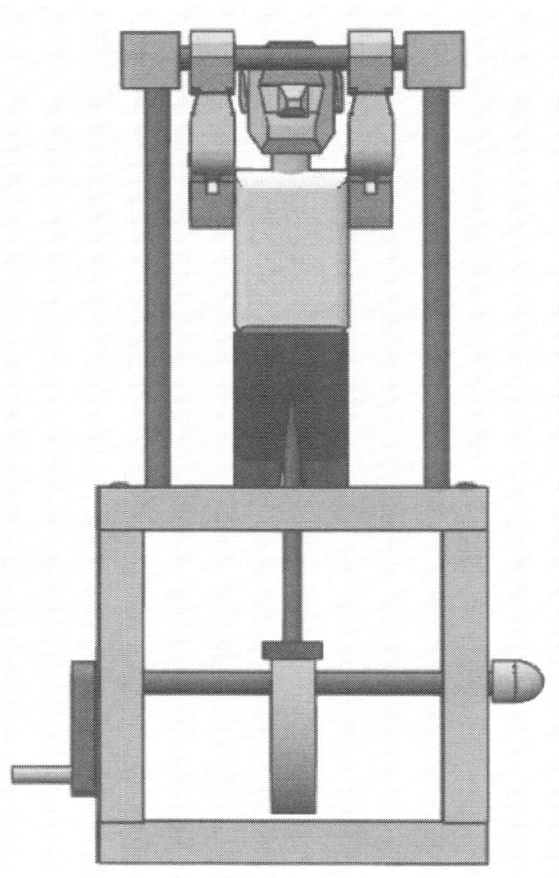

Main frame

The frame is made from standard ¾″ stock. The dimensions are shown below.

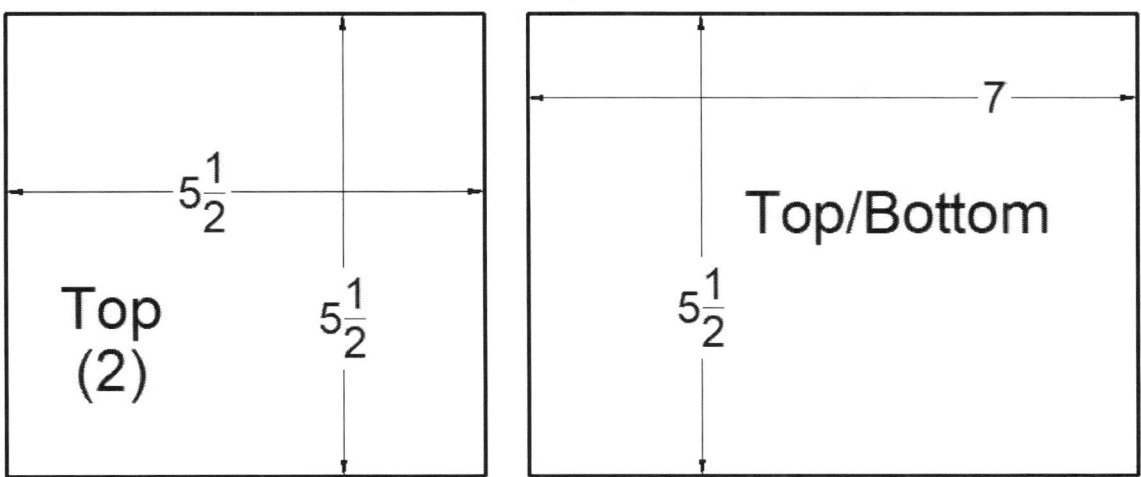

The top and bottom pieces will have four 1/8" mounting holes.

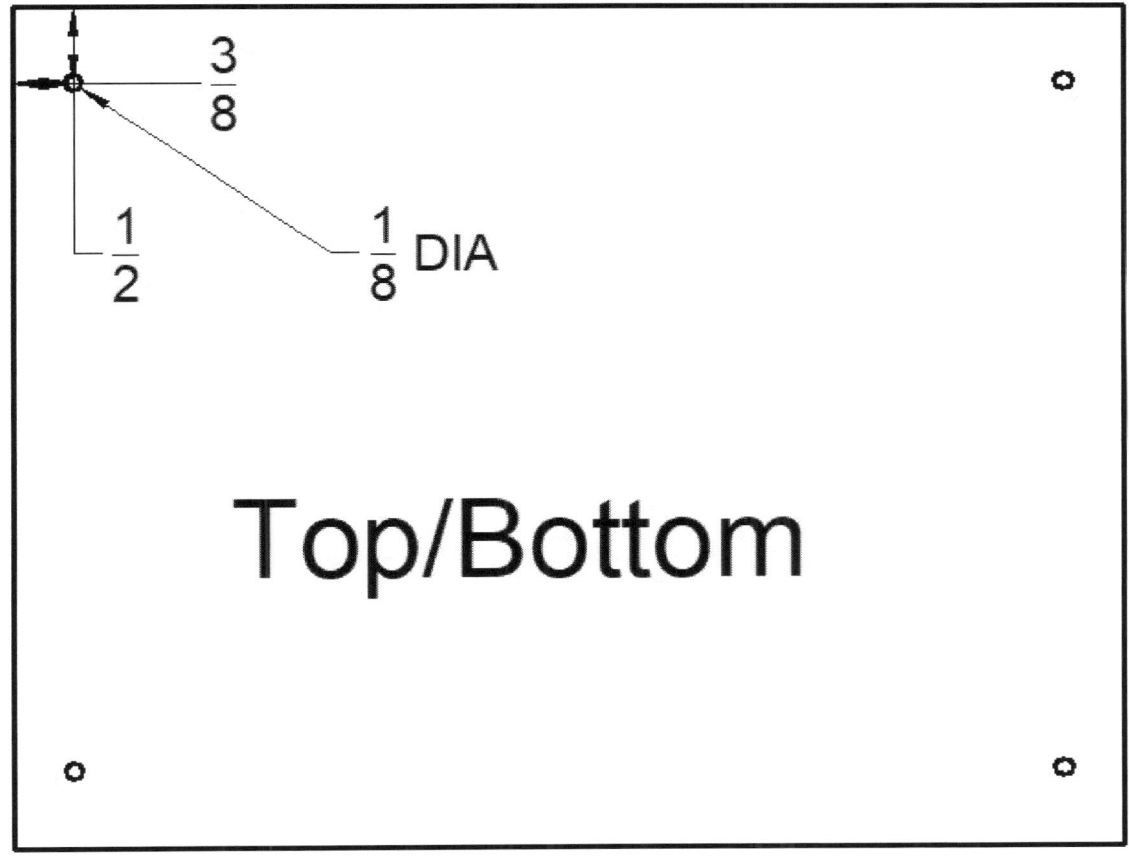

Countersink the holes on the bottom of the bottom piece to recess the screw heads That will allow the project to sit on a smooth flat surface.

The top piece has additional holes. There is a 17/64" hole in the exact center of the top piece for the action figure push rod.

There are two holes to mount the upright bars. Each of these holes should be ½" deep.

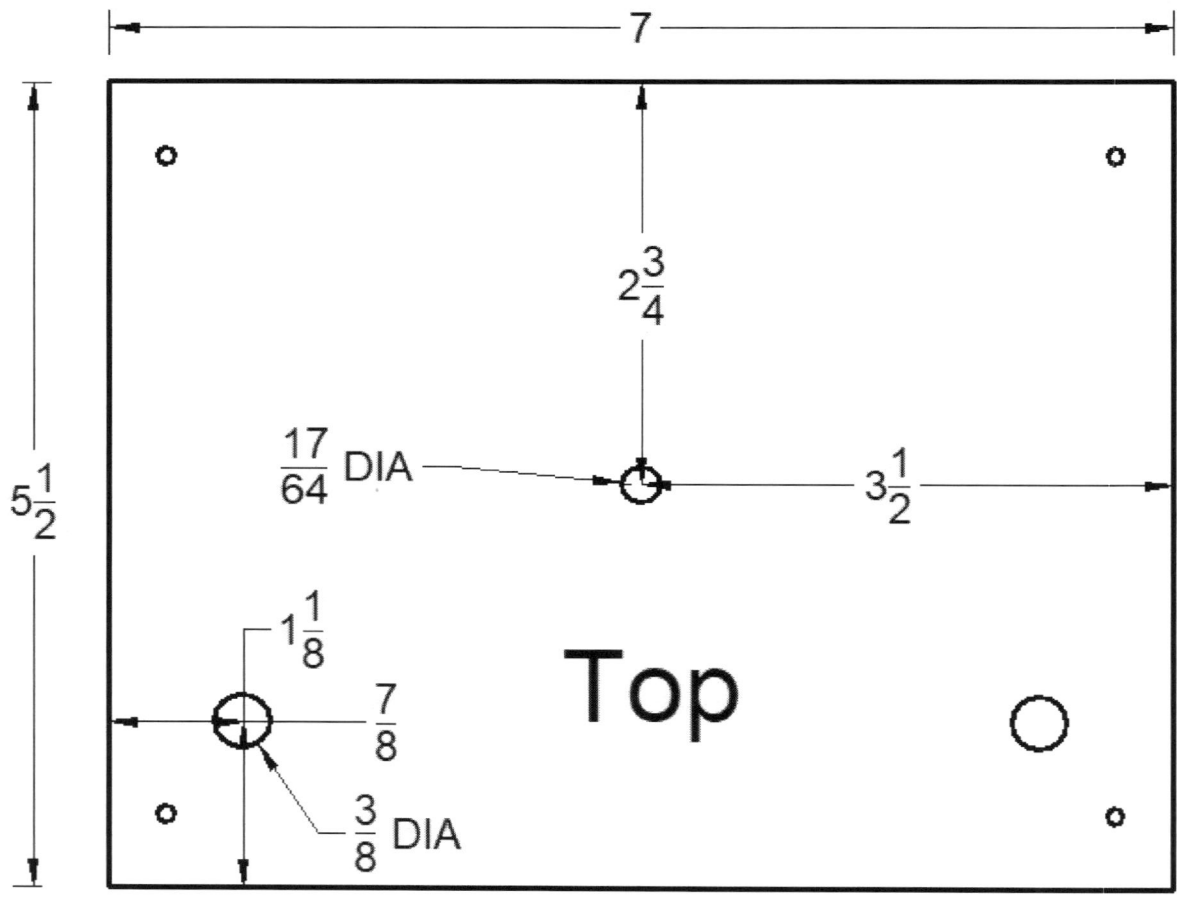

Both frame side pieces have an opening for the drive axle.

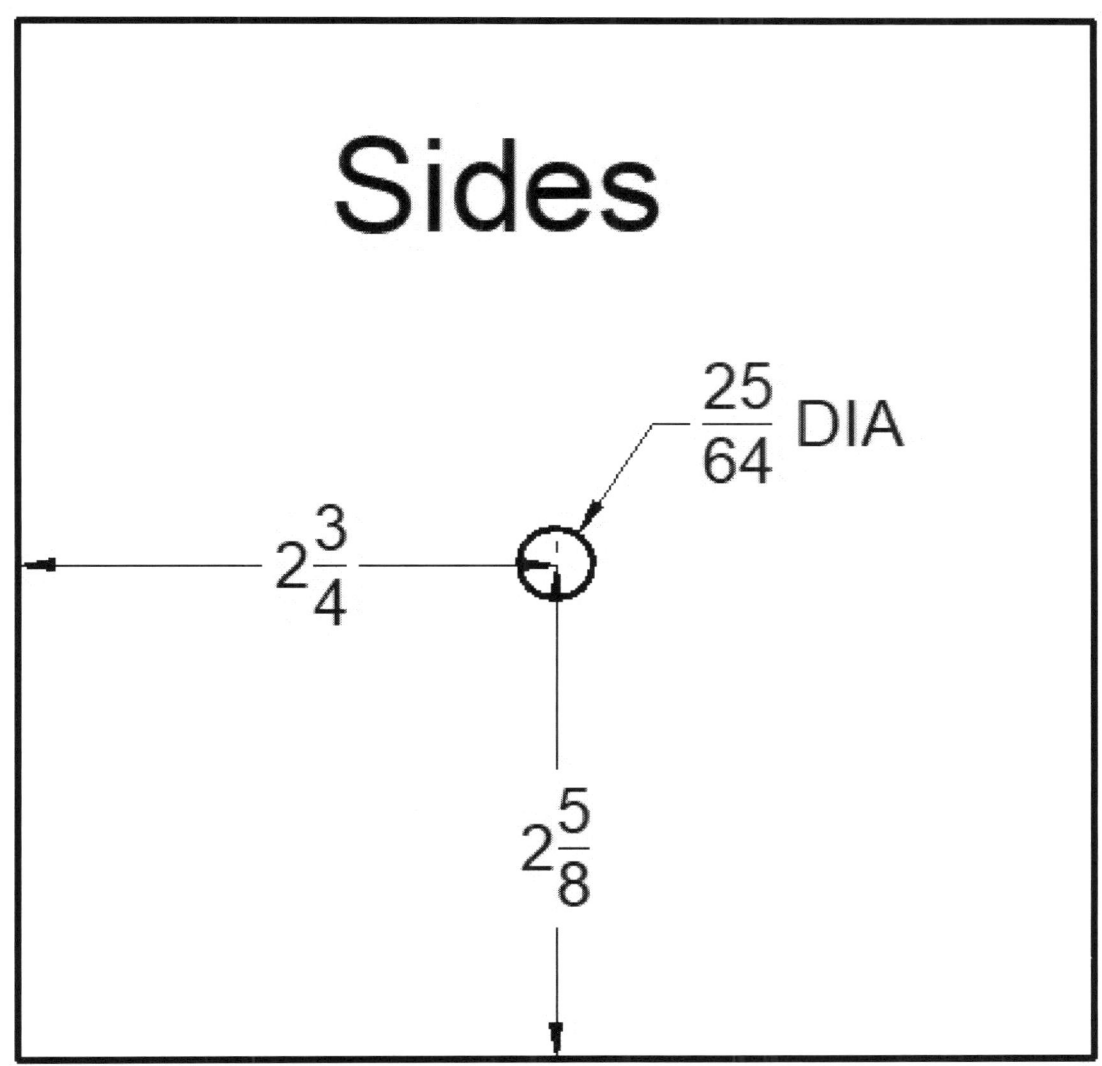

Sides

$\frac{25}{64}$ DIA

$2\frac{3}{4}$

$2\frac{5}{8}$

Assemble the frame with whatever screws you have available. I used 1 ½" panhead screws. Pre-drill the mounting holes to help prevent splitting the sides.

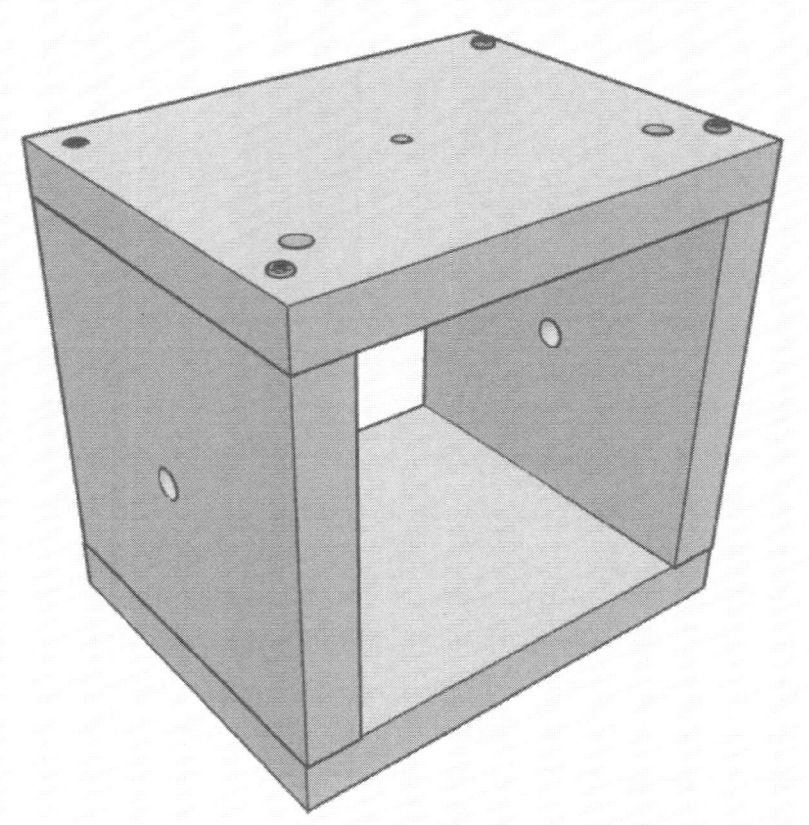

Drive train

We'll make the drive system next.

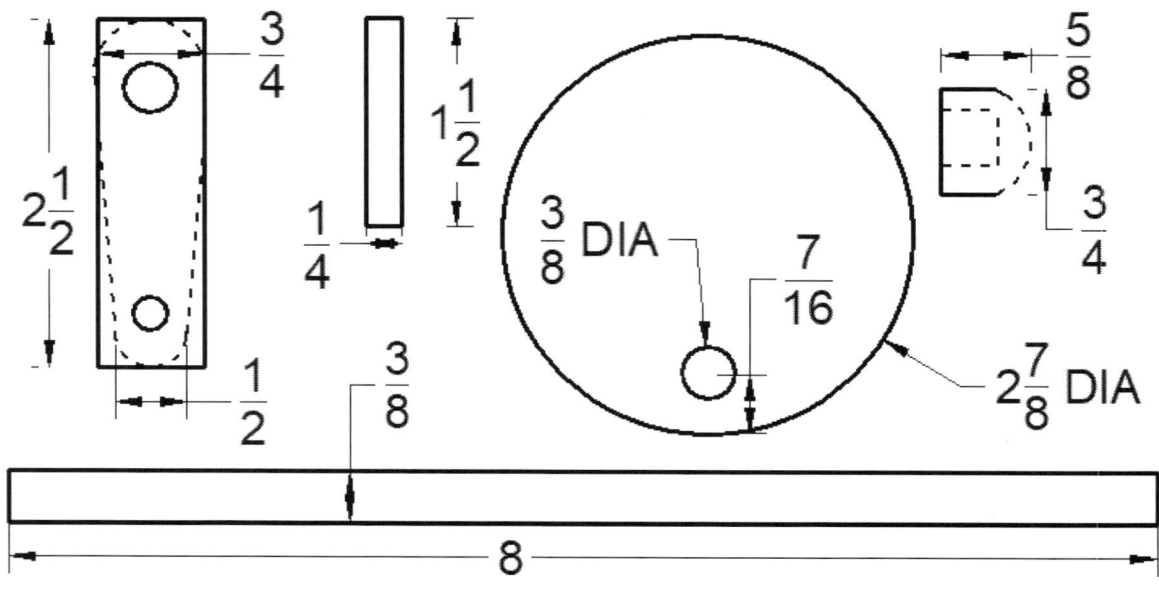

The assembled drive system is shown below.

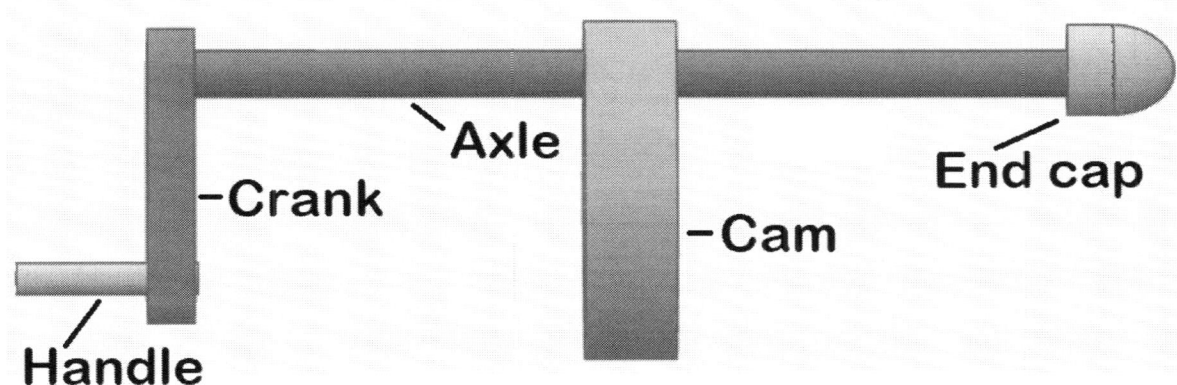

The axle is an 8" piece of 3/8" dowel. The final axle length will be determined during the assembly. Insert the axle into the frame and make sure it spins easily.

The cam is made from a piece of ¾" wood.

Temporarily install the cam onto the axle. Insert the axle into one of the side pieces. Rotate the cam. There should be a small amount of clearance between the the bottom edge of the side piece and the cam. The cam should have enough room on the top to allow a ¼" wood pad to fit between the cam and the top edge of the side.

The crank is made from a piece of 3/8" wood.

The crank handle can be a decorative knob from a hobby store or in this example, a piece of ¼" dowel, ~1 ½" long.

On the other end of the axle we will add an endcap made from ¾" dowel. Drill a hole ~3/8" for the axle. Round one end.

Insert and glue the crank handle into the crank. Glue the crank onto the axle.

Insert the axle into the frame. The crank should be ~1/16" away from the side of the frame.

Temporarily attach the end cap to the axle. Adjust the length of the axle so the end cap has ~1/16" clearance from the frame side. Do not glue the end cap in place yet.

Temporarily install the cam. Drop a scrap piece of ¼" dowel through the frame top access hole down to the cam. Line up the cam so it is centered on the ¼" dowel. You may have to remove the frame top and end cap side to move the cam.

Slide the cam over and apply glue to the axle. Slide the cam back into position.

The last piece in the frame is the push rod.

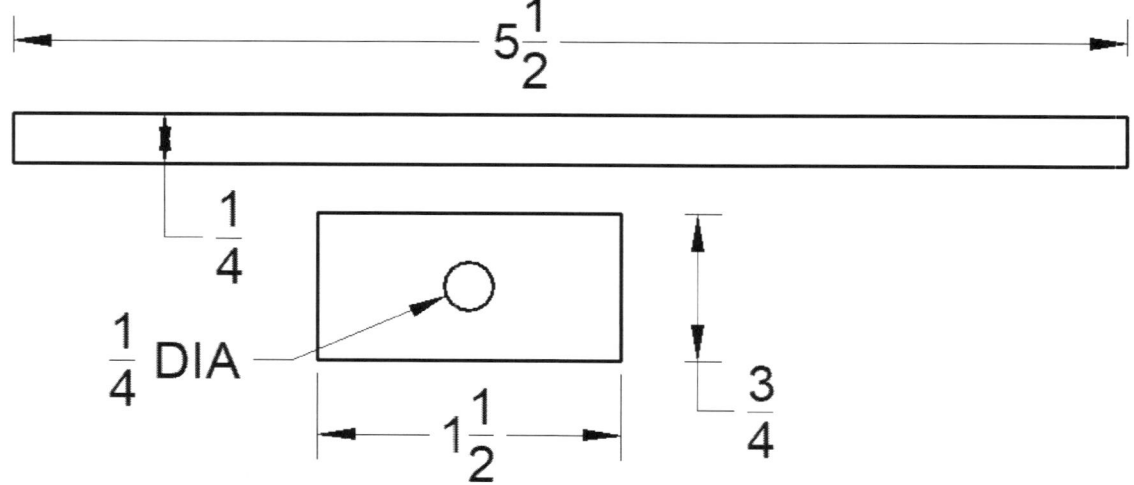

The push rod pad is 1/4" thick. Drill a ¼" hole in the center of the pad. Lightly sand all the edges.

Insert the push rod into the access hole in the frame top. Glue the push rod into the center of the pad, flush with the bottom. Sand the bottom of the pad.

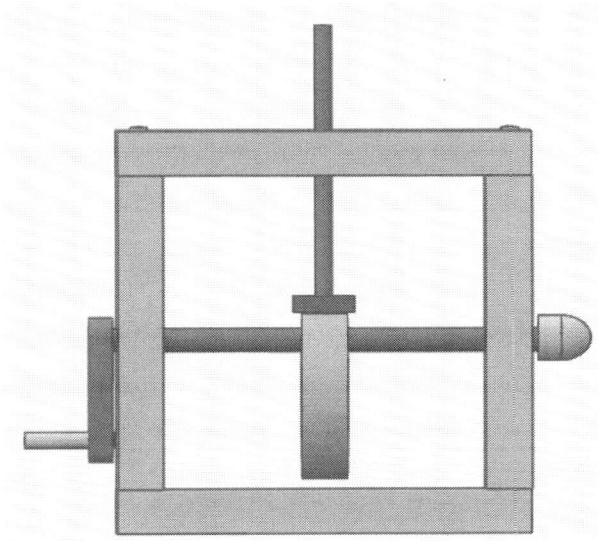

Action figure

Now we can make the action figure. The action figure is made from a scrap piece of standard 2 x 4, 2 x 6, etc. which is normally 1 1/2" thick.

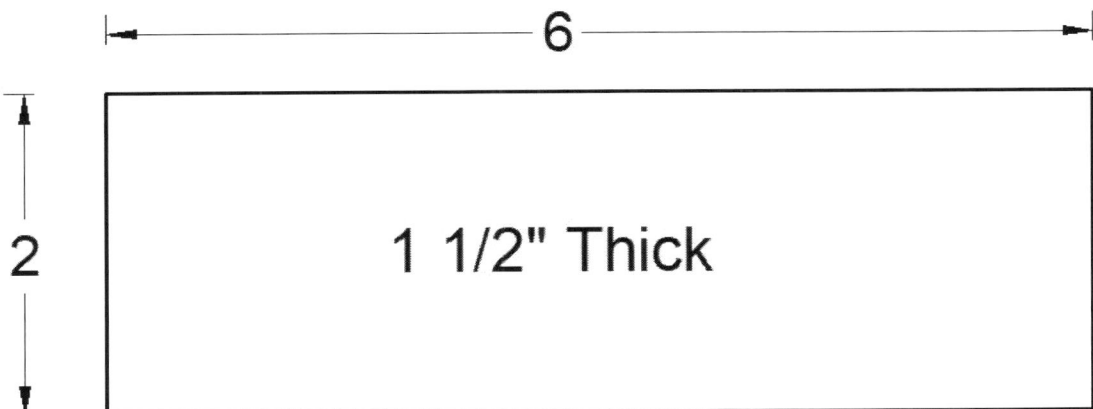

Next is the hole for the neck. That will allow us to create the head separately. That in turn will allow us to try a variety of heads and to turn the head as desired. Drill the neck hole on one end of the body block. The hole should be ~3/4" deep.

That is deeper than we need but it also allows you to set the length of the neck to whatever looks best for you. You can either measure for the hole or draw diagonal lines from the corners.

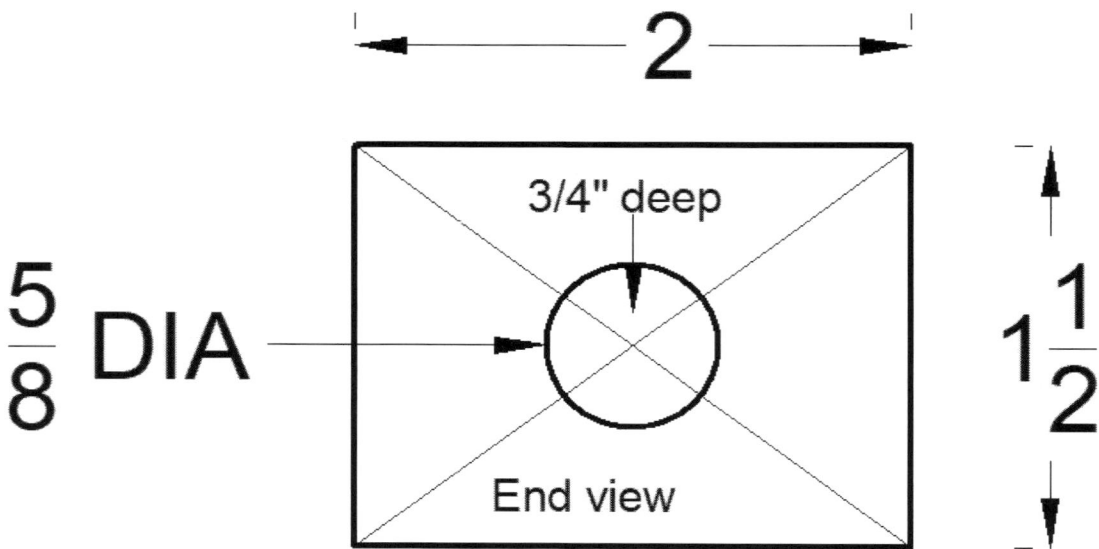

A push rod will be used to lift the Pull up guy. The push rod will be mounted in the center of the bottom of the action figure. You can either measure or use diagonal lines to find the center. Drill a ¼" hole 3" deep.

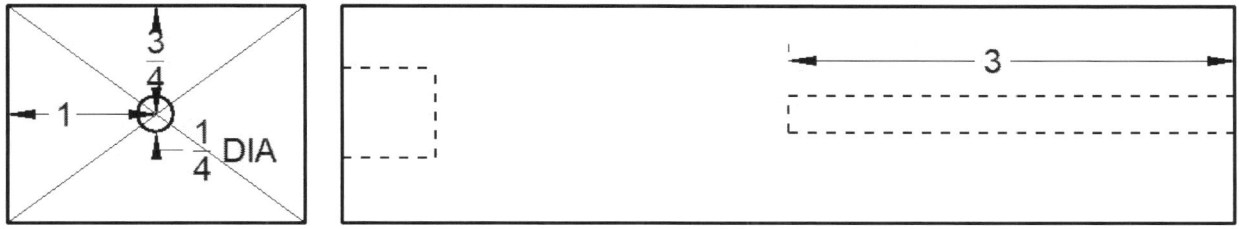

Shape up the body. The small diagonal cuts on each side are to show the beltline. The large diagonal cuts define the legs.

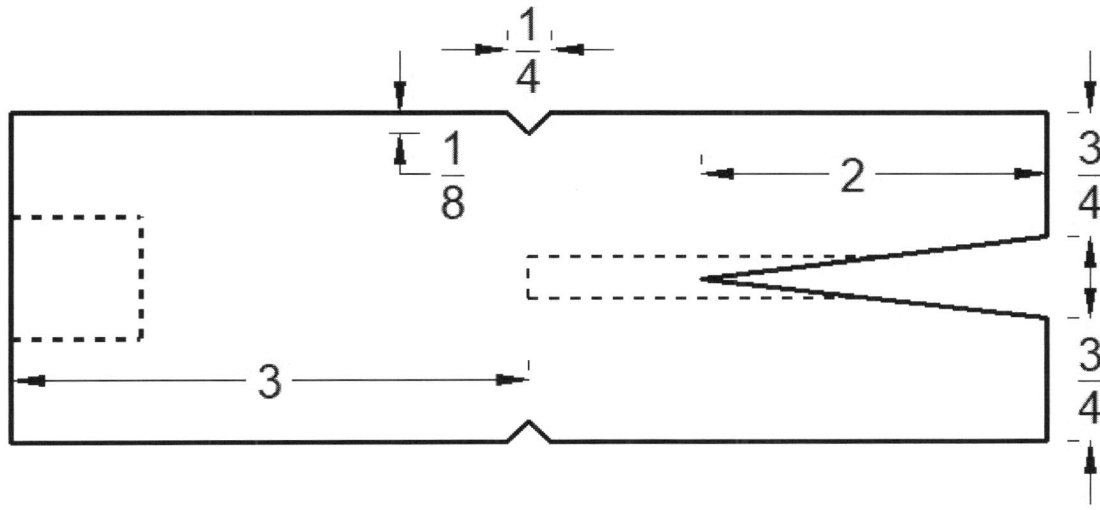

The next step is to trim the legs to make the shoes.

Tip: you may find it easier to make the shoes separately. Then you can make them slightly smaller and rounded to make it look like the pants are hanging over them. It will also be much easier to paint the shoes and the legs. If you choose that option, make the main block 5 ½" long rather than 6". Then cut two pieces ¾" wide, 1 1/2" long, and ½" thick for the shoes. Glue them to the bottom of the legs when complete.

The diagonal cuts on the front and back are to show the belt line and are at the same position as the side cuts.

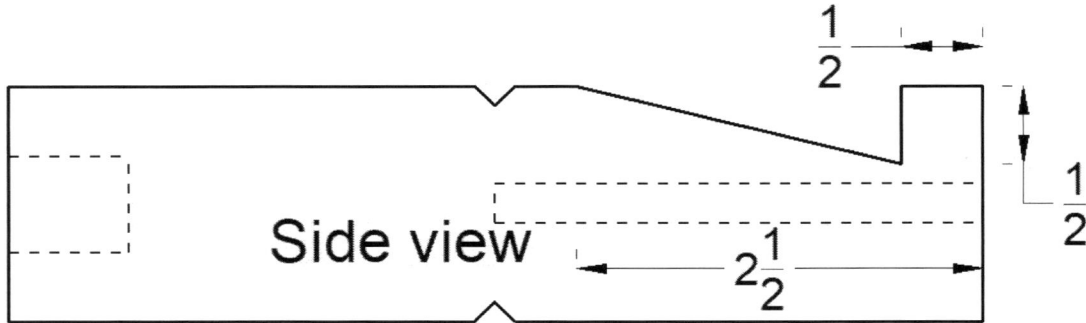

This is what the body should look like so far.

Round off all the corners except the top of the shoulders to make the body more realistic.

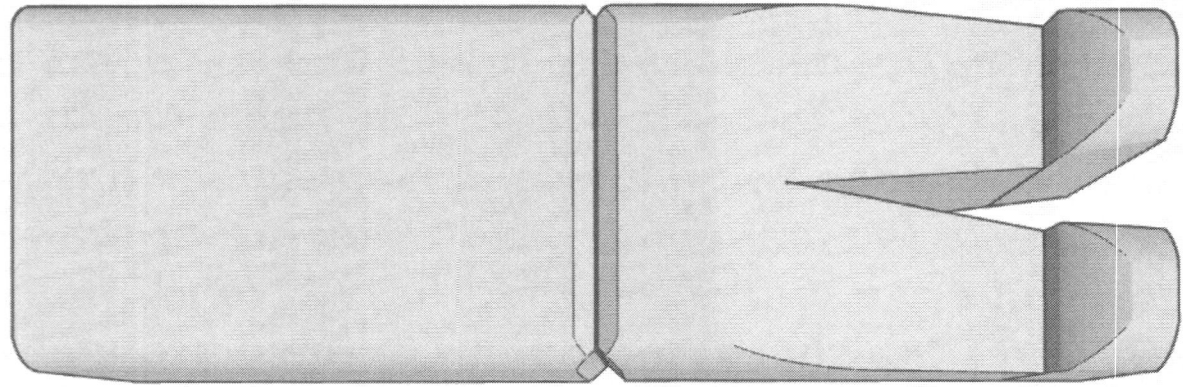

The shoulder tops will be rounded after we attach the arms.

At this point you may want to consider painting on some clothes and shoes or whatever cosmetics you have the time, skill, or desire to add. Of course, if you have any wood carving skills you can add a lot to the figure.

The arms will be made from two pieces, upper arm and forearm. The hand will always be aligned with the forearm so the hand and forearm will be one solid piece. Try to make all the arm pieces from the same piece of wood.

We'll start with the upper arm.

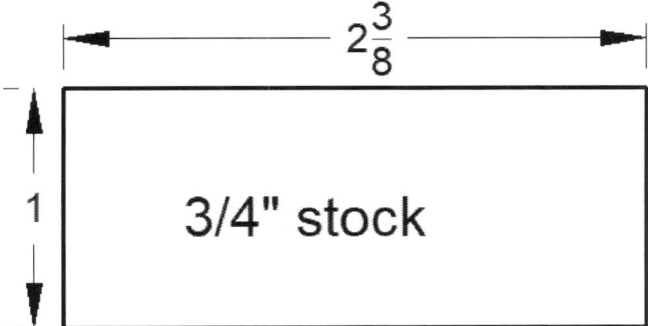

Drill the mounting holes next. The 3/8" hole is only a countersink to help hide the mounting screw. Drill it deep enough so the screwhead will be below the arm surface.

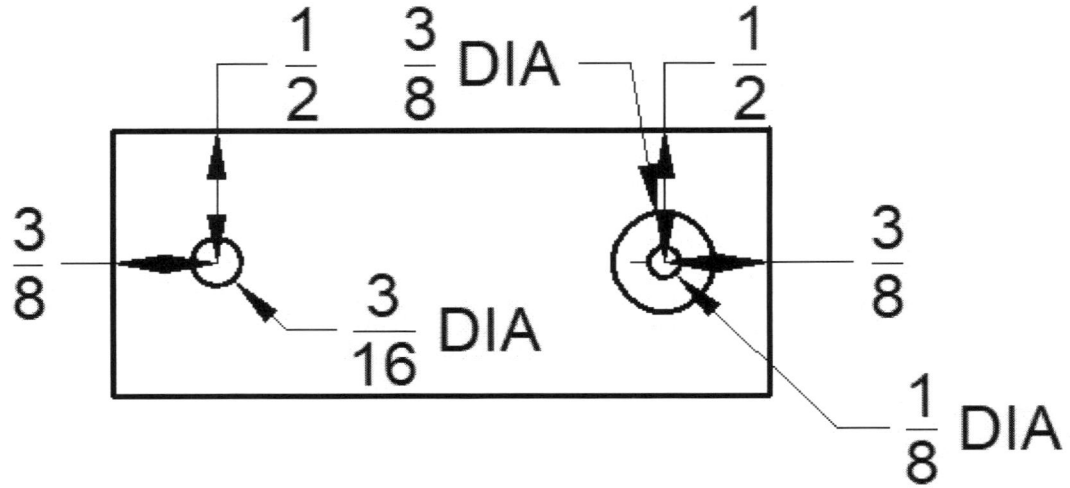

Cut the slot next to attach it to the forearm.

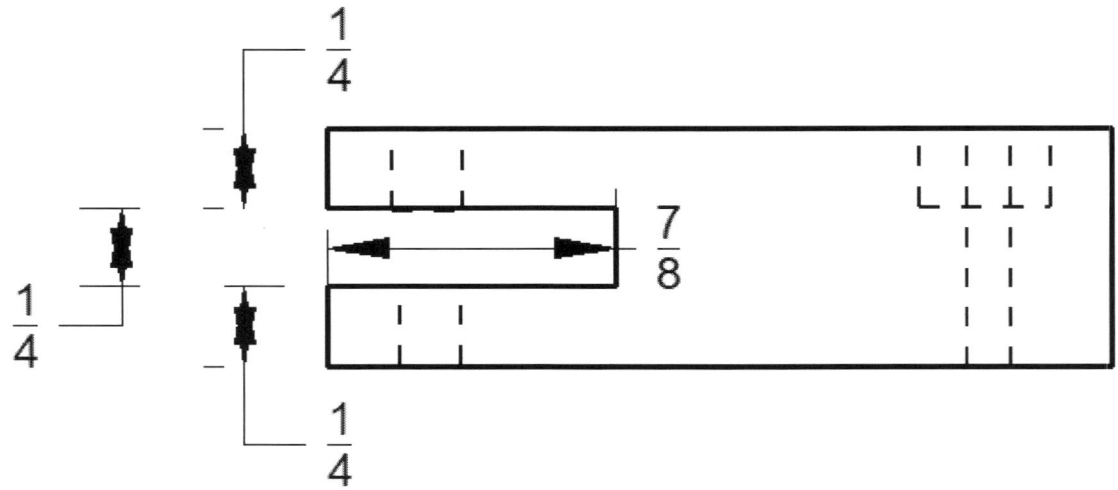

Shape the upper arm as shown.

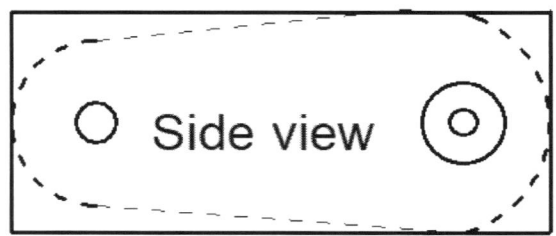

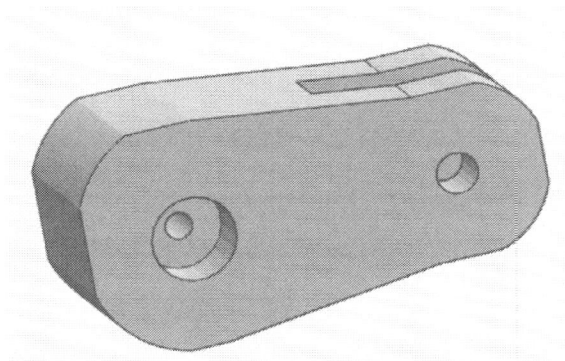

Sand all the edges except the area that will make contact with the chest.

The forearm will be hinged together with the upper arm. We'll start the forearm with the basic block. The forearm is made from ¾" stock.

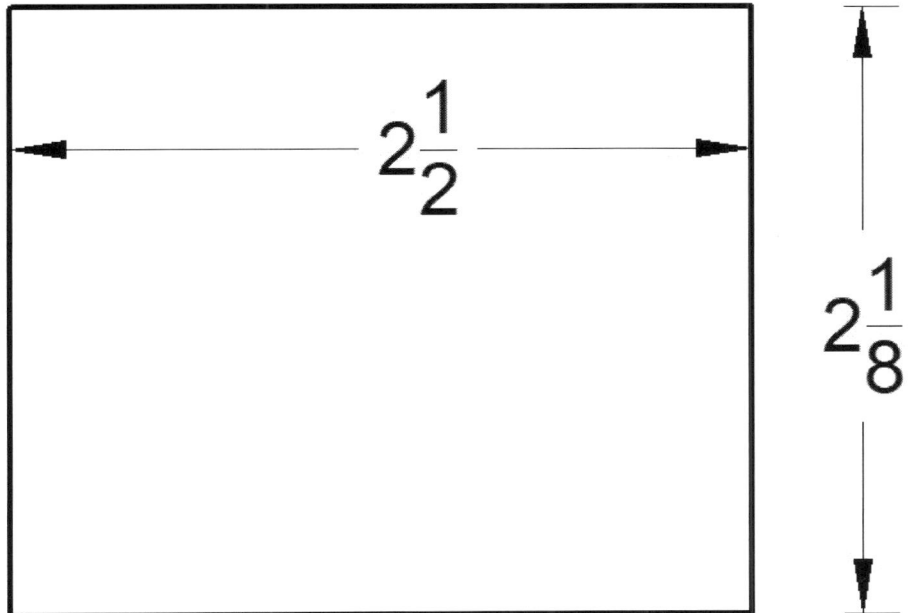

There are two holes required, one for the pull-up bar and one for the connection to the upper arm.

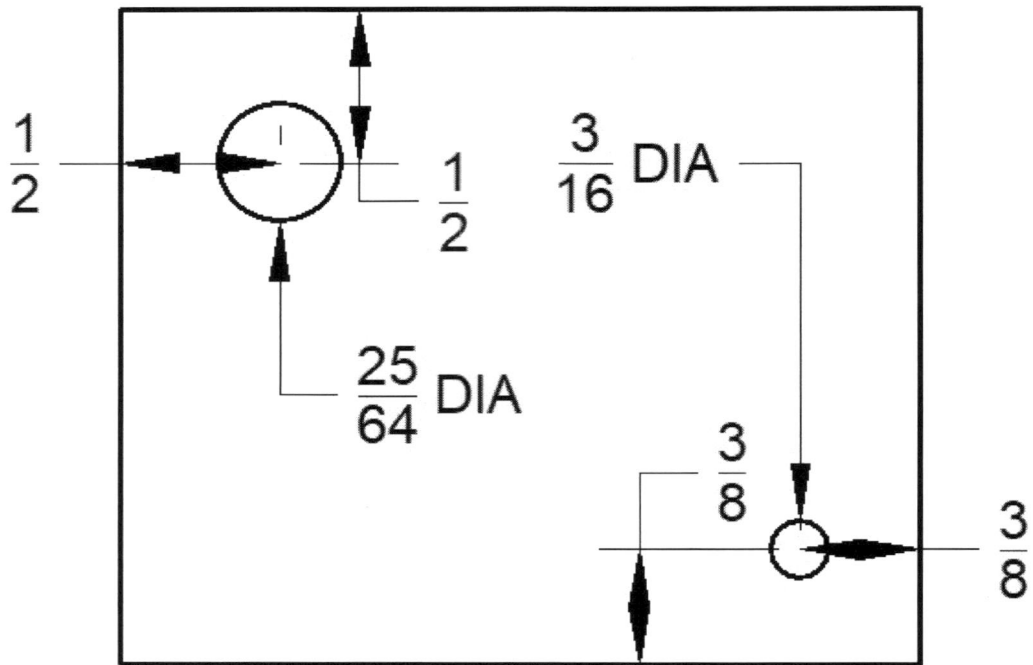

Insert a scrap piece of 3/8" dowel into the 25/64" hole. It should rotate with ease.

Start shaping the arm.

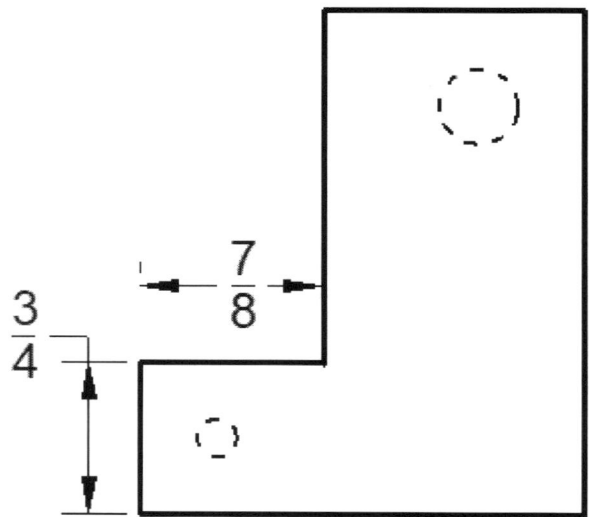

Stand the forearm on end and narrow down the connector part of the forearm. Round off the connector.

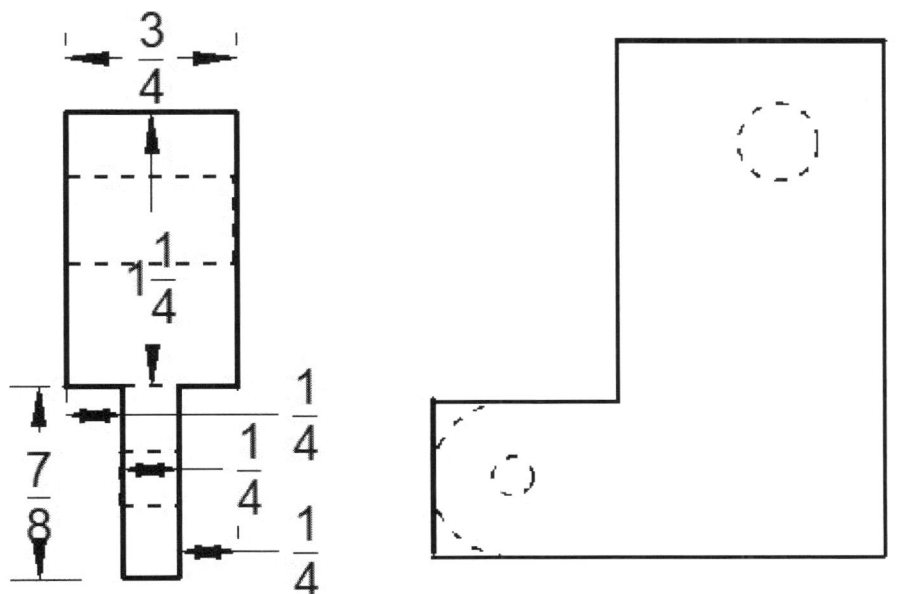

Make the rest of the side cuts.

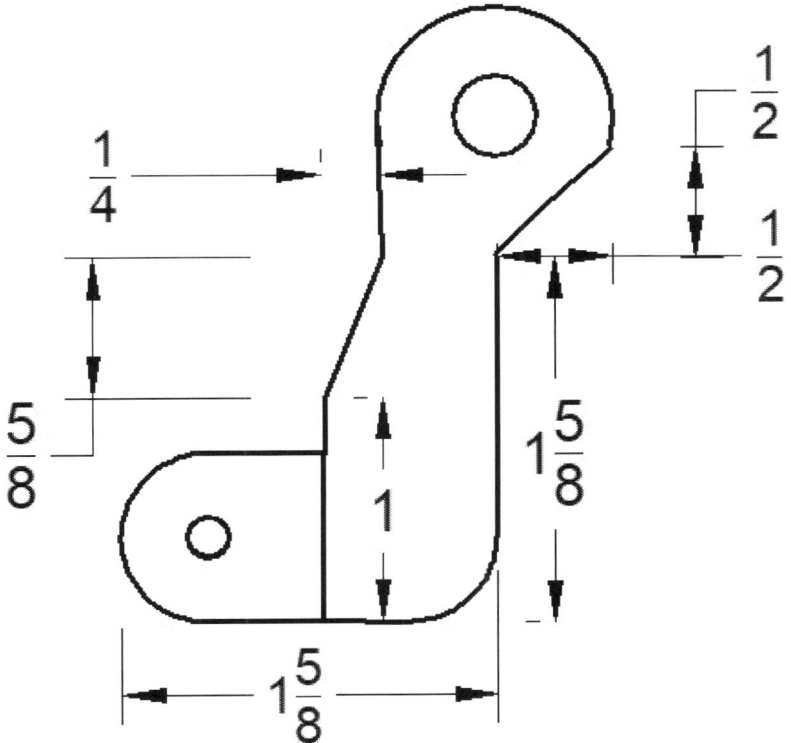

Lay the arm with the connector facing up and make the following cuts.

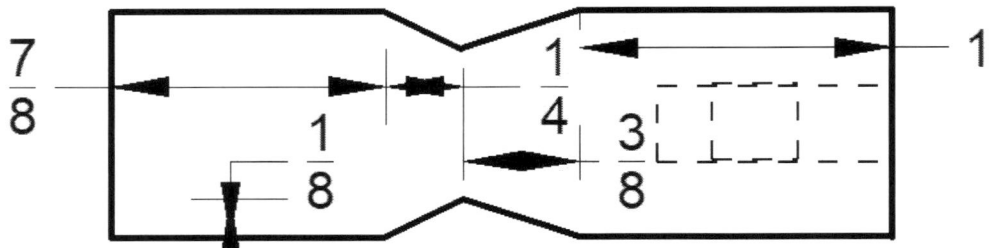

Temporarily insert the connector into the slot in the upper arm. Insert a scrap piece of 3/16" dowel through both the upper arm and forearm. Rotate the pieces to make sure they rotate easily.

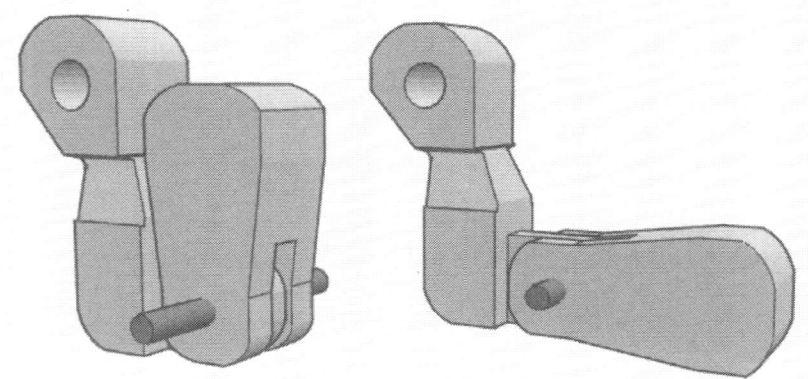

Sand all the edges.

This would be a good time to paint or stain the figure if desired.

Attach the upper arm to the lower arm with a ¾" long piece of 3/16" dowel. Attach the upper arm to the body with a 1 ½" screw.

The head instructions are located on page 177.

Your Pull up guy should now look like this:

Insert a scrap piece of 3/8" dowel into both hand openings. Make sure both arms rotate easily.

Pull up bars

The pull up bars are next. The bars are 3/8" dowel. The two uprights are 8" long and the cross piece is 4 ¾" long.

The corner connectors are made from ¾" wood. Cut the pieces as shown below.

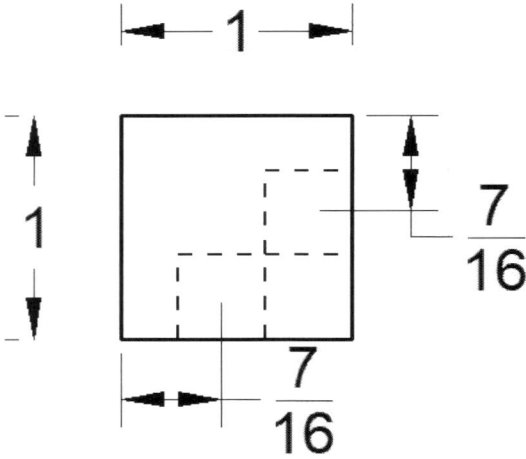

Drill 3/8" holes, 3/8" deep.

Temporarily insert the cross bar through both hands and into the corner pieces. Insert the two side bars. Take extra time to make sure the pull up bars are square with each other. There is very little clearance between the pull up guy nose and the cross bar.

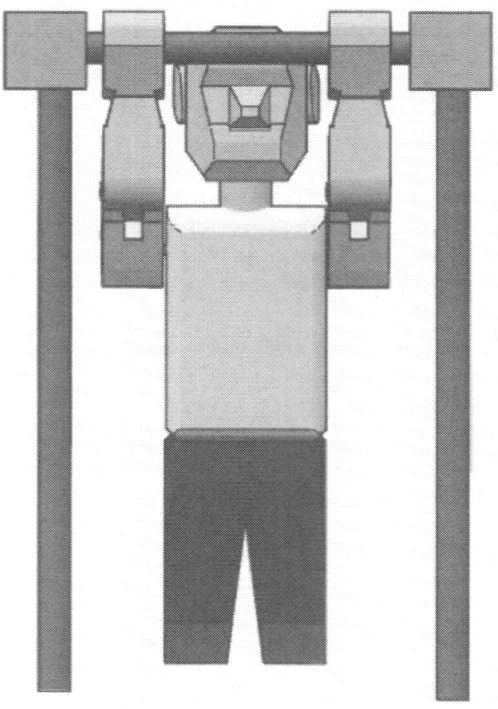

Stand the assembly onto the frame top piece with the side bars inserted into the frame holes. Insert the push rod into the pull up guys legs.

Turn the crank. If everything looks like it is working as expected, glue everything in place.

Your project is now complete!

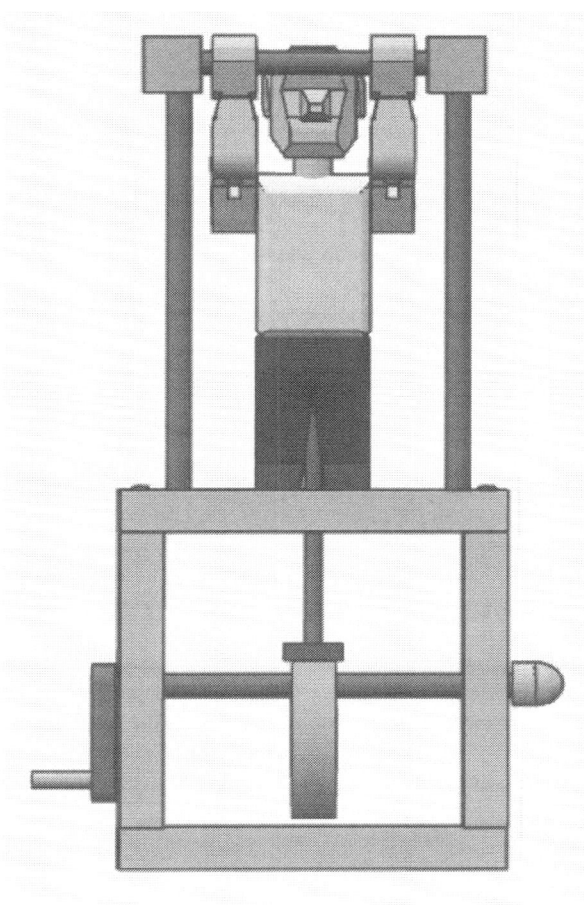

Bench Press

*****

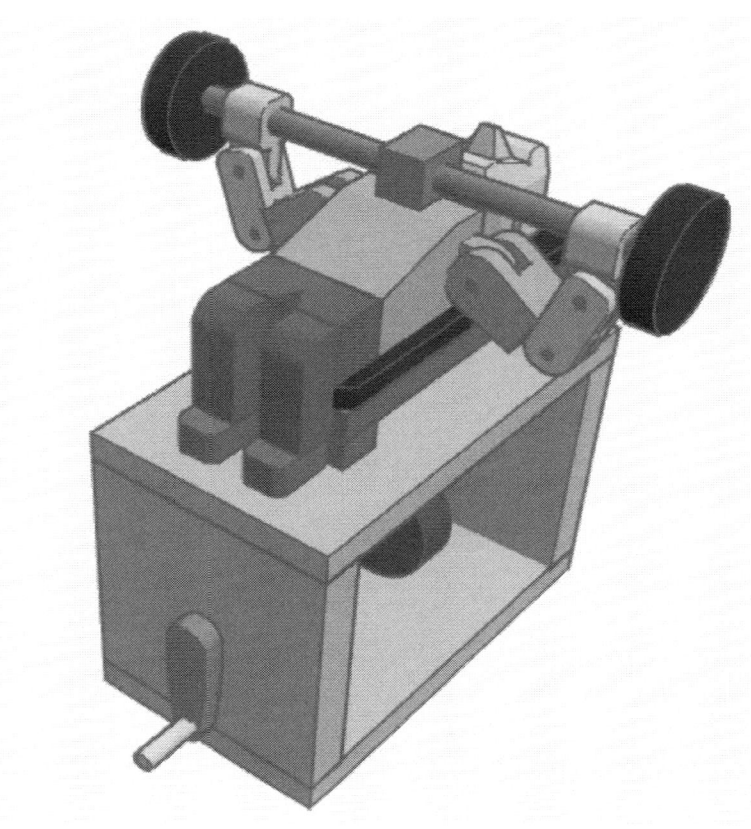

Main frame

We'll start with the frame. The top and bottom are ½″ thick. The sides are ¾″ thick.

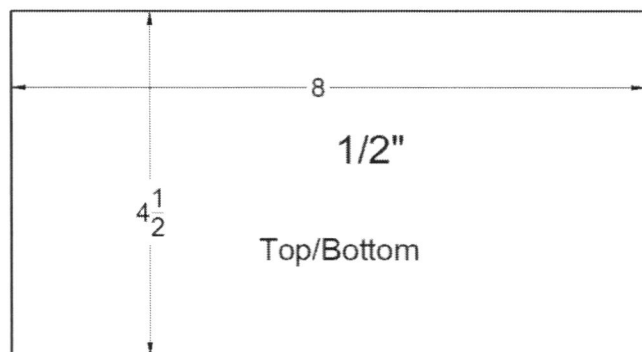

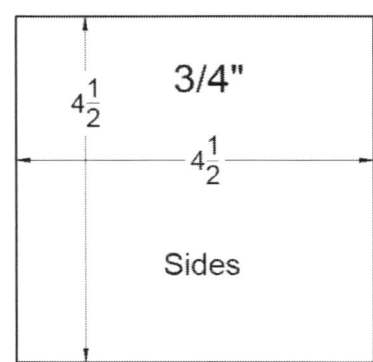

The drive axle is supported by the two sides. Make a mark on the bottom of each side to identify the bottom since the hole is not exactly in the middle.

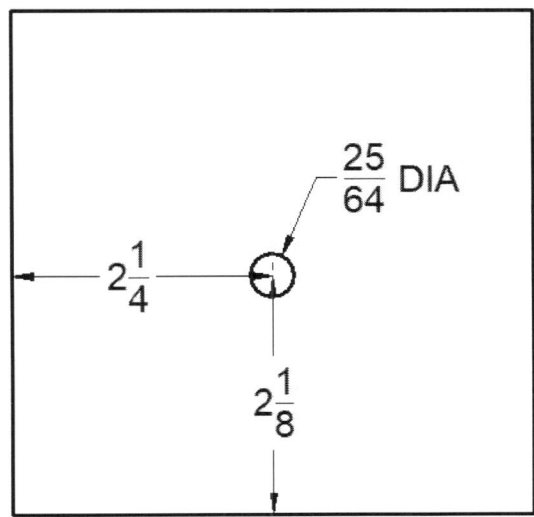

Assemble the frame with screws. I used 1 ½" pan head because I happen to have some.

Pre-drill the hole to prevent splitting the sides. Countersink the holes on the bottom of the bottom piece to recess the screw heads.

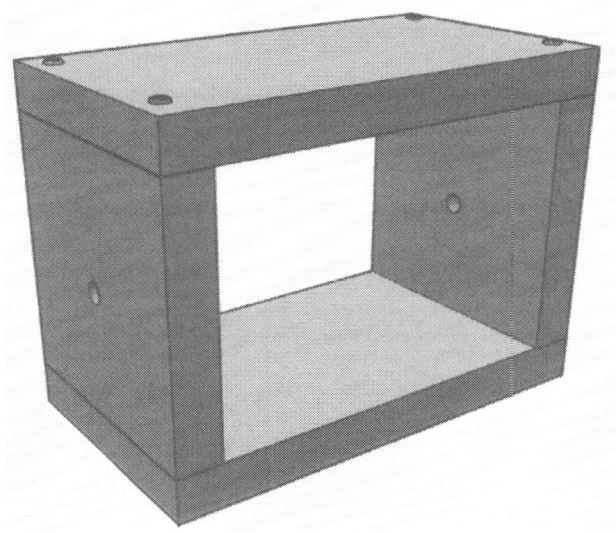

The bench top and legs are made from 1/2" wood.

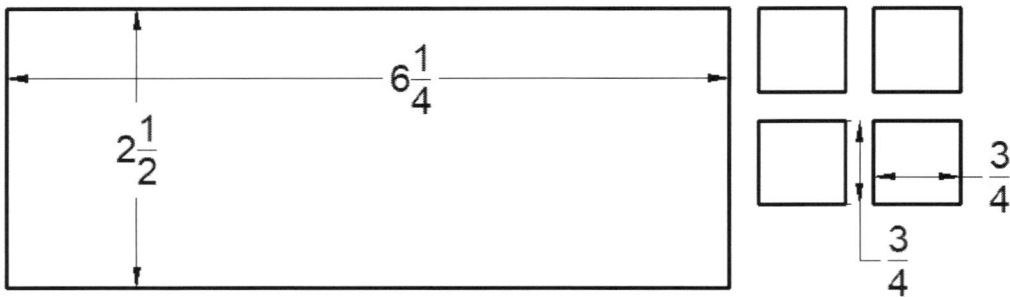

Glue the legs onto the four corners.

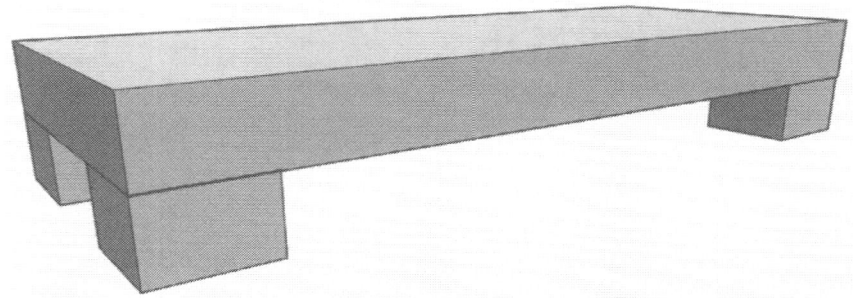

A "pad" will be added to make it look more real. The pad is made from 3/8" wood. I made mine from Black Walnut to make it look more real without having to paint it.

The pad is the same size as the bench top (6 ¼" x 2 ½"). Round the corners.

Glue the pad to the bench top.

To finish the frame, glue the bench to the basic frame. One end is flush with the edge of the frame.

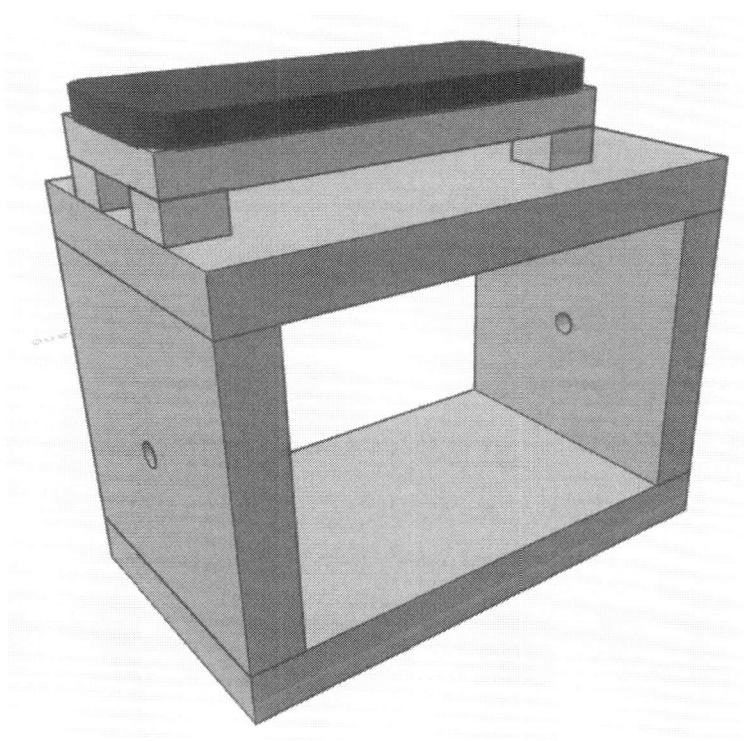

Action figure

Now we can do the action figure. We'll start with the upper body. This is what the completed upper body should look like.

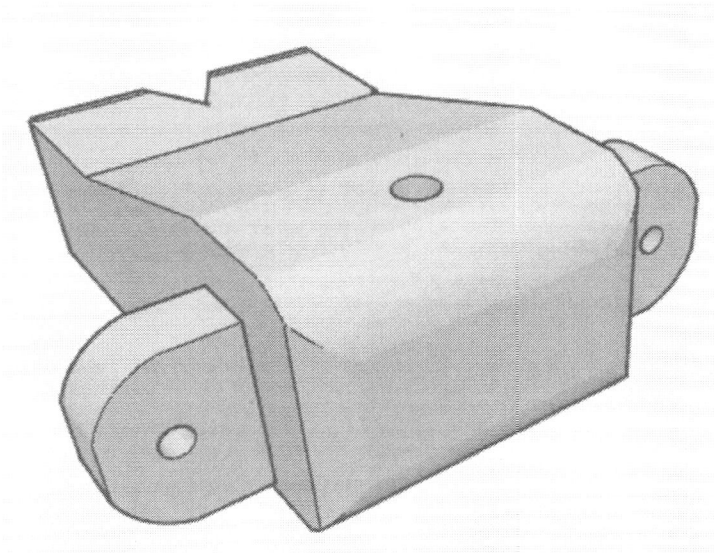

The upper body can be cut from a standard 2 x 4.

However, I would recommend using a scrap piece of 2 x 6 or larger to allow the grain to be oriented as shown. The body is 1 ½" thick.

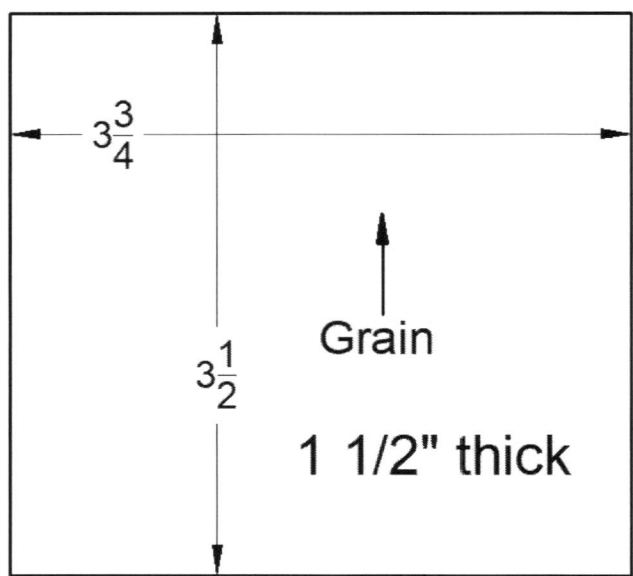

Drill the hole for the push rod.

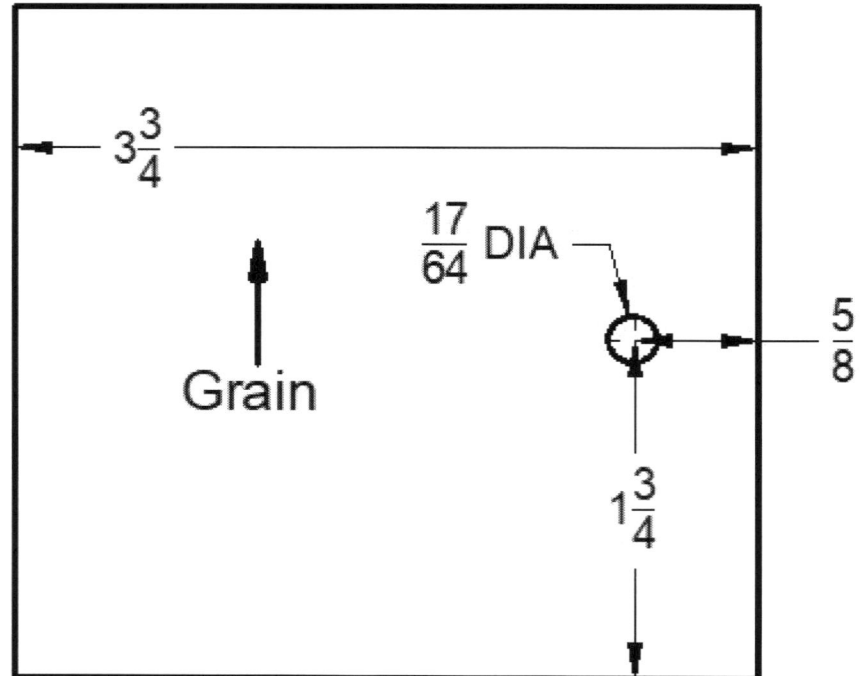

Draw the lines for the arm connectors.

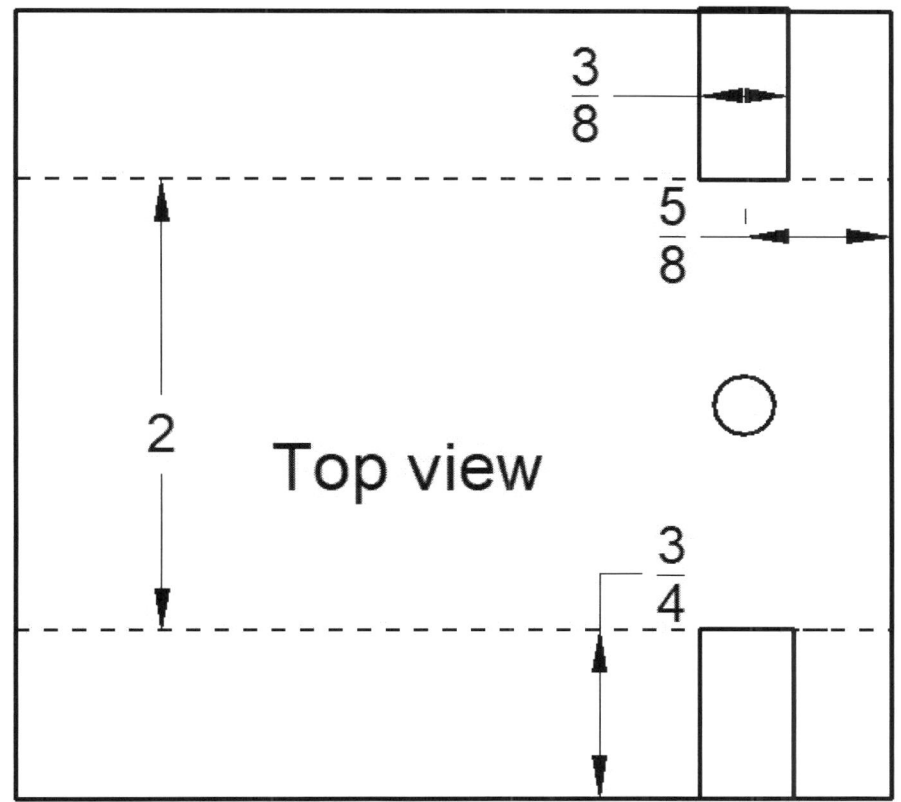

Stand the block on end to drill the two holes for the arm connectors. Drill the holes ~1" deep.

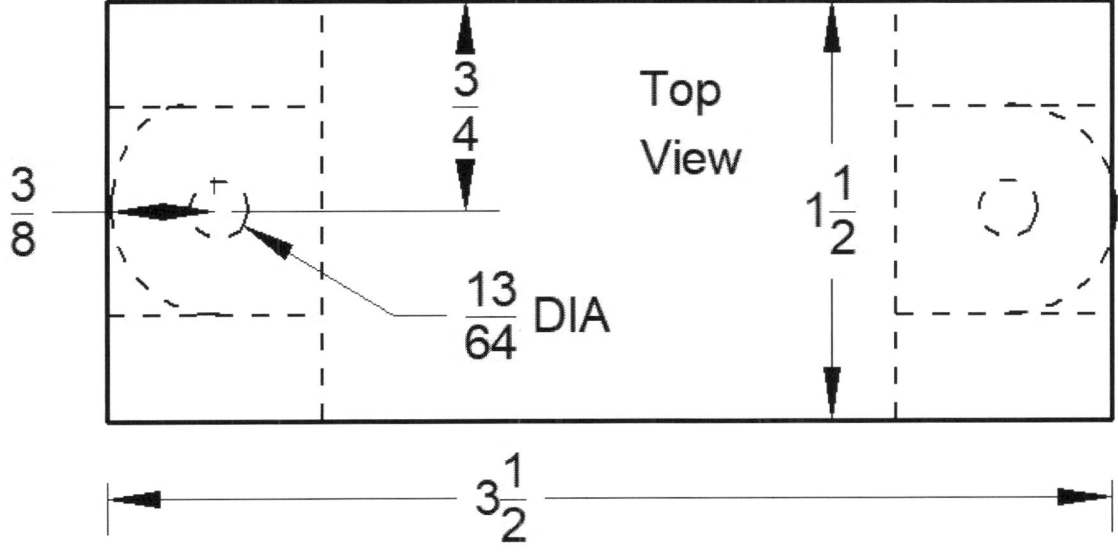

Round the upper end of the chest.

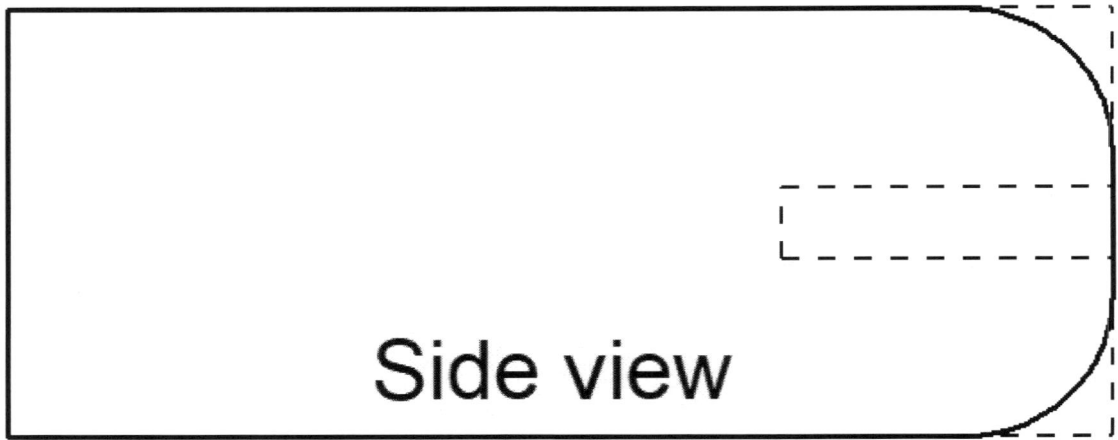

Side view

Trim the upper body down to the waist line. As an option you can make small diagonal cuts on the top and both sides to identify the belt line, which is 1" from the bottom.

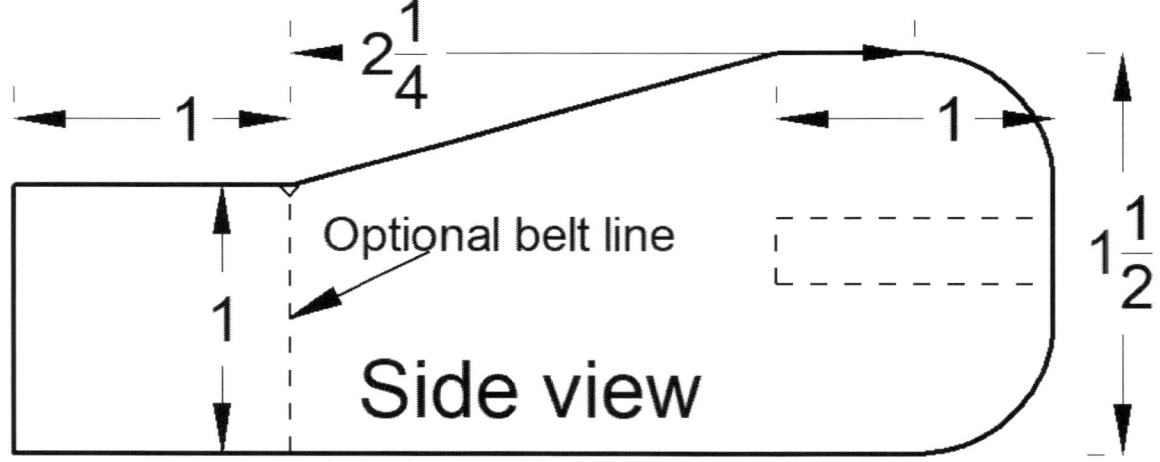

Optional belt line

Side view

Trim off the excess wood around the arm connectors. Slightly round the top of the shoulders.

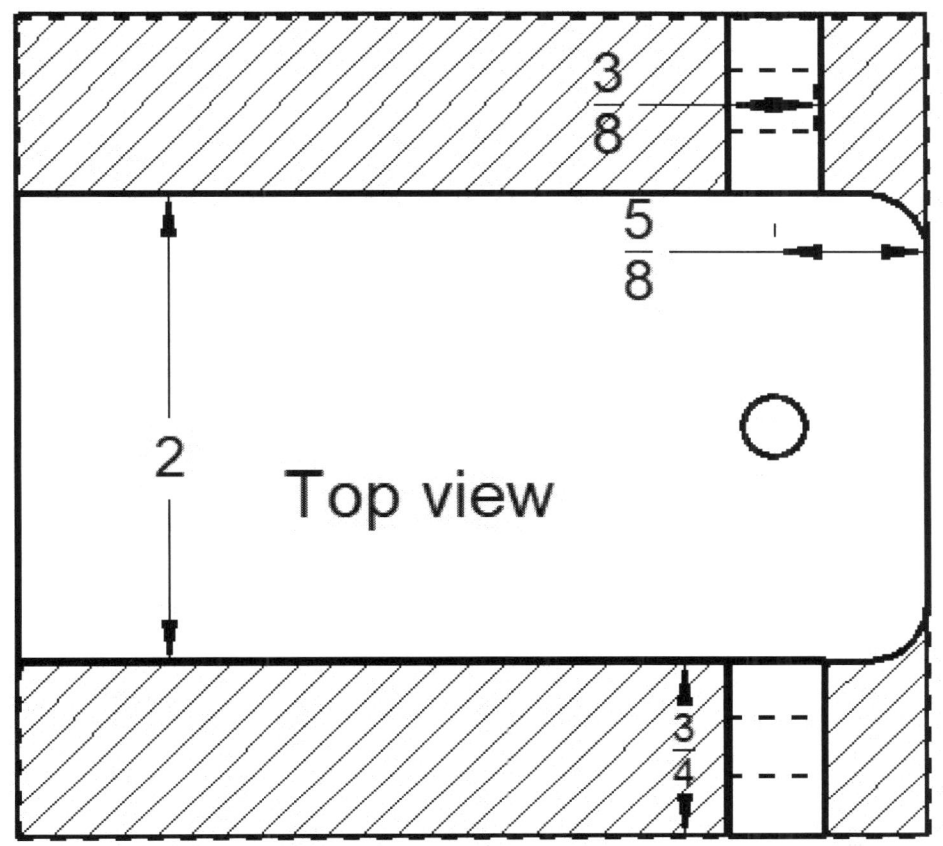

Stand the upper body on the head end. Trim the arm connectors. Round the end of the connectors.

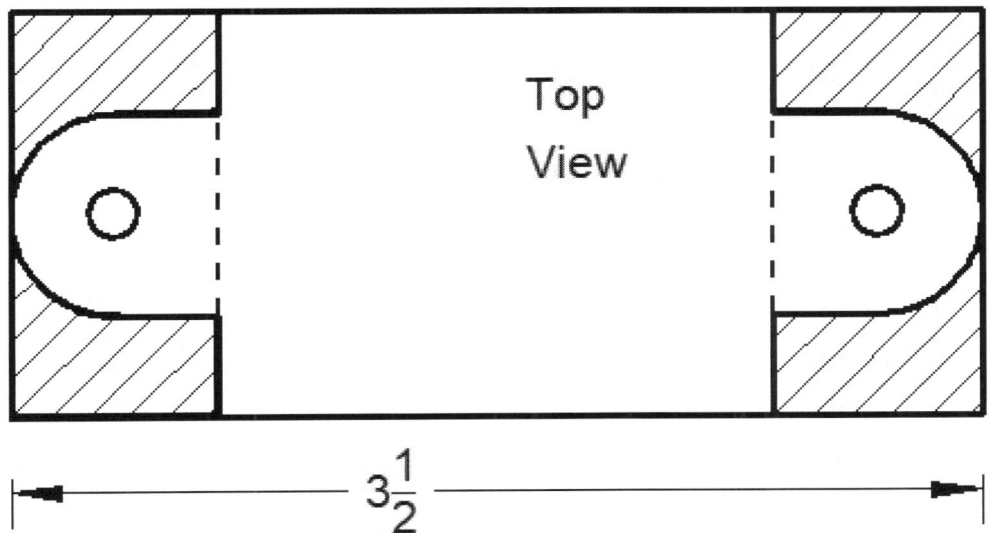

The bottom of the chest piece is actually also the start of the legs. The legs will need a notch cut to identify the leg portion.

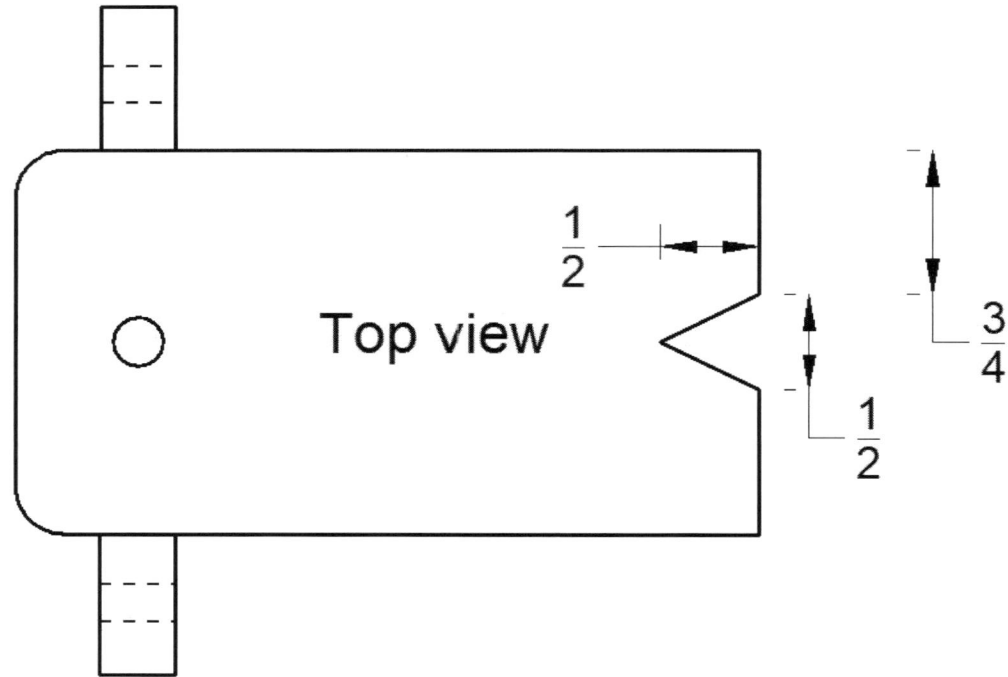

The completed upper body should look like this.

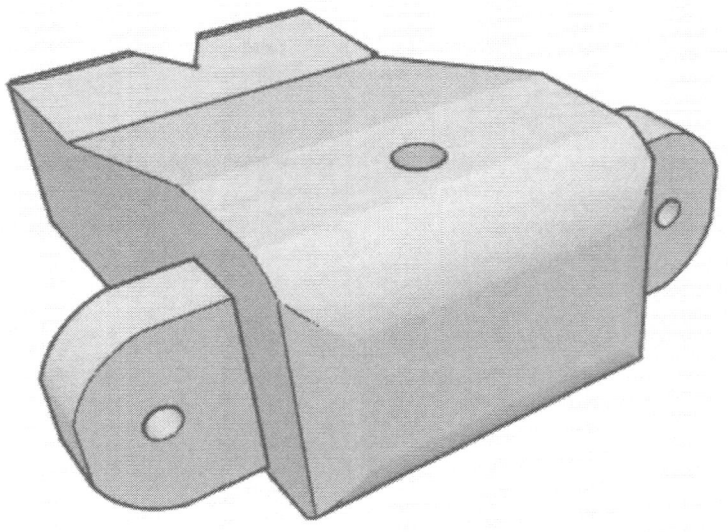

The legs are made from ¾″ wood.

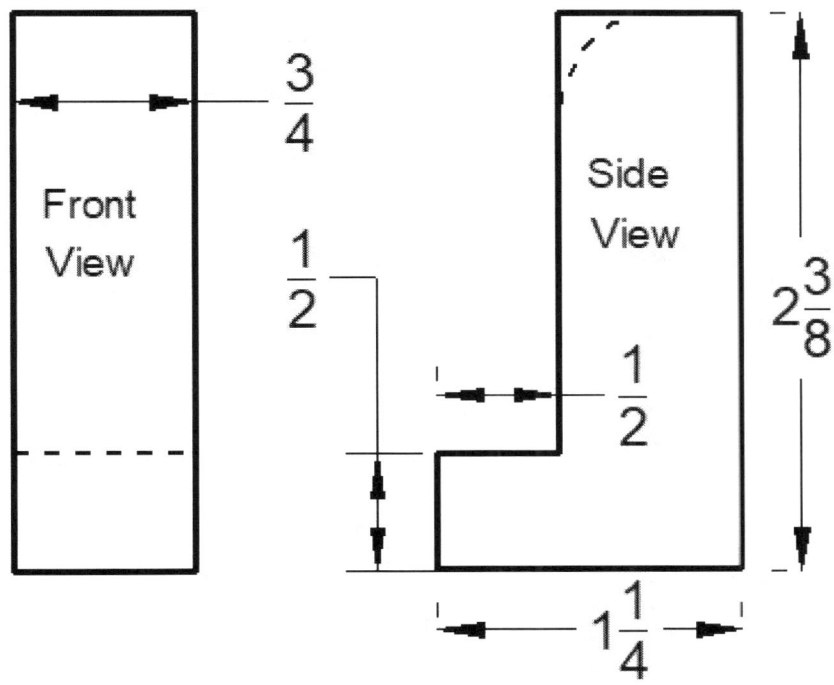

Make two of the legs.

Round the knee part of the legs. Round and sand the front edges of the legs. Round and sand the front of the shoe part of the legs.

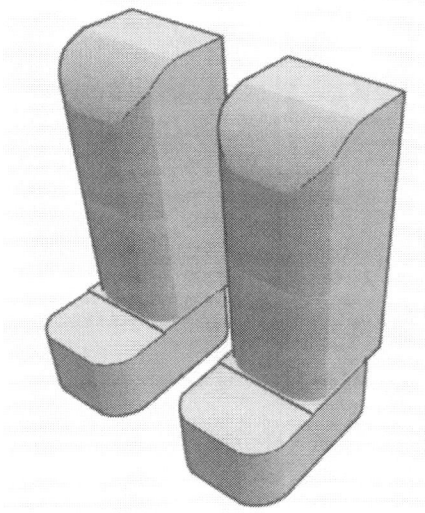

We need to assemble everything we have at this point.

Do not glue anything until all the pieces are matched up and in alignment.

Place the body on the bench pad, centered left to right. Make the bottom of the chest piece flush with the end of the bench.

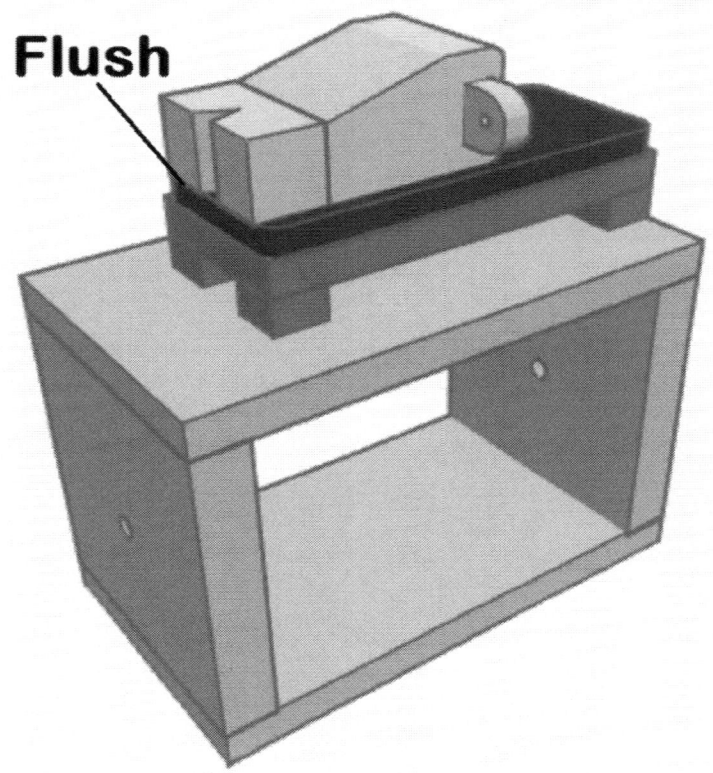

Set the legs in place. Sand as necessary to align the legs with the body edges.

Glue the legs to the end of the chest. Do **not** glue the bottom of the shoes to the frame. Sand all the glue joints.

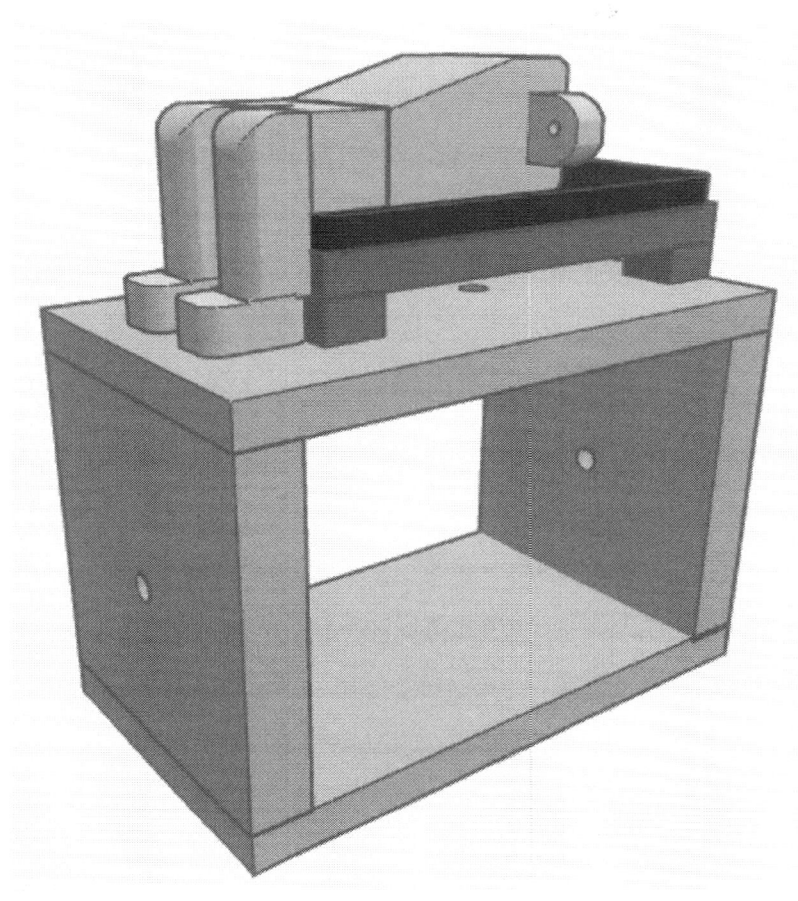

The head is next. Details on making the head are provided on page 177. Insert a piece of 1/2" dowel into the head for the neck. There should be ~3/8" extending out from the head for the exposed part of the neck.

Now would be a good time to paint the body if desired.

Glue the body to the bench. It is important to have the body in the middle of the bench side to side. Apply glue to the end of the neck and the back of the head. Glue the neck to the body and the head to the pad.

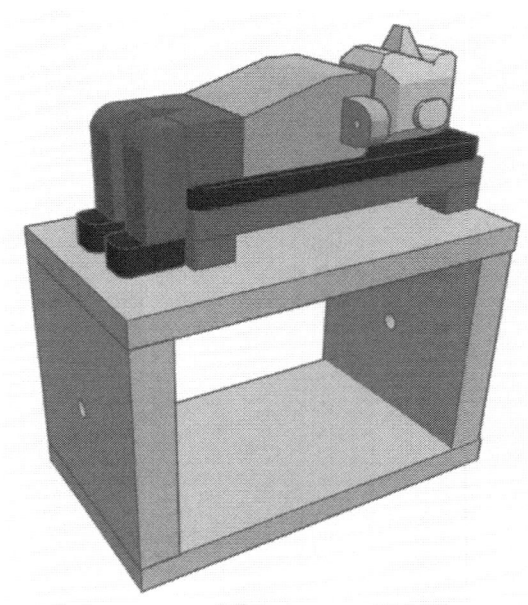

The barbell will be lifted by a cam under the frame. There should already be a 17/64" hole in the chest for the pushrod. Continue drilling that hole through the pad, bench, and frame top.

Insert a scrap ¼" dowel in the push rod hole. Lift the dowel and let it drop. The dowel should drop through the hole without any restriction.

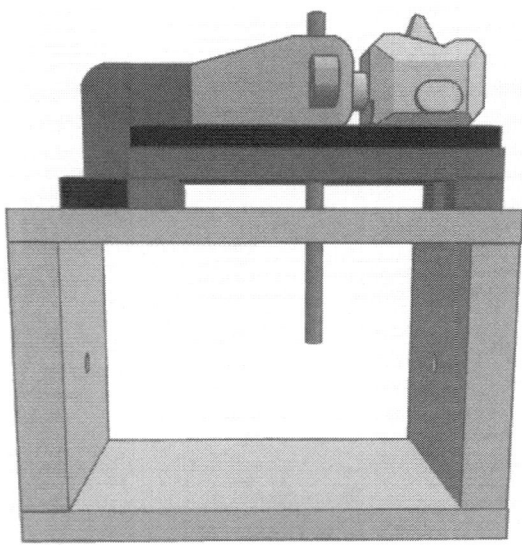

Now we can add the arms. The arms have three parts, upper arm, forearm, and the hand.

The upper arm is 1" thick. A hole is required on both ends of the upper arm. There is a 13/64" hole on one end and a 3/16" hole on the other end with identical placement.

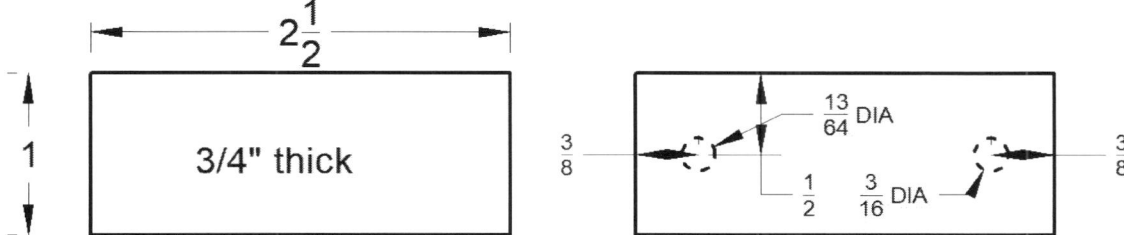

The upper arm needs to be reduced from 1" to ¾" to match up with the ¾" forearm. Draw the lines but do not make the cut yet.

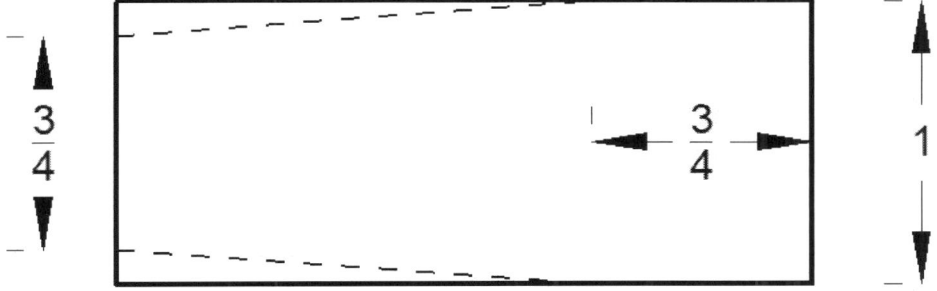

The upper arm has a slot on one end and a connector on the other end.

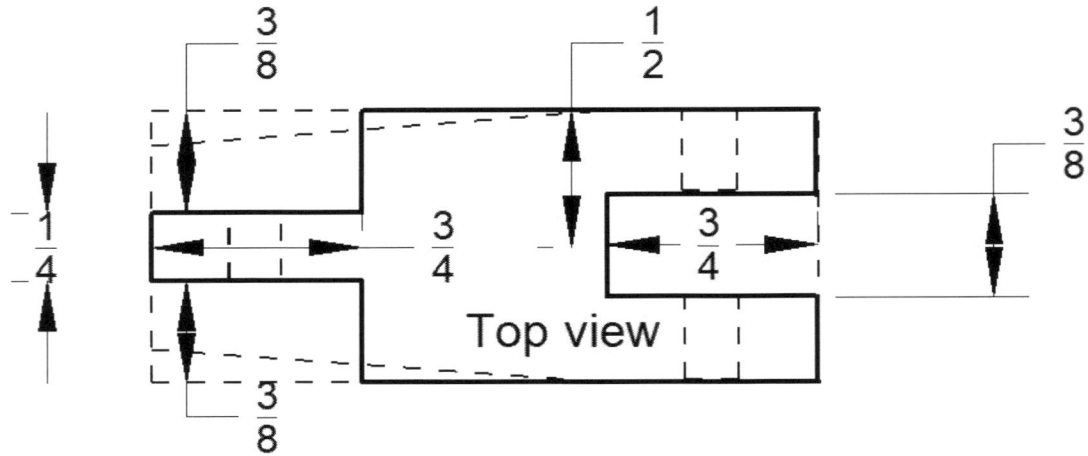

Top view

Remember to make two of these, one for each arm.

Round both ends. The notch cut is necessary to allow the arm to bend more than 45 degrees.

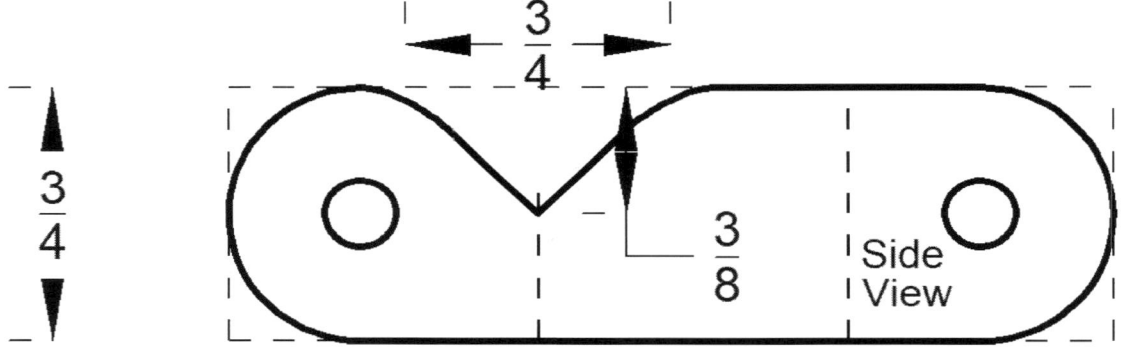

Side View

The final upper arm should look like this.

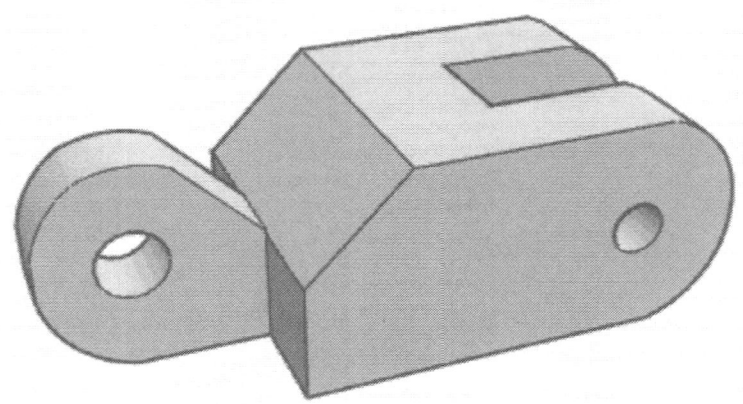

The forearm is made from ¾" stock. The print below shows the progression of the build.

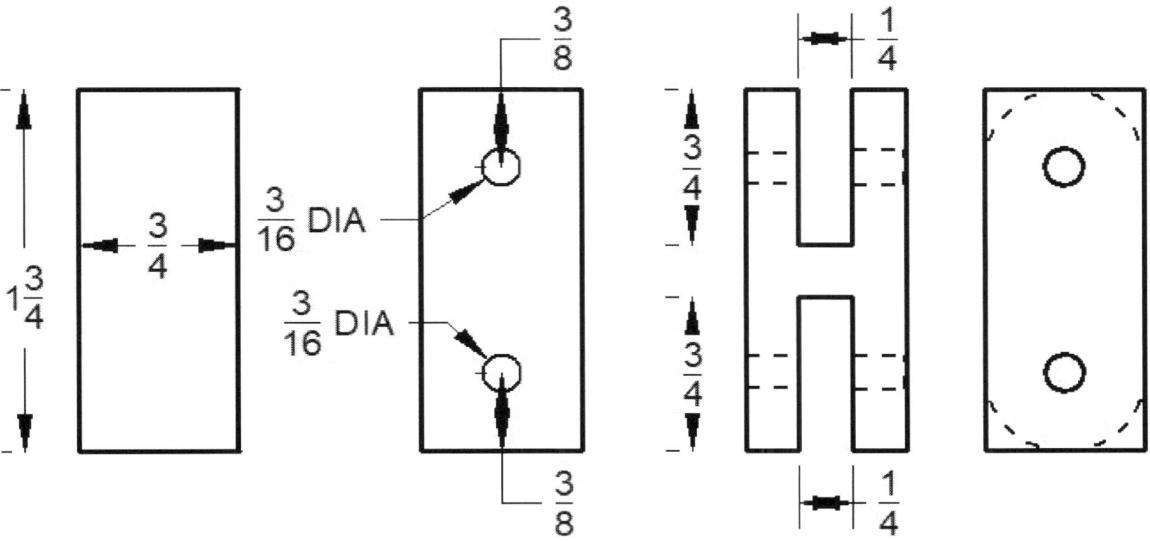

We start with a basic block cut from a piece of ¾" stock. Then drill the holes. Turn the piece on its side and cut the slots. Finally, round off the ends.

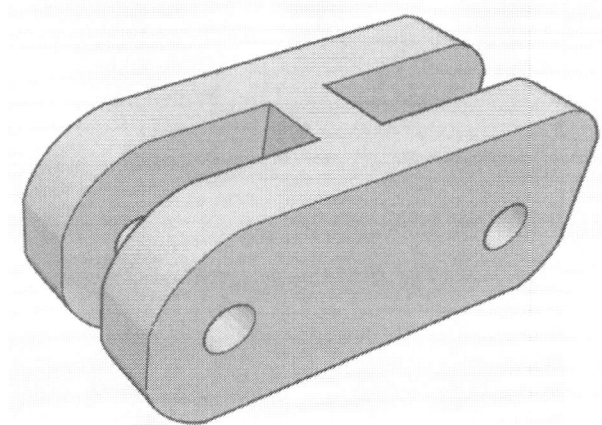

Temporarily connect the forearm to the upper arm with 3/16" dowel and adjust as needed to make them flex easily.

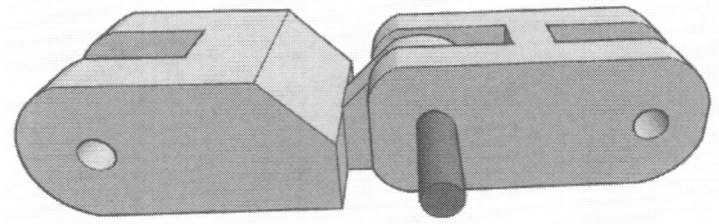

Follow the progression for the hand build as shown below. Start with a piece of ¾″ stock.

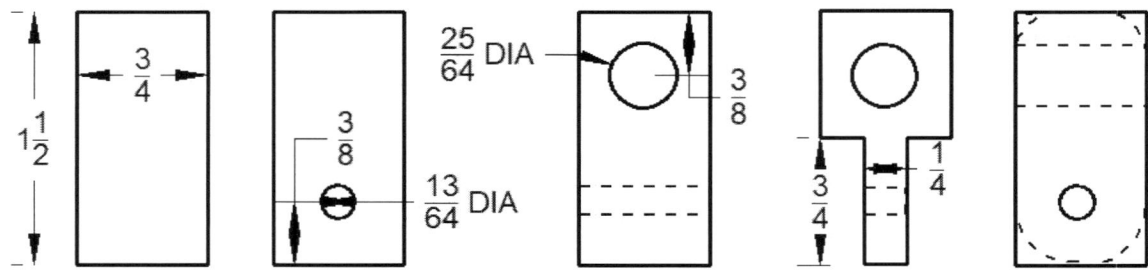

Drill the 13/64″ hole for the connector. Turn the hand on its side and drill the 25/64″ hole for the bar.

Narrow the connector. Round the connector. Make a slight round to the top of the hand.

Assemble the entire arm. Use 3/16″ dowels for all the joints. Cut the dowels to length so they are flush with both sides.

Add any paint desired.

Attach the arms to the connectors on the body. Insert a piece of 3/8" dowel 9" long through both hands. That will be the bar for the weights. Lift the bar to manipulate both arms. You should be able to lift the bar approximately 1 ½" without any flex problems with the arms. It is normal at this point to have to spend extra time to sand and maybe adjust the notches to get all the joints to work as desired.

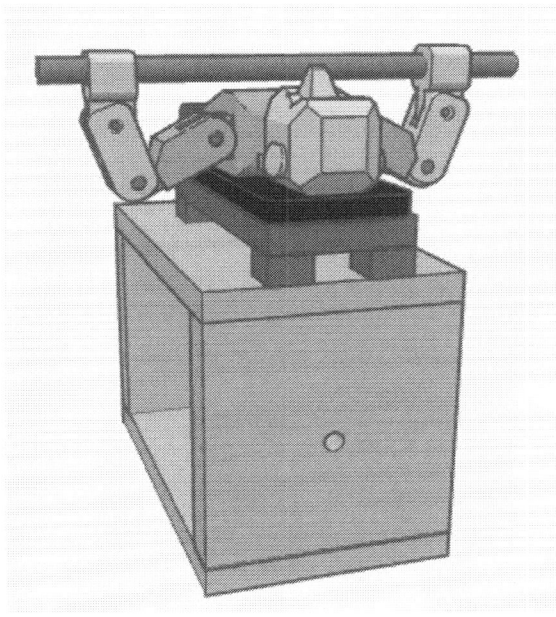

Remove the bar. Now we'll add a piece to connect the bar to the pushrod.

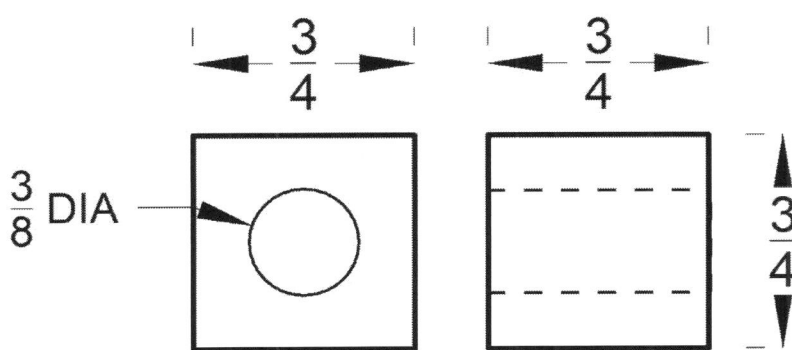

Cut a small block ¾" x ¾" for the connector. Drill a 3/8" hole through the center of the connector. Slide the connector to the middle of the bar (4 ½").

With the connector in the middle of the bar, drill a ¼" hole, 3/8" deep, in the bottom of the connector. Note that the hole will extend into the bar.

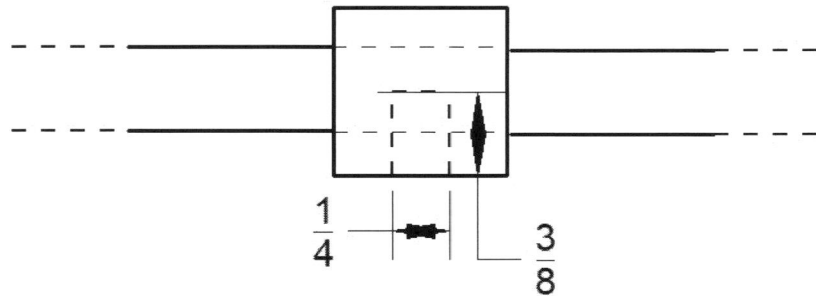

The push rod should be ~6" long to start with. It will be trimmed to size later.

Insert the push rod into the chest. Slide both hands onto the weight bar. Temporarily insert the push rod into the connector. Move the push rod up and down by hand approximately 1 ½ inches to insure both arms are flexing. Also make sure the push rod will easily drop back down without hanging up. Do not glue the push rod or weight bar in place yet.

The weights for the ends of the bar are 2" disks. You can cut ½" from a 2" dowel or cut the disks from ½" wood. Drill a 3/8" hole in the center to mount the weights on the bar.

Drive train

Now we can move to the lower section of the frame.

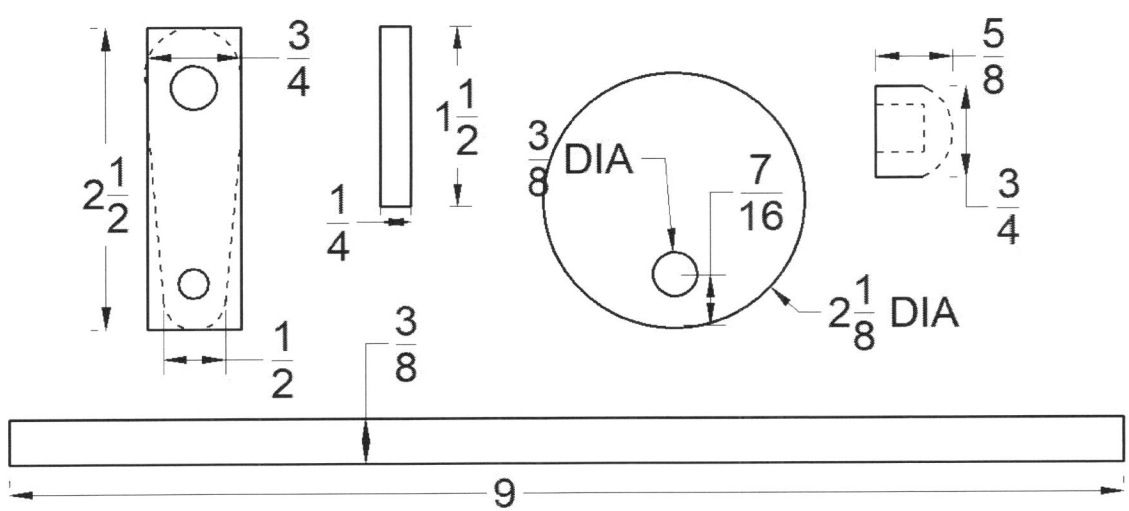

This is the assembled drive system with the part names.

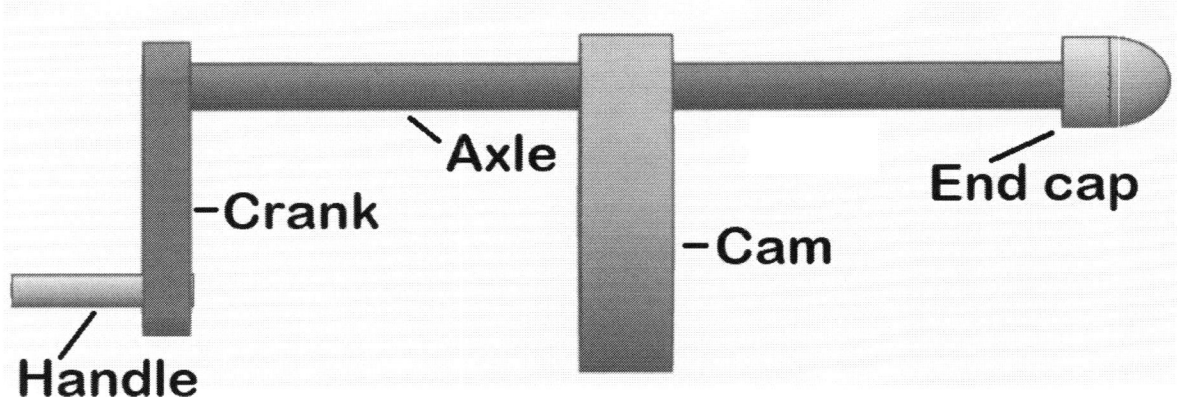

The axle is an 9" piece of 3/8" dowel. The final axle length will be determined during the assembly. Insert the axle into the frame and make sure it spins easily.

The cam is made from a piece of ¾" wood. Insert the axle into one of the side pieces. Temporarily install the cam onto the axle. Rotate the cam. There should be a small amount of clearance between the the bottom of the frame and the cam. There should be at least 3/8" clearance between the cam and the top frame piece.

The crank is made from a piece of 3/8" wood.

The crank handle can be a decorative knob from a hobby store or in this example, a piece of ¼" dowel, ~1 ½" long.

On the other end of the axle we will add an endcap made from ¾" dowel. Drill a hole ~3/8" for the axle. Round one end.

Insert and glue the crank handle into the crank. Glue the crank onto the axle.

Insert the axle into the frame. Temporarily attach the end cap to the axle. Adjust the length of the axle so that both the end cap and crank have ~1/16" clearance from the frame sides. Do not glue the end cap in place yet.

Remove the end cap and install the cam. Line up the cam so it is centered on the ¼" push rod. You may have to remove the frame top and end cap side to move the cam.

Slide the cam over and apply glue to the axle. Slide the cam back into position.

The last piece to add for the project is a pad at the bottom of the push rod. It is highly unlikely the cam will turn with the push rod rubbing against it by itself. The pad is made from ¼" stock.

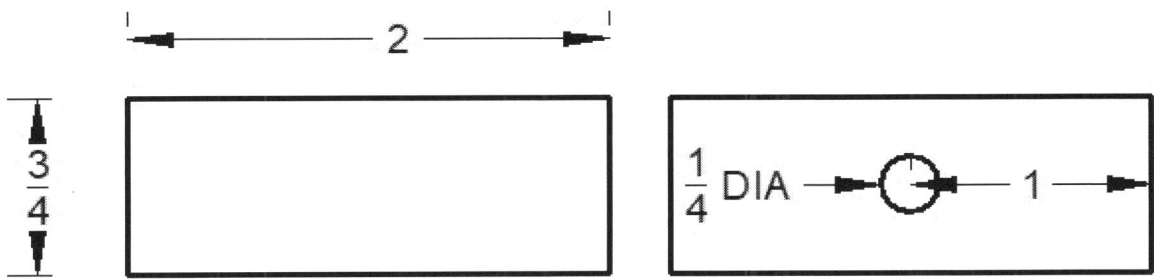

Drill a ¼" hole in the center to attach the push rod. Lift the push rod and temporarily attach the pad. Rotate the crank to lift the weights. At the cams lowest point the weight bar connector should be ~1/16" above the chest. Adjust the length of the push rod as needed.

At this point the project should be fully operational. Glue all remaining parts in place.

Project complete!

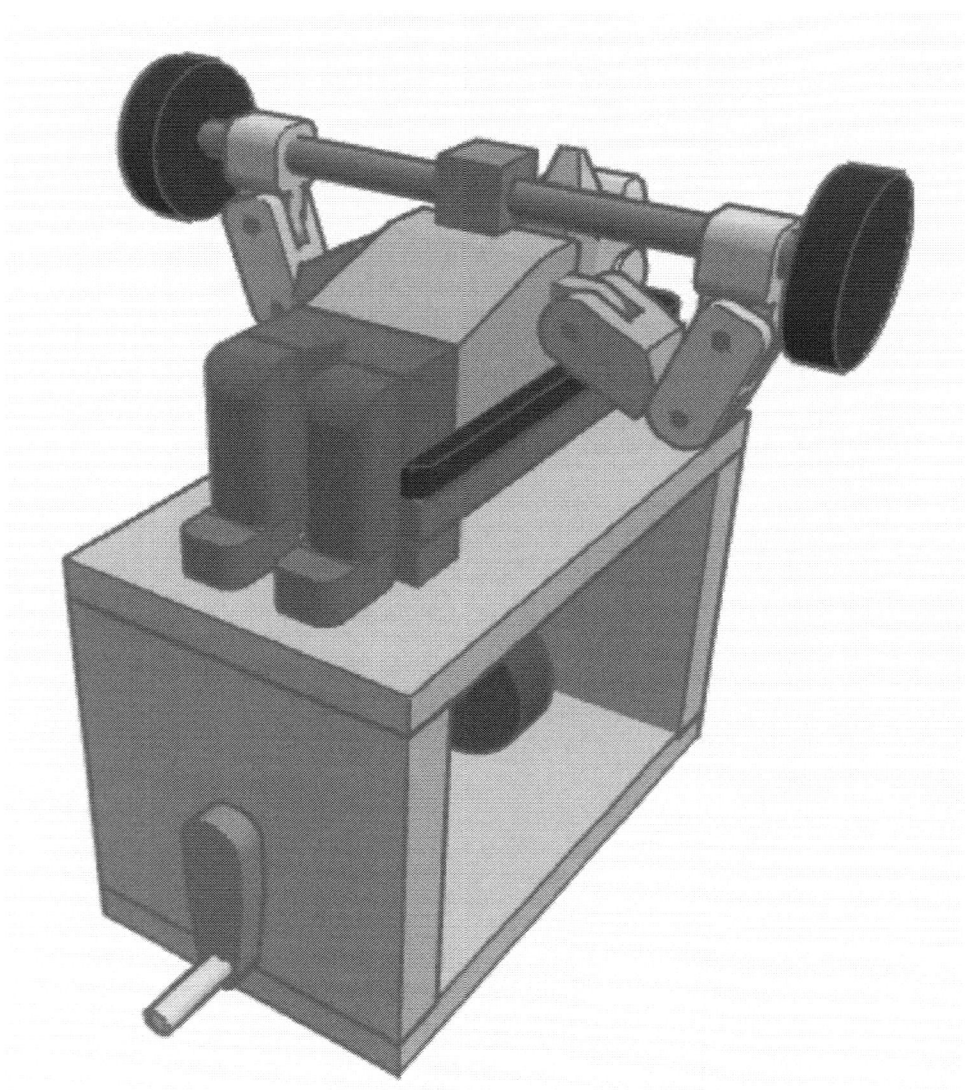

Exercise Bike

An exercise bike is normally driven by the rider moving the pedals. In this project we will use a "friction" wheel underneath to drive the wheel which will move the rider legs.

We'll make the frame first, the drive train, the bike, and then finish with the bike rider.

Main frame

Let's make the main frame. The top and bottom frame pieces are made from ½" wood. The top and bottom pieces have the same basic dimensions.

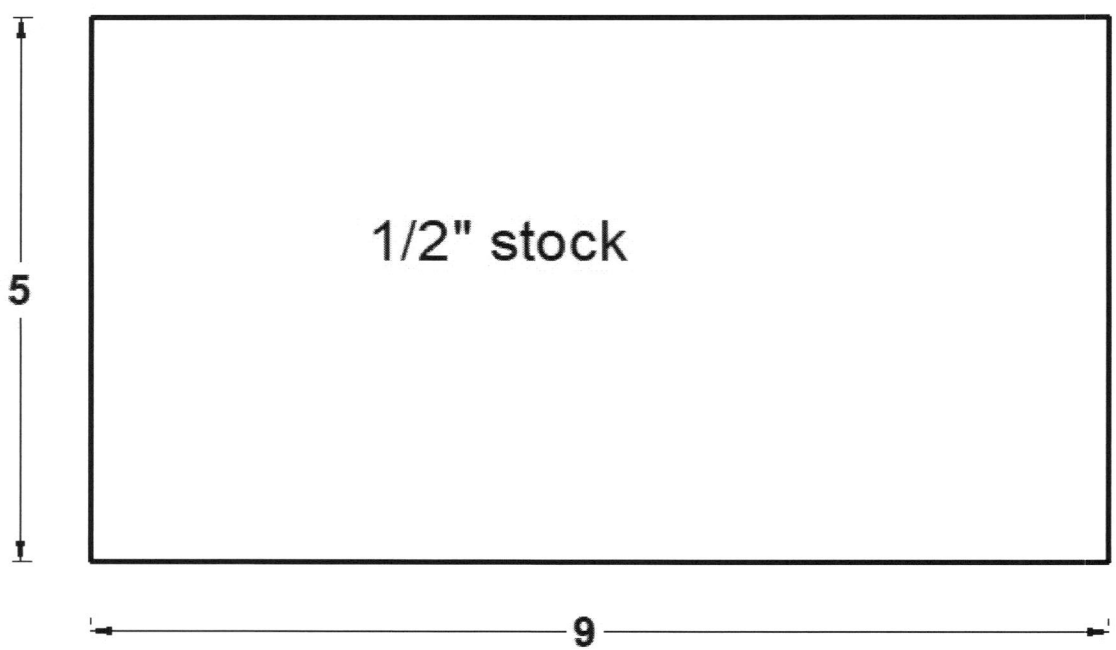

1/2" stock

5

9

Drill the mounting holes and round the corners.

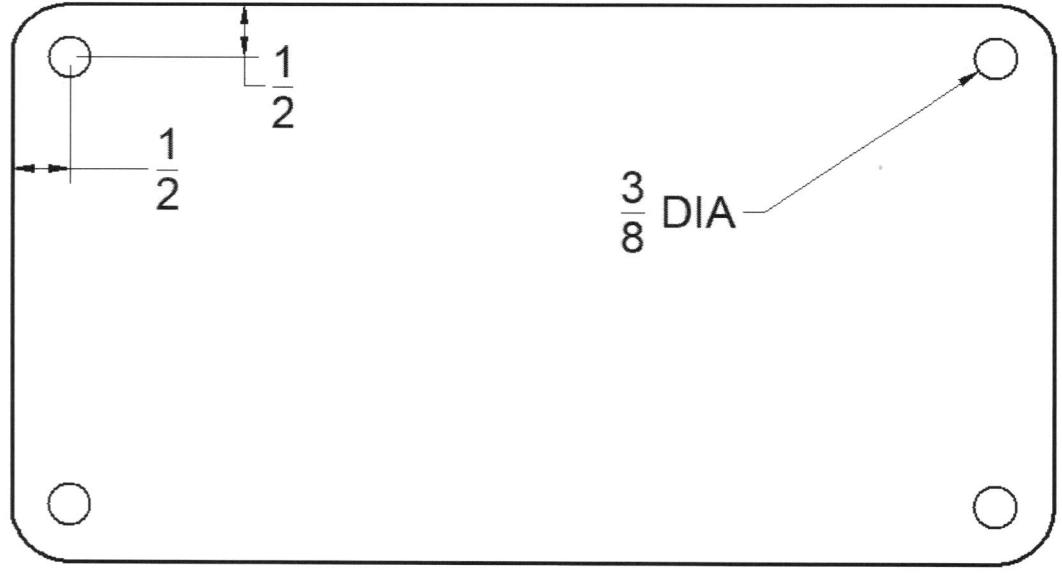

$\frac{1}{2}$

$\frac{1}{2}$

$\frac{3}{8}$ DIA

The bottom frame piece is now complete.

The top frame piece requires a slot for the wheel to ride in.

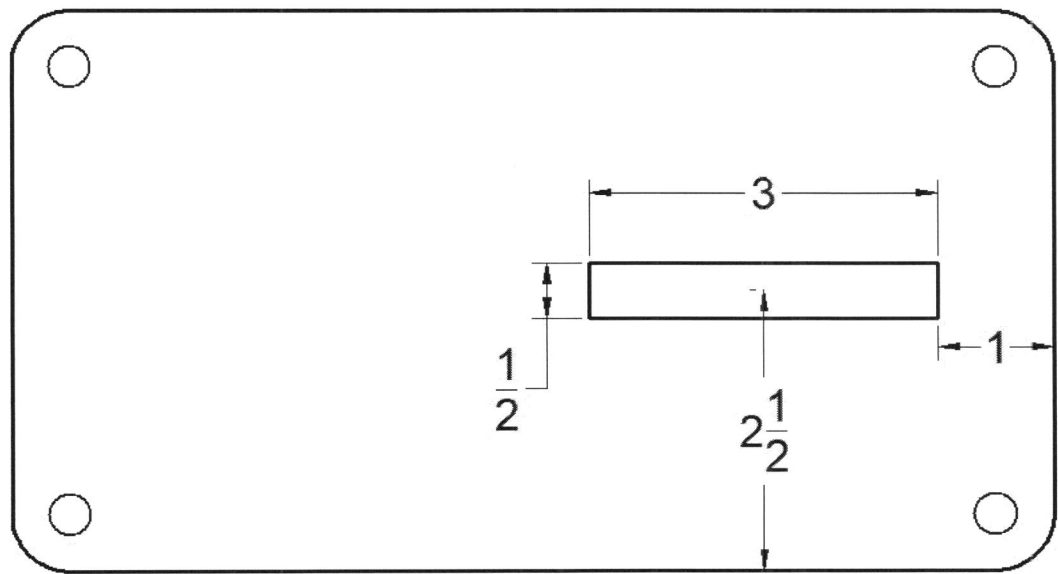

The mounting post are made from 3/8" dowel. Cut four pieces each 4 ½" long. Glue all four corner posts into the top frame piece only. We will be separating the top and bottom frame pieces many times during the assembly.

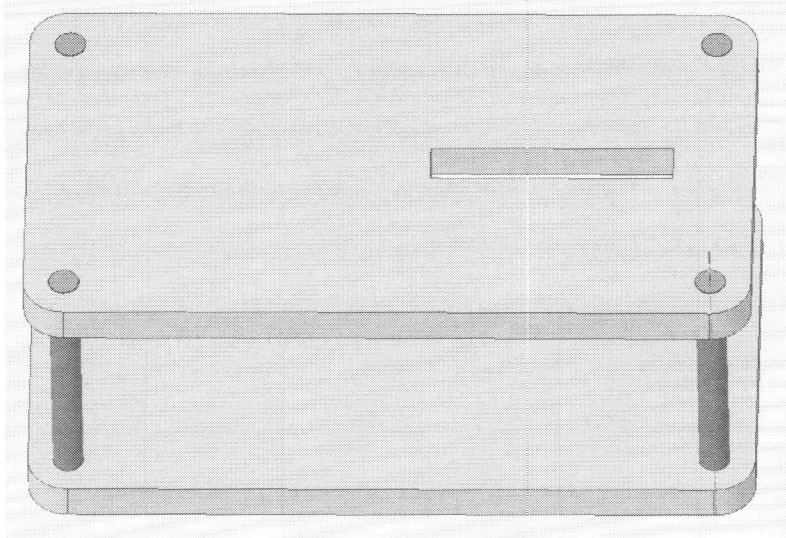

Drive train

The drive train is next.

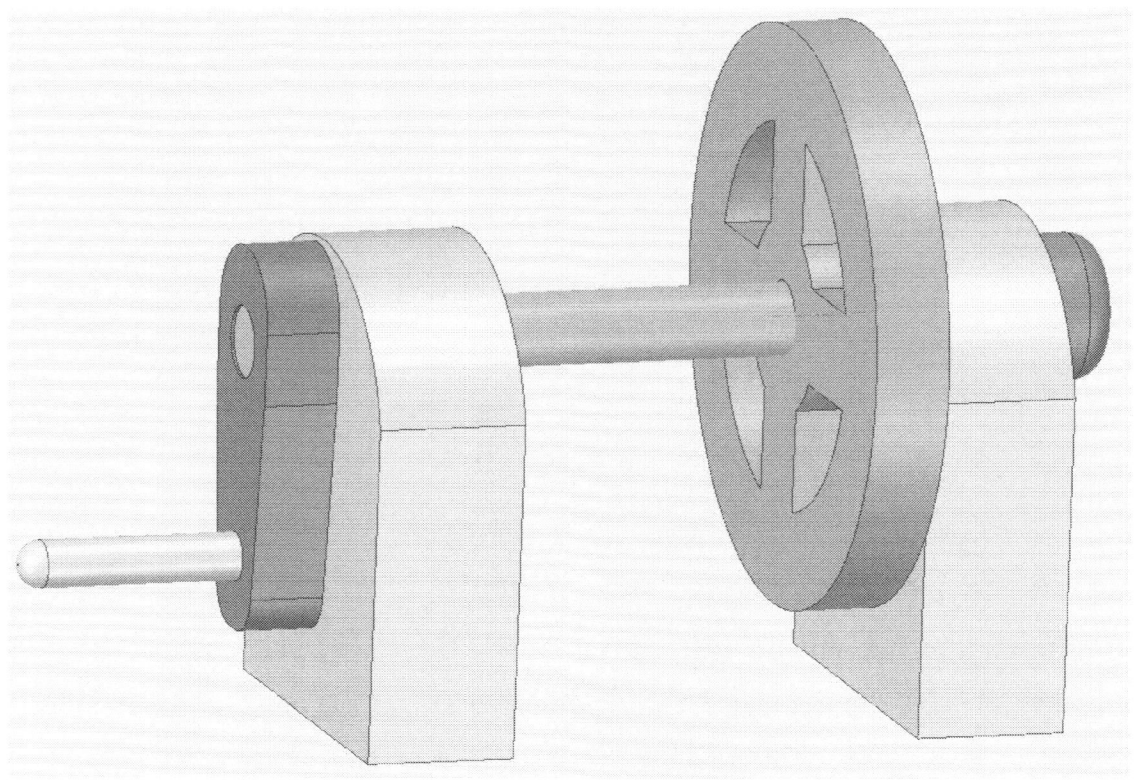

A "Friction wheel" is used to drive the bike wheel. This wheel will rub against the bike wheel above it.

The wheel is made from 3/8" stock.

If you prefer, you can make it a simple 3" diameter wheel with a 3/8" hole in the center.

In my example I added "Spokes" in the center to make it look a bit more professional.

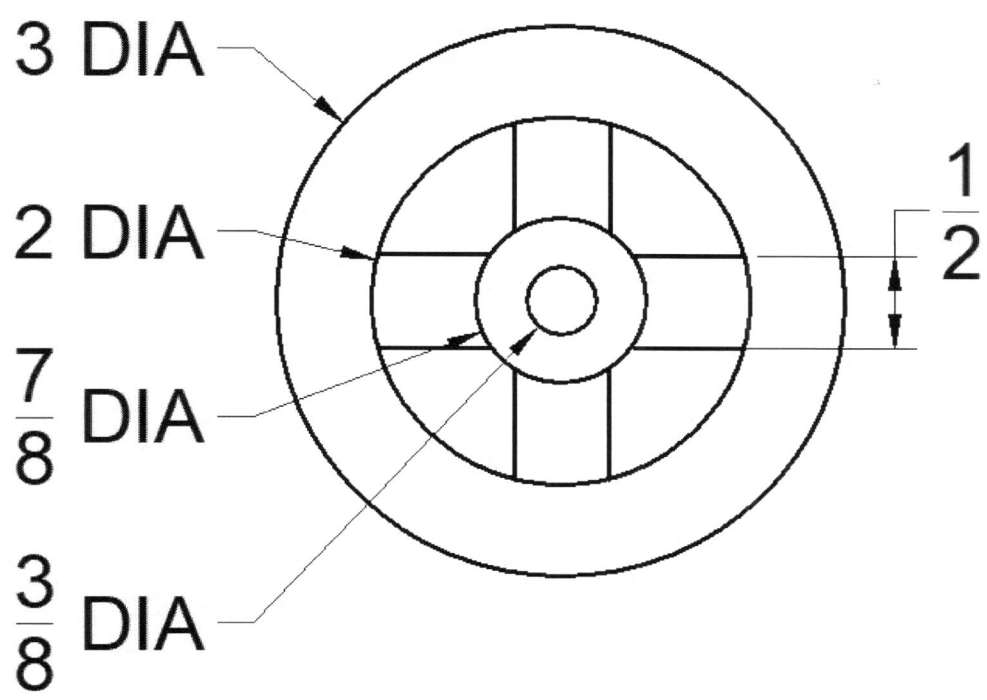

3 DIA

2 DIA

$\frac{7}{8}$ DIA

$\frac{3}{8}$ DIA

$\frac{1}{2}$

Slightly sand all the edges.

The Drive axle is a piece of 3/8" dowel, 4 ¼" long.

The drive train is supported with two supports.

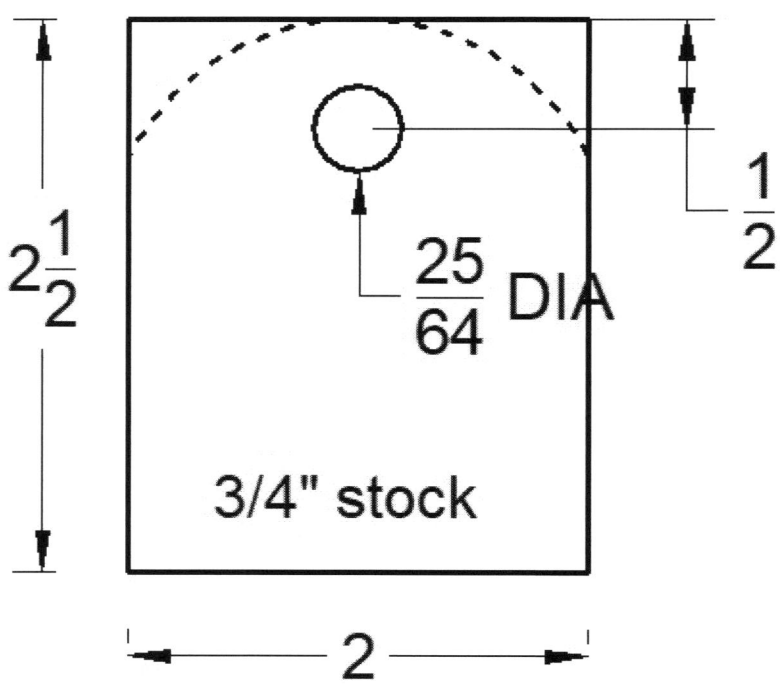

$2\frac{1}{2}$ $\frac{25}{64}$ DIA $\frac{1}{2}$

3/4" stock

2

Round the corners as shown with the dotted lines.

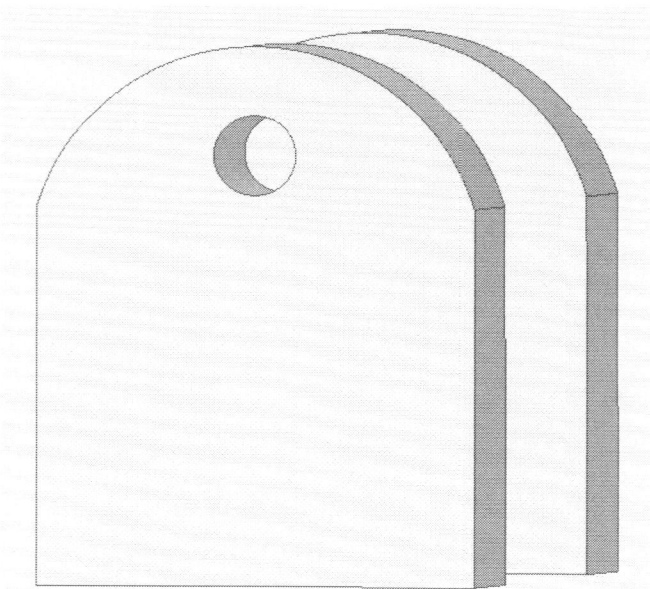

The crank is made from 3/8" stock. The handle is a piece of ¼" dowel.

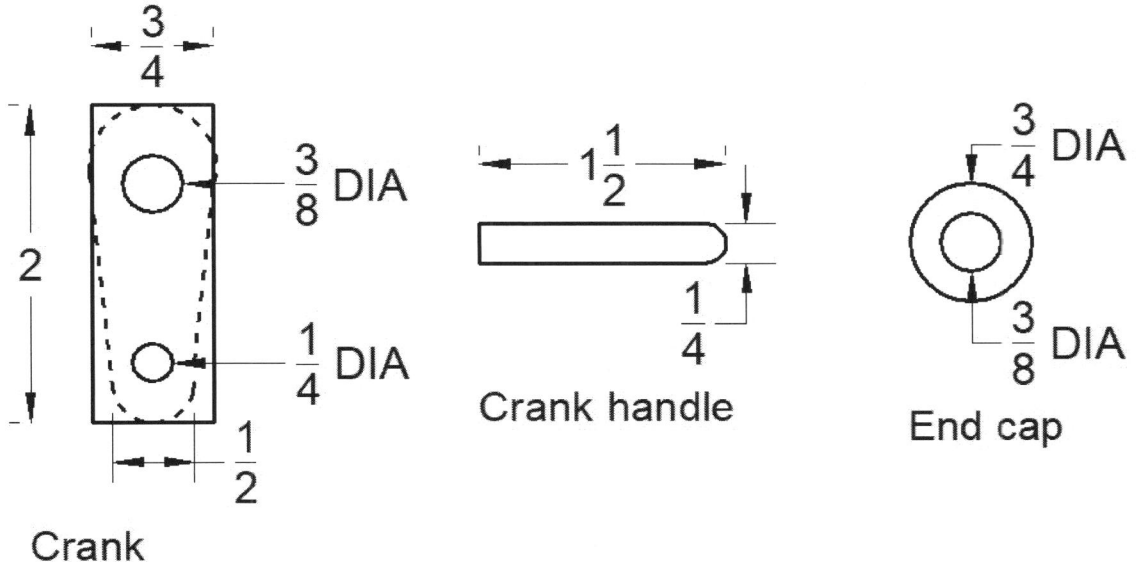

Crank

Crank handle

End cap

The end of the handle should be flush with the crank.

The last piece for the drive train assembly is an end cap to install on the end of the drive axle. The cap is made from ¾" dowel, 1/2" long. Drill a 3/8" hole ~ 3/8" deep in the center. That should complete all of the components for the drive train assembly.

Loosely assemble all the components.

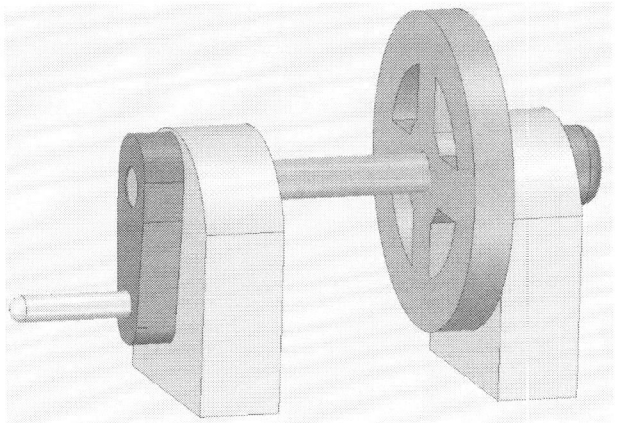

Hold down both drive train supports and turn the crank to make sure the drive axle does not bind.

Set the drive train in place as shown below. Align the friction wheel with the slot in the top frame piece. Center the wheel in the slot. The crank should be beyond the edge of the bottom frame piece.

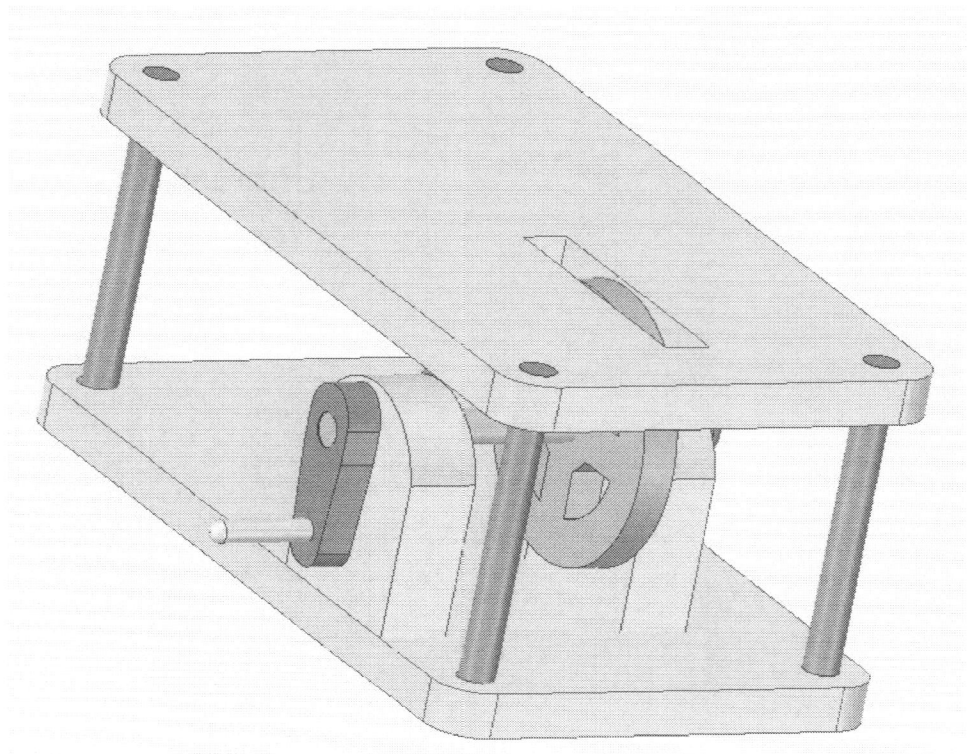

Insert the drive axle. Glue the drive train supports to the bottom frame piece. You can use screws to install the supports if you prefer.

Glue the crank onto the drive axle. Glue the end cap onto the other end of the drive axle.

Turn the crank to make sure the friction wheel turns parallel to the slot in the top frame piece.

This completes the Drive train part of the project.

Bike

The bike assembly begins with the main bike platform.

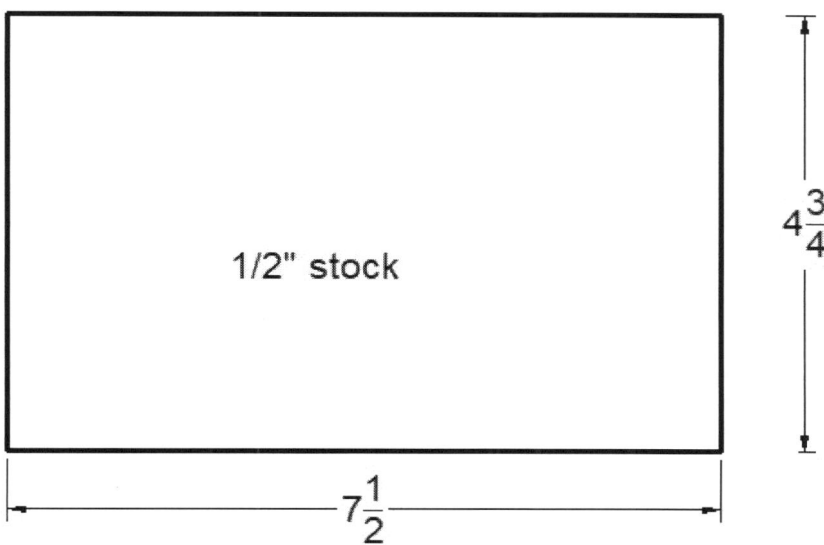

1/2" stock

$4\frac{3}{4}$

$7\frac{1}{2}$

Add the cuts and holes.

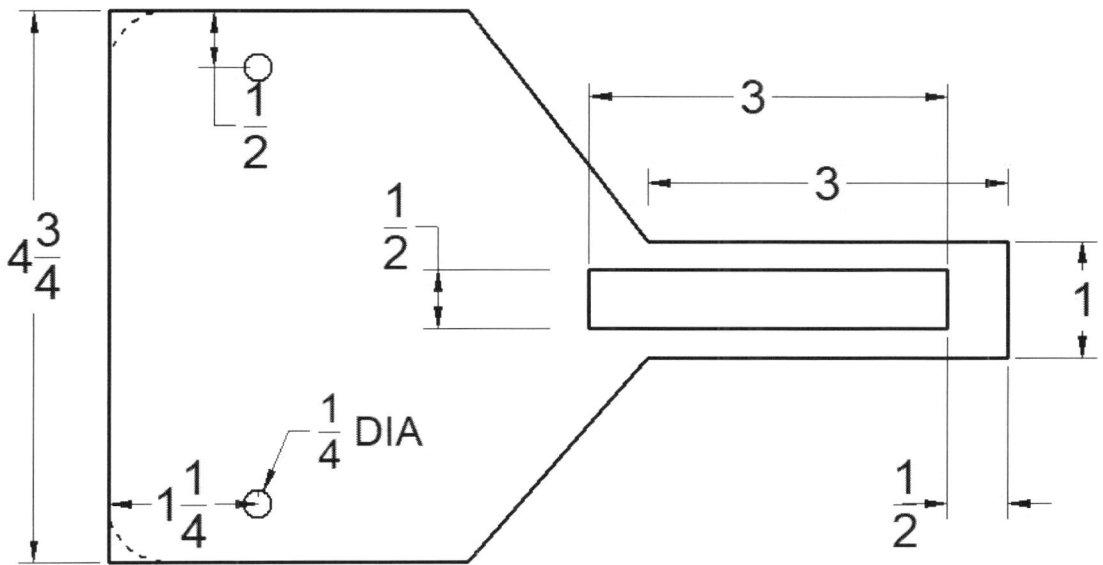

$4\frac{3}{4}$

$\frac{1}{2}$

$\frac{1}{2}$

$\frac{1}{4}$ DIA

$1\frac{1}{4}$

3

3

1

$\frac{1}{2}$

Round off the corners on the main body.

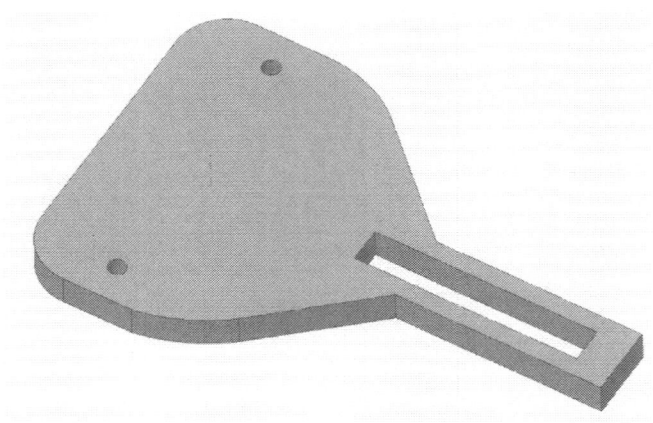

The stands for the wheel are next.

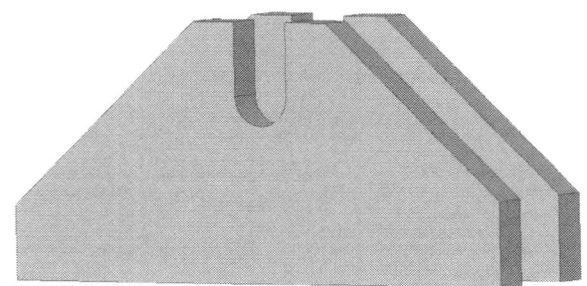

The stands are made from ¼" wood. Start with the basic blocks. Make two of them.

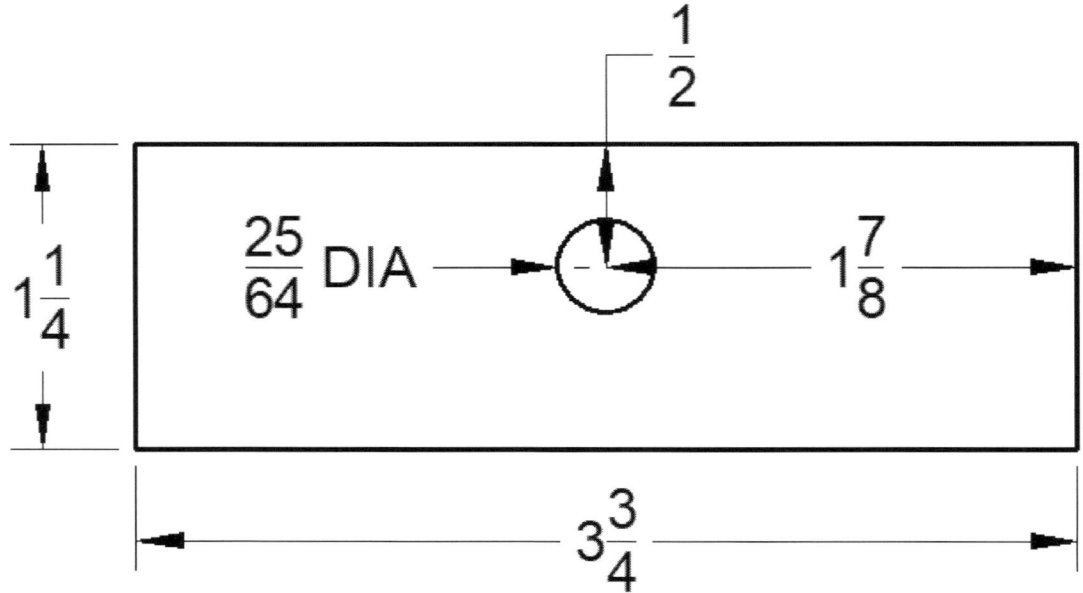

Trim the wheel mounts with the cuts as shown below.
Cut straight up the sides of the hole to form the slot.
Then cut the angle dimensions.

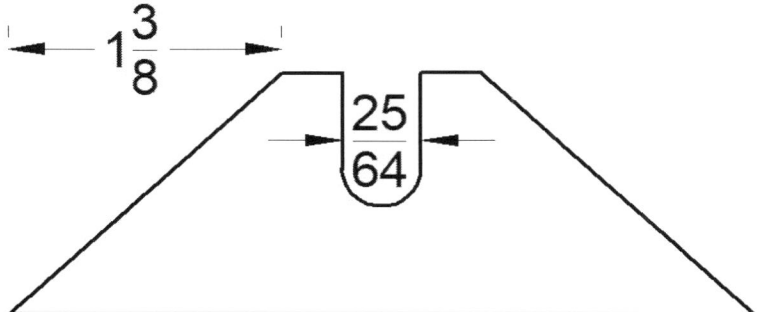

Glue both wheel mounts on to the bike frame. The end of the mounts should be even with the narrow end of the bike frame and the sides flush with the sides of the slot in the bike frame.

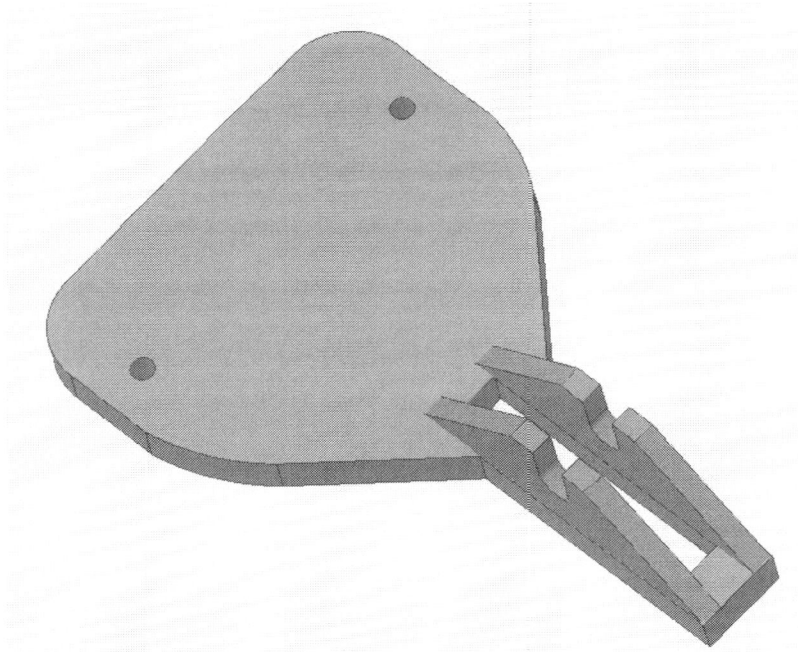

The bike wheel is made from 3/8" stock.

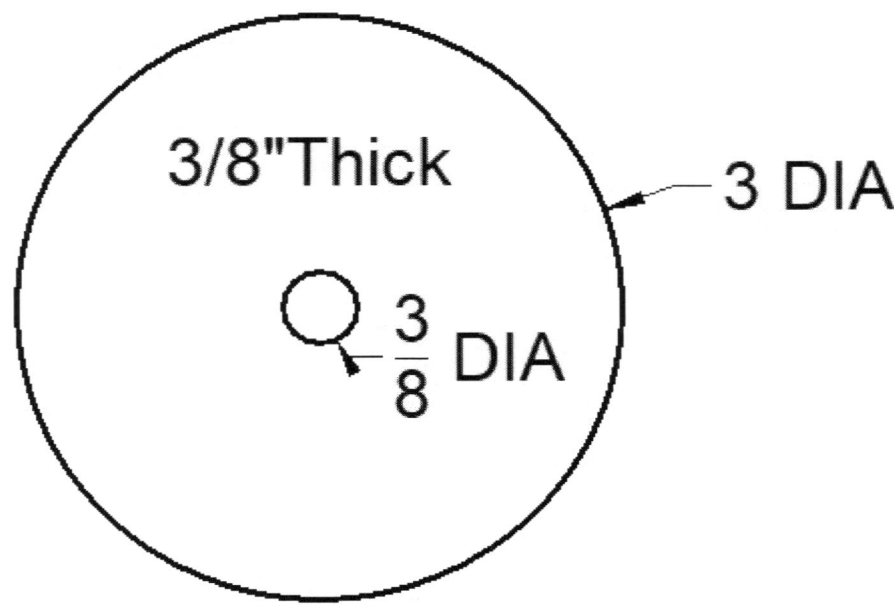

This wheel does not require any cosmetic "spokes" because the exercise bike wheels are usually solid to help provide centrifugal force.

The drive wheel axle is a piece of 3/8" dowel, 1 ½" long. Make the axle a little longer than 1 ½" so you can trim it back to the exact size needed when the other parts are added. Center the bike wheel on the axle and glue it in place.

Set the bike wheel in the wheel mounts. Spin the wheel. Check to make sure it does not touch the sides or the ends of the bike frame and spins easily.

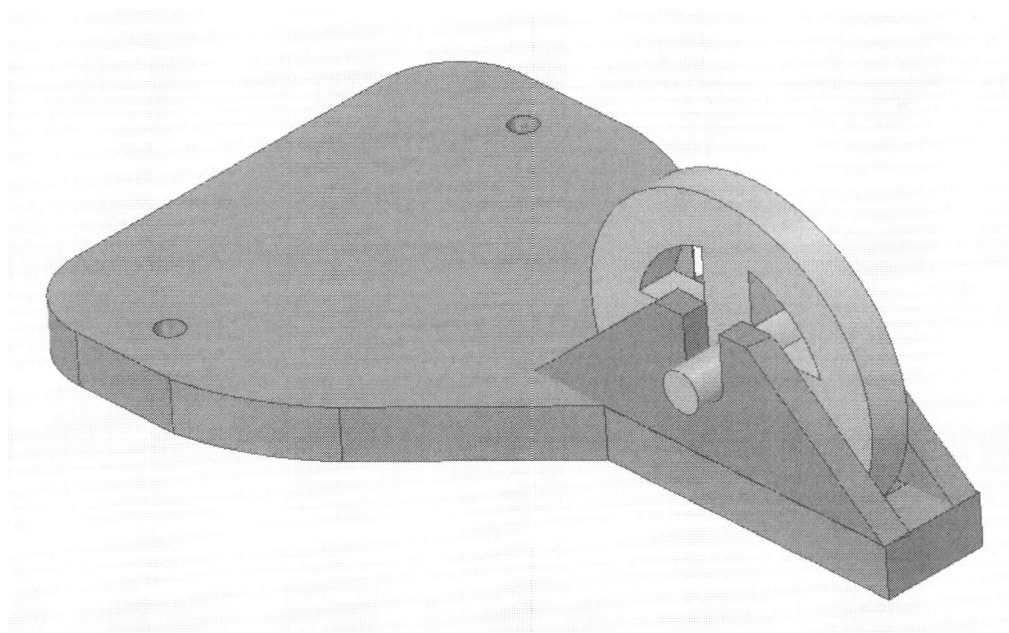

Set the bike frame on top of the main frame. Line up the wheels. Because the drive wheel "floats" in the bike wheel mounts, the drive wheel should be resting on the friction wheel underneath it. Turn the crank to make sure both wheels turn easily.

Do not glue the bike frame to the main frame yet.

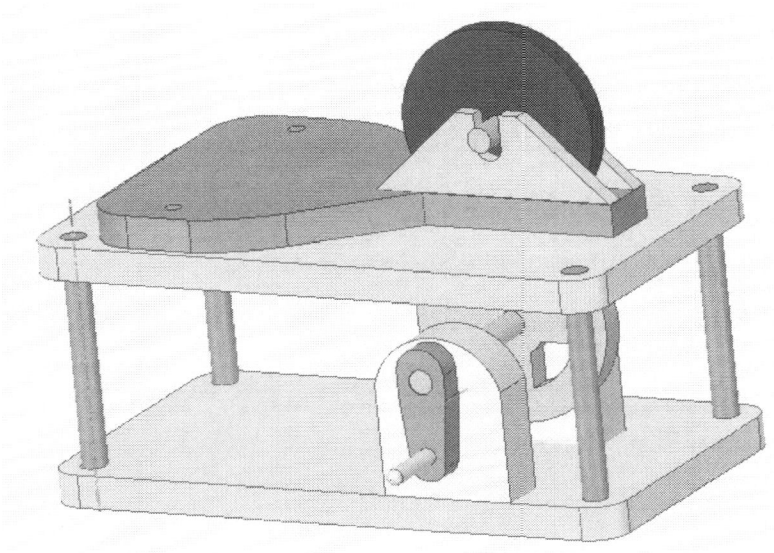

The pedal attachments are next. These pieces will be made from ¼" stock.

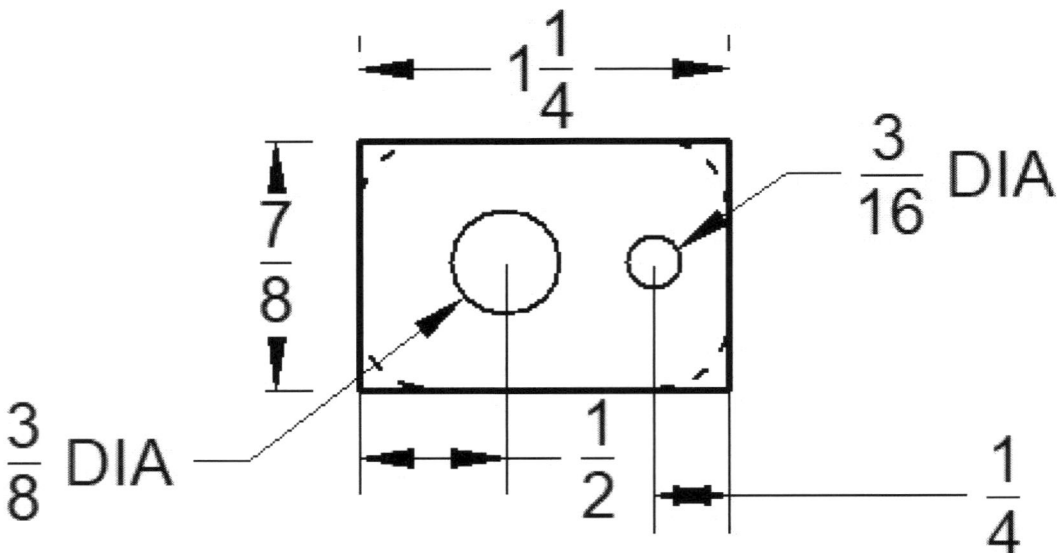

Round off the corners. Glue a ¾" piece of 3/16" dowel into the 3/16" hole, flush to one side.

Glue the pedal attachments onto the bike wheel axle. Slide the pedal attachments as close to the wheel mounts as you can get and still allow the wheel to spin without rubbing.

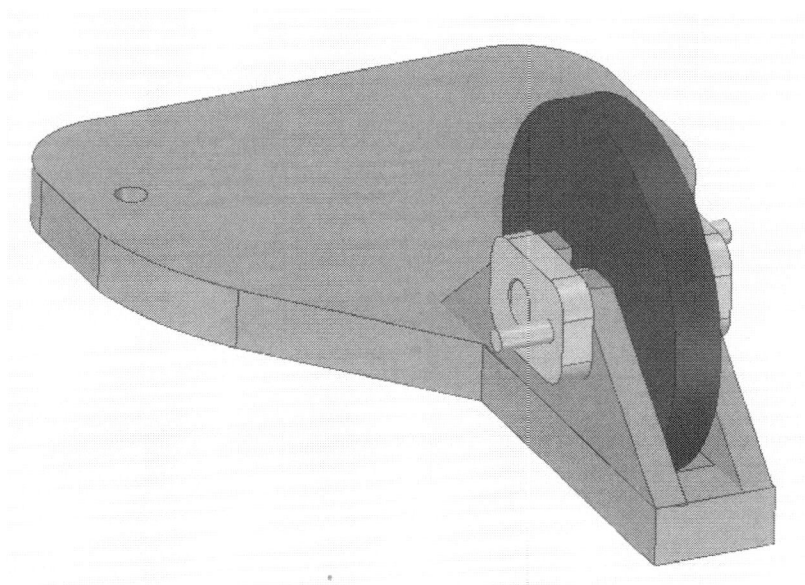

We need to make a small cap to hold the pedal on to the pedal attachment. The cap is a 3/8" long piece of 3/8" dowel. Drill a 3/16" hole on one end, ¼" deep. Round off the other end.

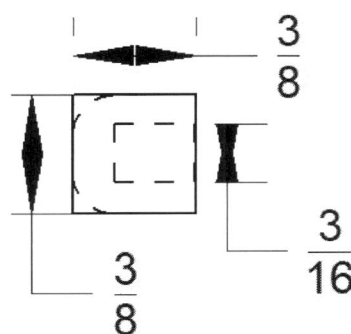

Temporarily install the caps.

Your bike frame should look like this at this point.

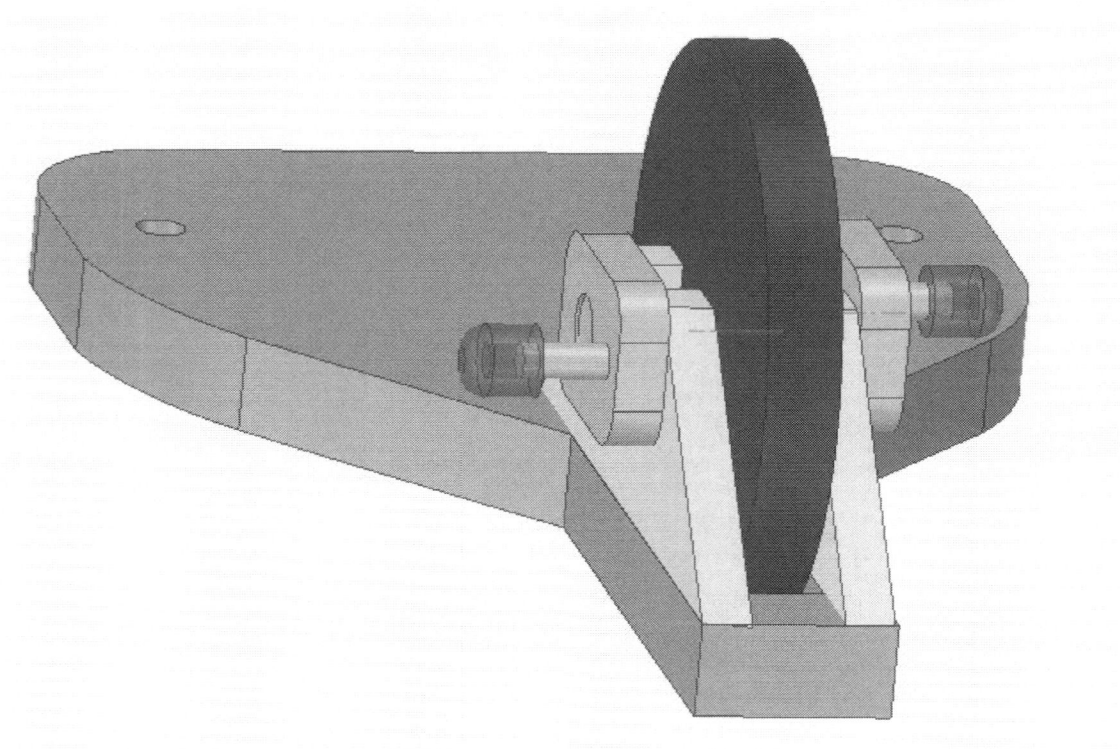

The bike seat is made in two parts.

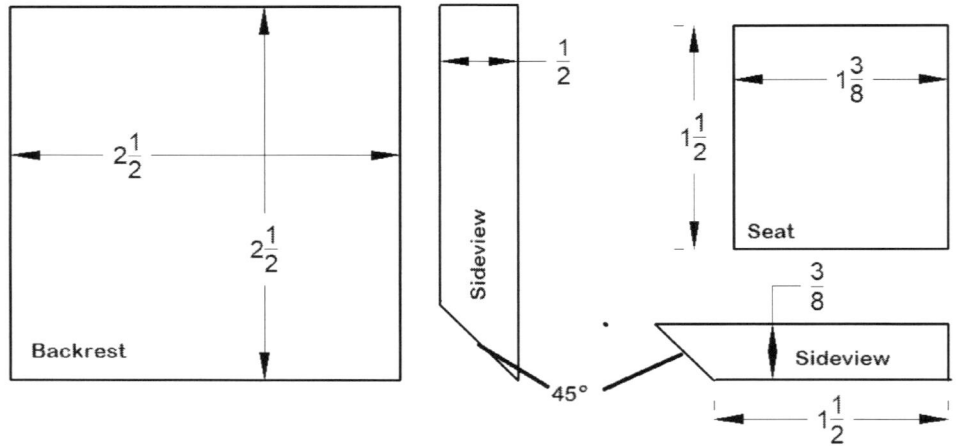

Glue the seat bottom to the center of the bottom of the backrest.

90

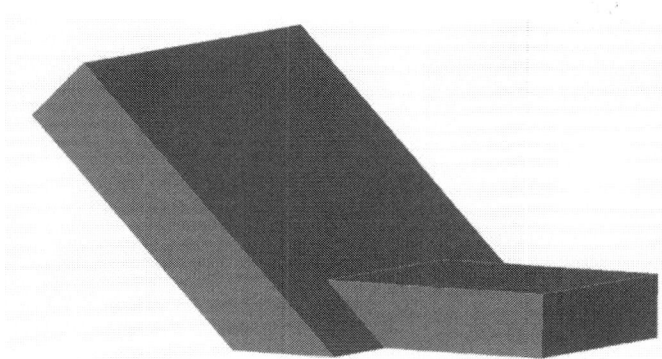

The seat post is made from ¾" dowel.

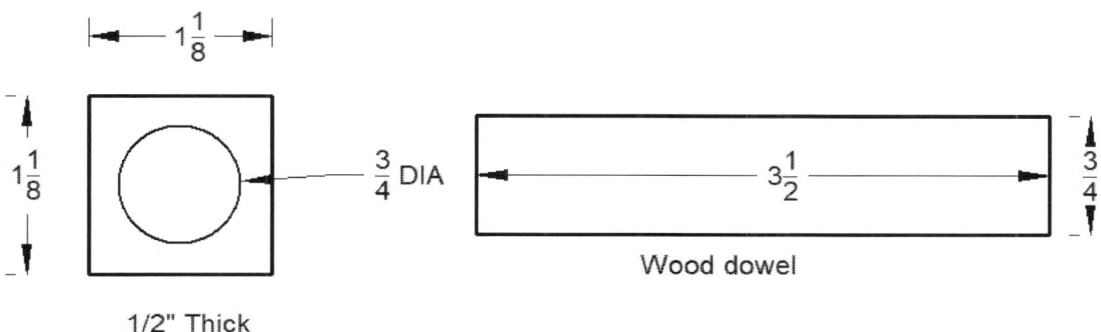

$1\frac{1}{8}$

$1\frac{1}{8}$

$\frac{3}{4}$ DIA

$3\frac{1}{2}$

$\frac{3}{4}$

Wood dowel

1/2" Thick

The post is glued flush into a small frame. The frame and post then are glued to the bottom of the seat. Locate the post near the center of the bottom of the seat.

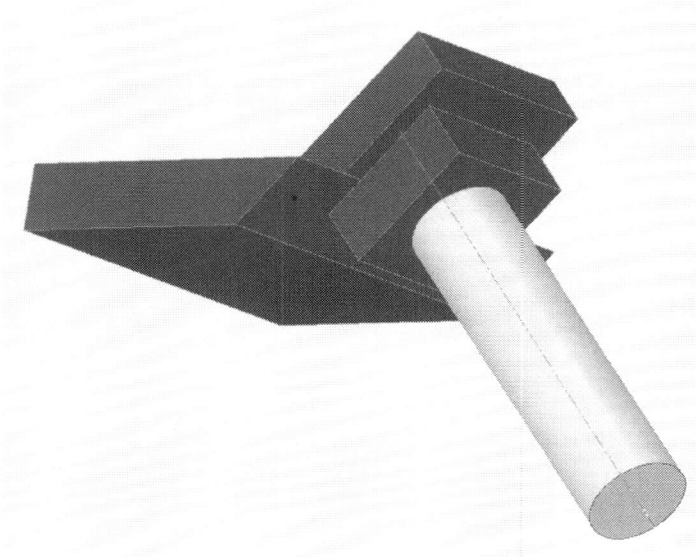

The seat will be attached to the bike frame after the action figure body is complete.

The bike handrails are the last part of the bike frame. The corner connectors are ¾" cubes and you will need 2 of them. Drill ¼" holes, 3/8" deep, on 3 sides as shown. Round all the edges. The uprights and rails will be added later.

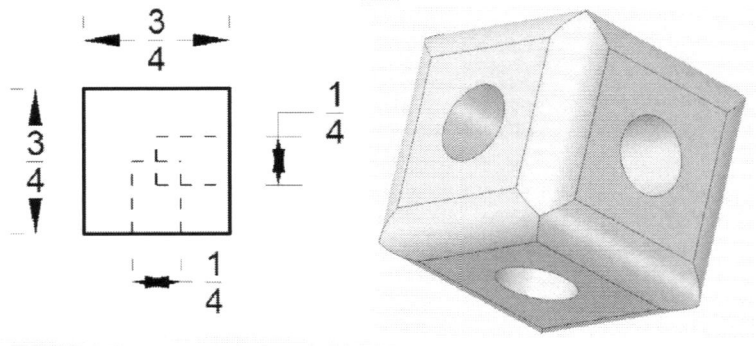

Action figure

The body is the last section for this project. We'll start with the chest.

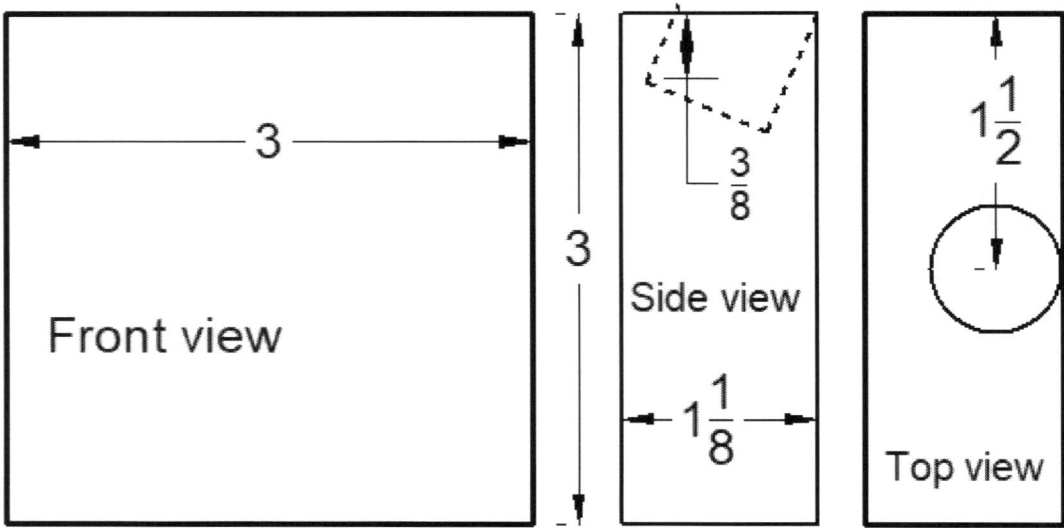

Cut a 3" x 3" piece of 2 x 4. Trim it down to 1 1/8" thick. Drill a ¾" hole for the neck at a 22.5°angle as shown. The depth of the hole should be about 3/8" on the short side.

Make the trim cuts as shown. Round the bottom.

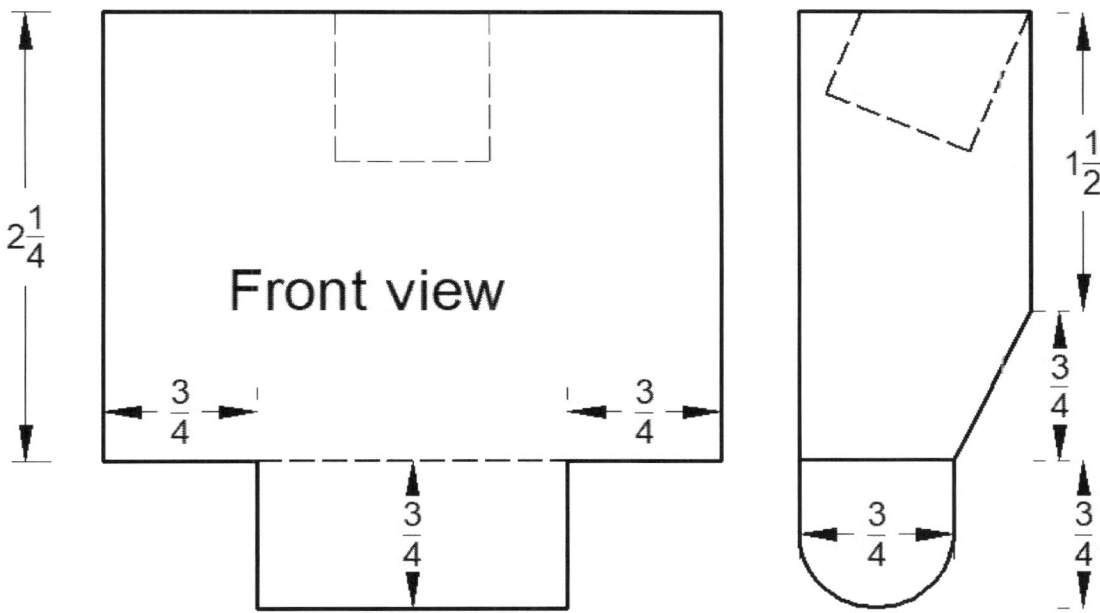

The head is the same one that is used on all the other actions figures as found on page 177. There is one exception however. The hole for the neck must be drilled at a 22.5°angle. The back rest for the bike seat sits at a 45°angle. The chest has a 22.5° hole for the neck. With a 22.5°angle for the neck on the head, the head should end up pointing straight to the front.

Cut a piece of ¾″ dowel for the neck. The length will depend on how deep you drilled the holes in the chest and the head. You should have about 3/8″ of exposed

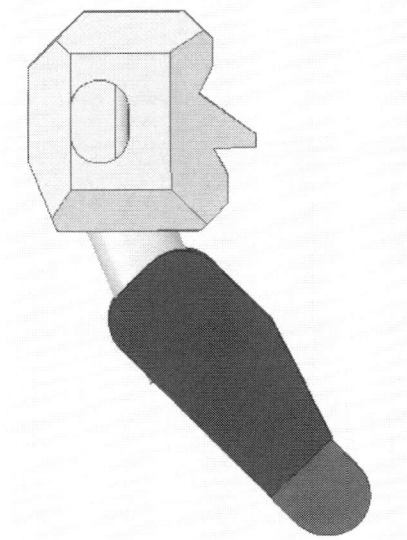

neck.

Now we'll move on to the arms. The arms are made from ¾″ wood. Both arms are identical so make two of them.

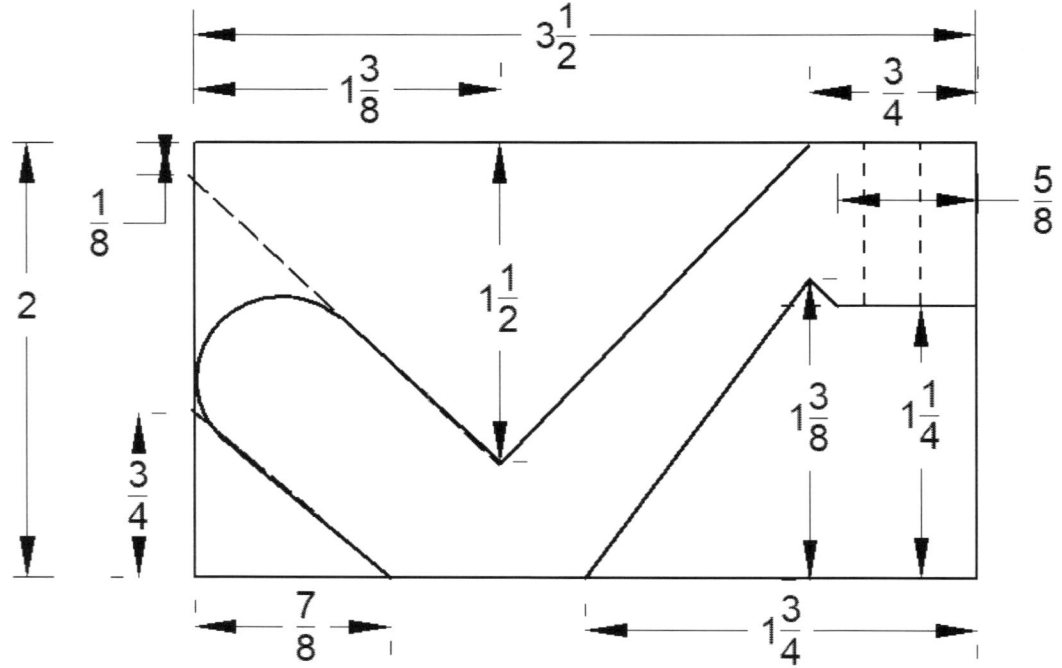

Drill a 9/32" hole, centered, through the hands indicated with the dotted lines.

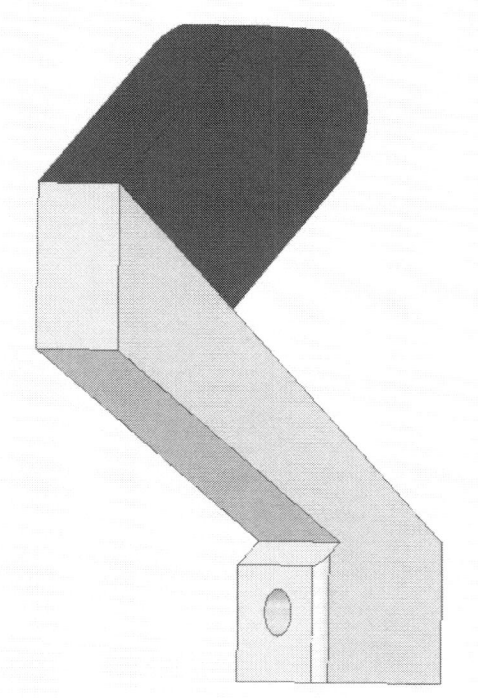

The arms will be attached after the hand rails are installed.

The image below shows the completed leg.

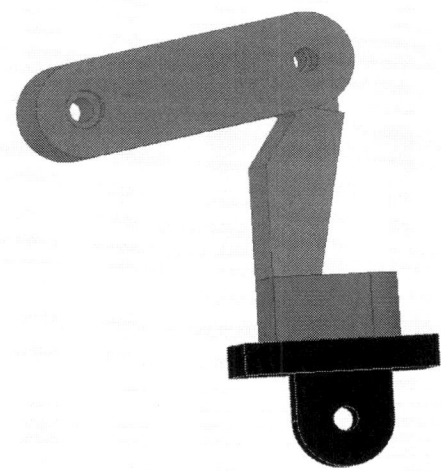

We'll make the upper leg (Thigh) first. Use ¾" wood.

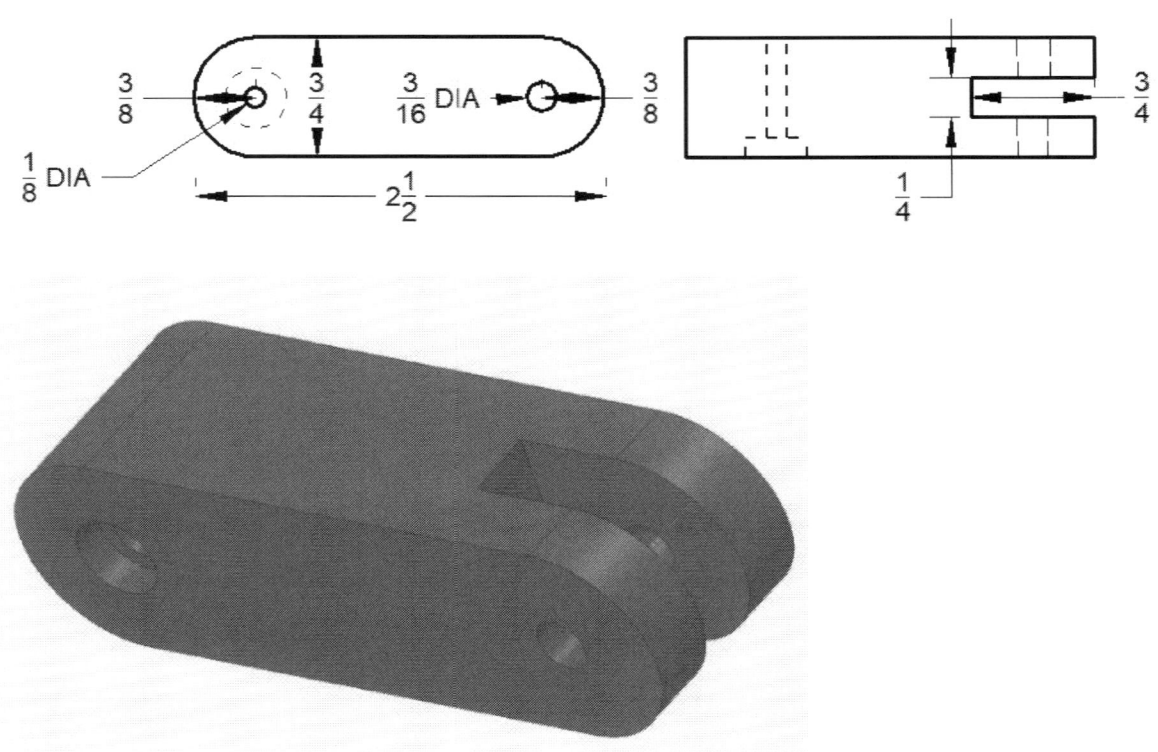

The lower leg requires a few more cuts.

Start with a basic block from ¾" wood.

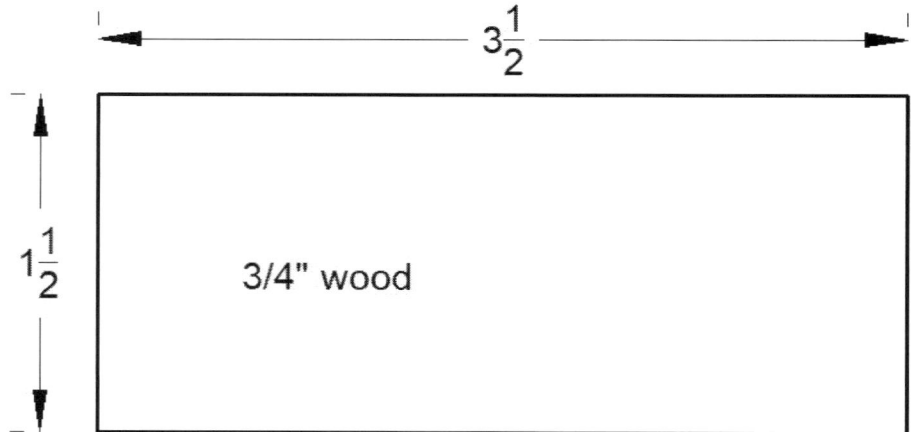

Make all the trim cuts. You may want to take look at the lower leg image below to better understand the cuts.

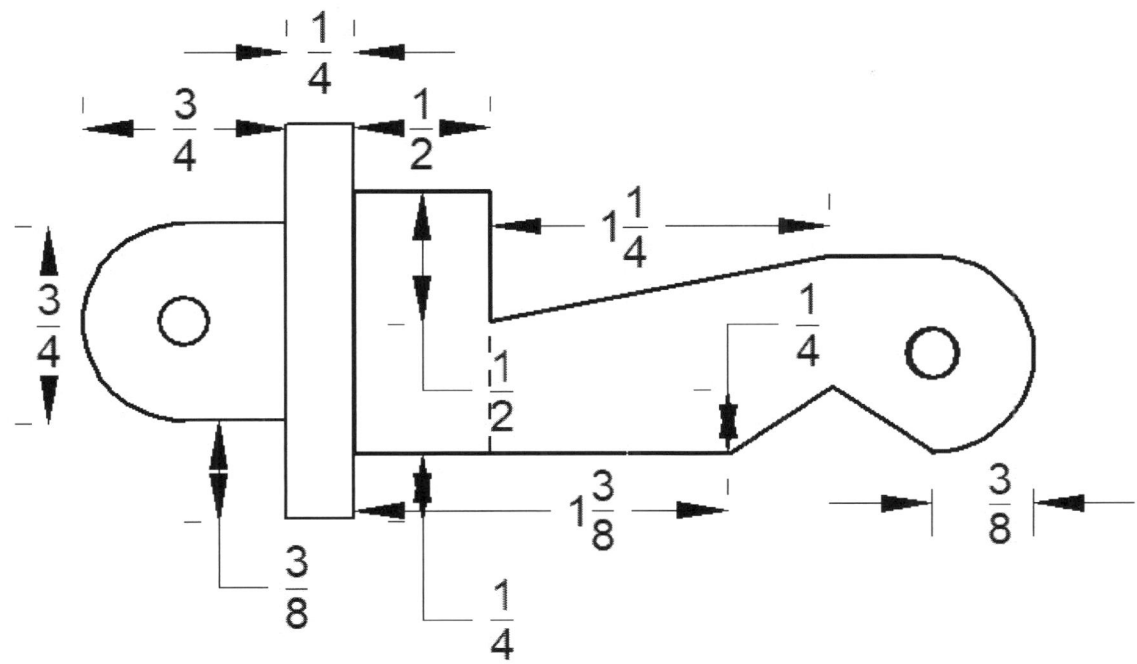

Make the final cuts using the top view.

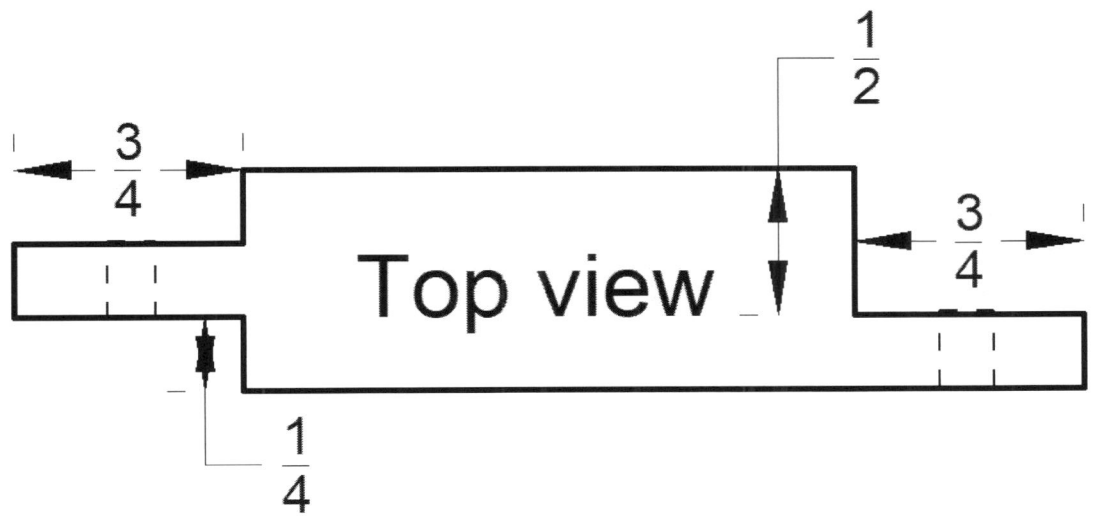

Round off the tip of the shoe.

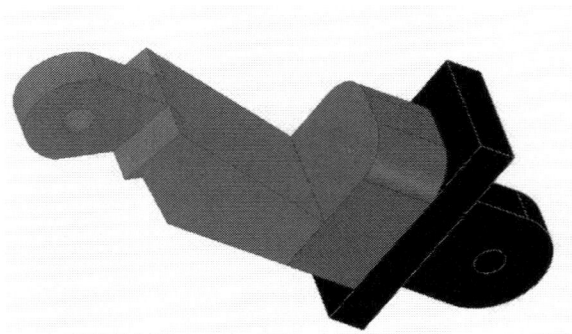

We now have just about everything we need to complete the assembly. If you prefer to paint any of the parts, now would be the time to do it. Sand all the edges.

Attach the upper and lower legs with a scrap piece of 3/16" dowel. Pay special attention to which side the leg will fit on. The countersunk hole on the upper leg has to be on the opposite side of the pedal attachment below the shoe.

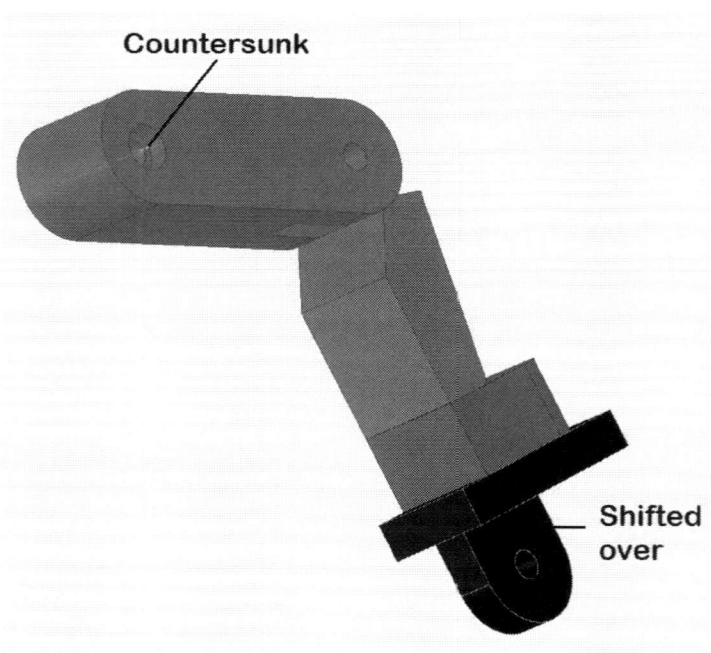

Countersunk

Shifted over

Attach both leg assemblies to the chest. The top part of the upper leg should be at least 1/16" from the body.

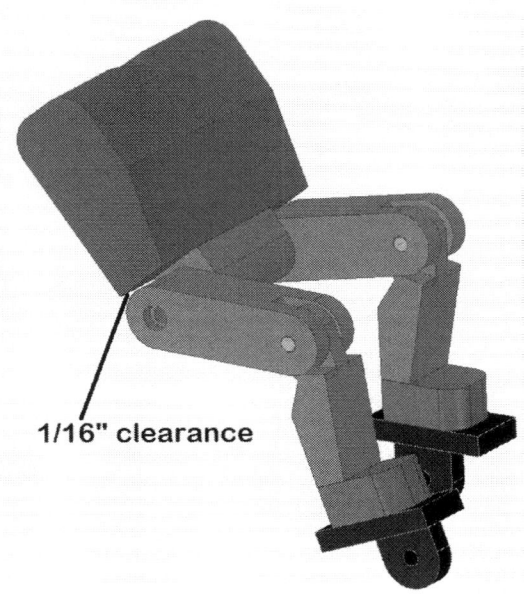

1/16" clearance

I used 8-32 x 1" panhead screws to attach the legs to the chest. Leave them loose enough so both legs move easily.

Attach the wheel to the pedal attachments on the bottom of both shoes. Temporarily attach the pedal attachment caps.

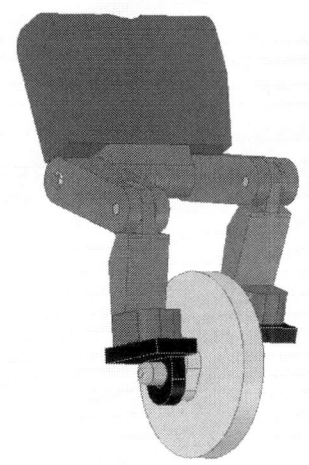

Set the chest onto the seat. The bottom of the chest should be touching the seat part and the back of the chest should be flat against the seat back rest. The bottom of the seat should be centered between the legs. You may have to shave off a little of the sides of the seat if the legs rub on the seat.

Glue the chest to the seat.

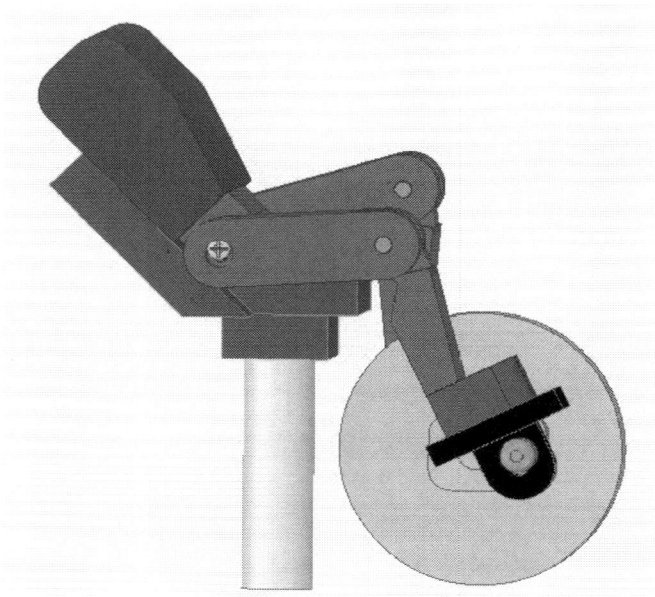

Now we will get our first view of the normal operation of this project.

While holding the body assembly, set the wheel into the wheel supports. Center the seat post in the middle of the bike frame. While turning the crank handle, move the seat post to move the body to find the position where the legs move easily with the rotation of the wheel. After you find the best position, mark the location of the seat post and remove the body assembly.

Using the mark you just made, drill a ¾" hole in the bike frame. Install the seat post in the ¾" hole just made. Don't glue it into position until you find a need to. You may have to remove the assembly to make corrections or changes.

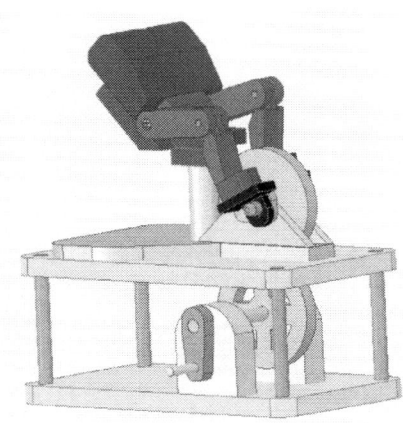

Turn the crank again to make sure the legs move easily.

Now that everything is in position, glue the bike frame to the main frame.

Glue the head and neck in place.

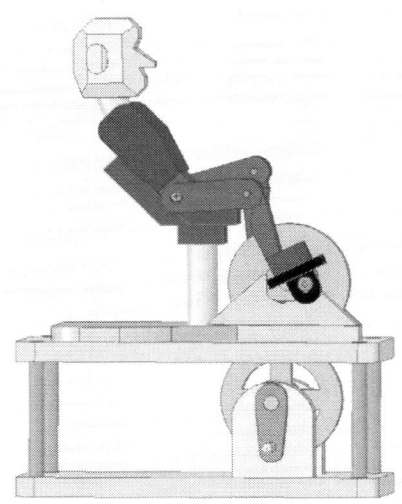

We need to assemble the handle bars before we can install the biker arms.

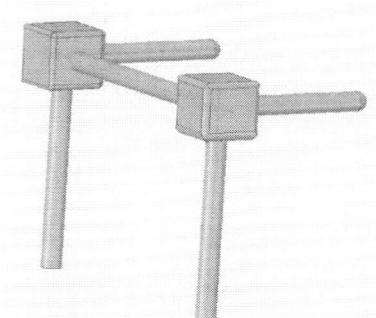

Cut a 3 ¾" piece of ¼" dowel for the cross piece across the back. Insert and glue the dowel 3/8" into a connector on each end (page 92). Orient the other two connector holes to face forward and down.

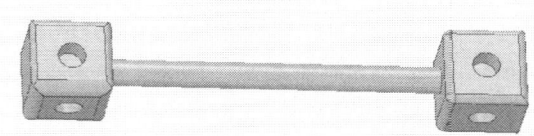

Cut two more pieces of ¼" dowel, each 1 ¾" long. These will be the actual handrails. Round off one end on each of them. Insert the handrails into the connectors (~1/4"). Do not glue than handrails yet.

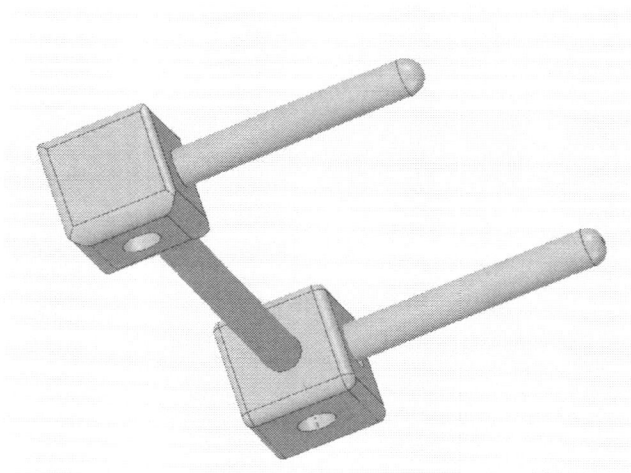

Hold or clamp both arms in place. They should be level with the top of the chest and slightly back from the front of the chest. Insert the hand rails through the hands. Reposition the arms as needed to get the hand rails parallel with the bike frame. Glue the arms in place.

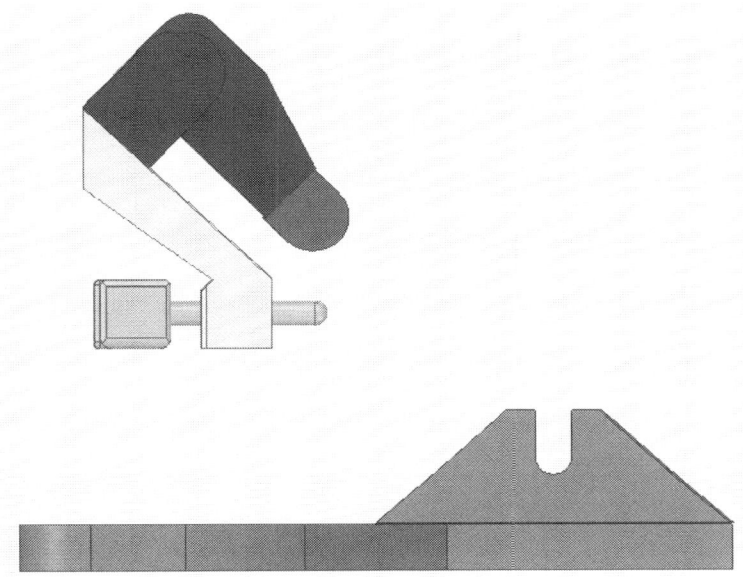

The last piece for this project is the hand rail upright posts. Measure the distance between the bottom of the connector and top of the bike frame. Add ½" for the bike frame and ½" for the insertion in the connector. Cut pieces of 3/16" dowel to length. Glue them into the base flush with the bottom and into the connector (~1/4").

Insert the hand rails through the hands into the connectors. Do not glue them if you don't have to. That will allow disassembly if needed.

This Bike project is complete!

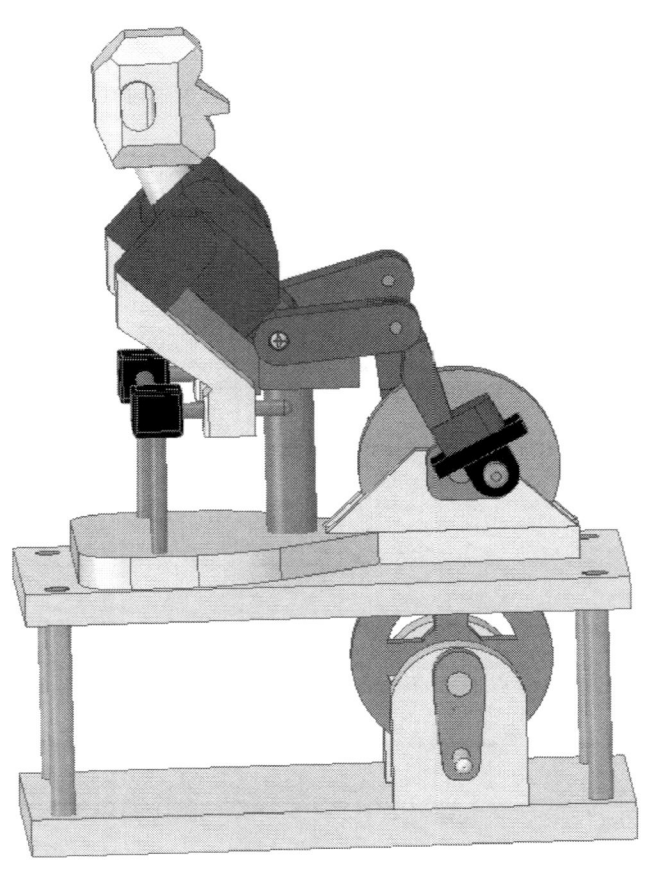

Treadmill

This project is an action figure walking on a treadmill. The action is provided with a two-journal crankshaft, very similar to a crankshaft found in automotive engines.

There are four major parts to the treadmill figure.

1 The main frame

2. The drive train

3. Treadmill

4. Action figure.

Main Frame
We'll start with the frame.

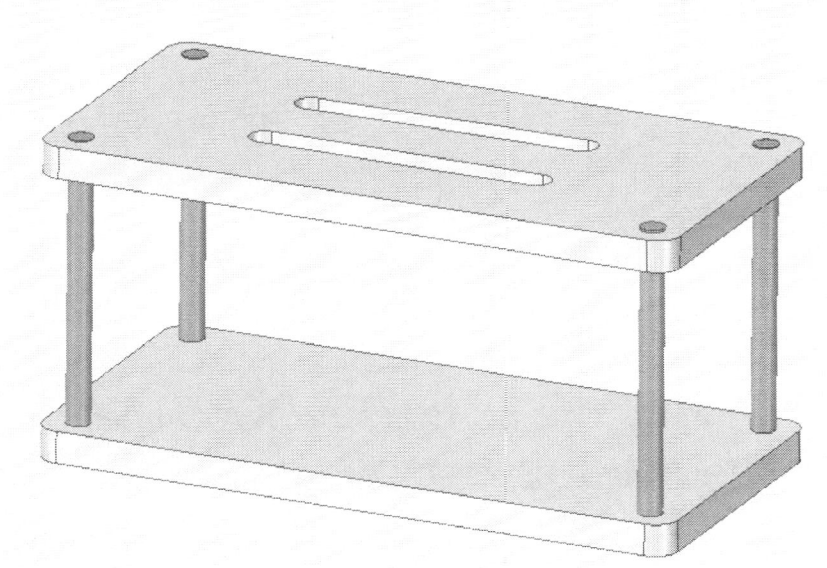

The top and bottom frame pieces are the same size.

Round the corners and slightly sand the edges.

The top frame requires two slots.

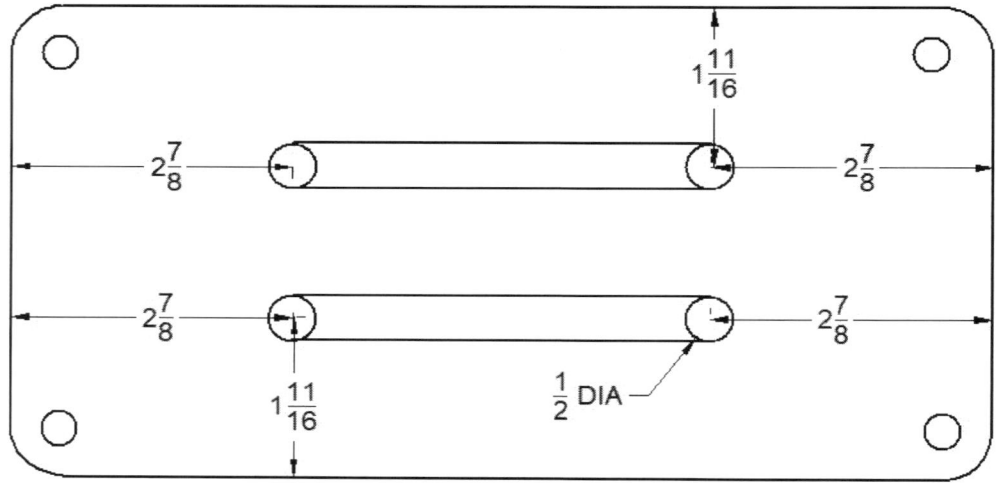

Drill ½" holes on each end of the slots as shown. Then draw lines to connect the holes on both sides. Cut out the space between the holes.

Cut four pieces of 3/8" dowel, each 5" long for the corner posts. Glue the dowel pieces into the top frame piece only. Temporarily mount the top frame onto the bottom frame piece to make sure everything fits ok.

Drive train

Now we can move on to the drive train.

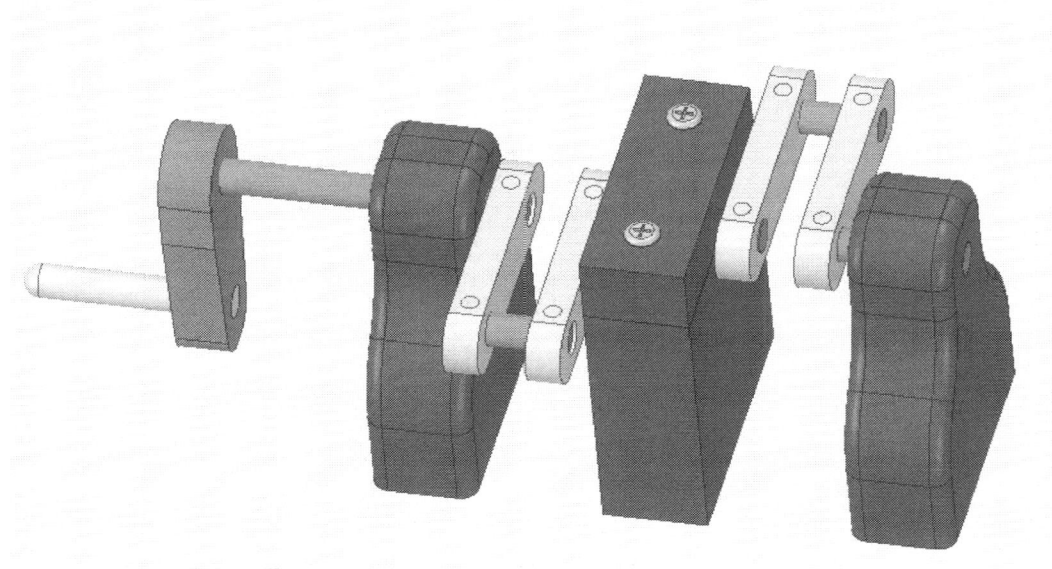

We'll start with the crankshaft.

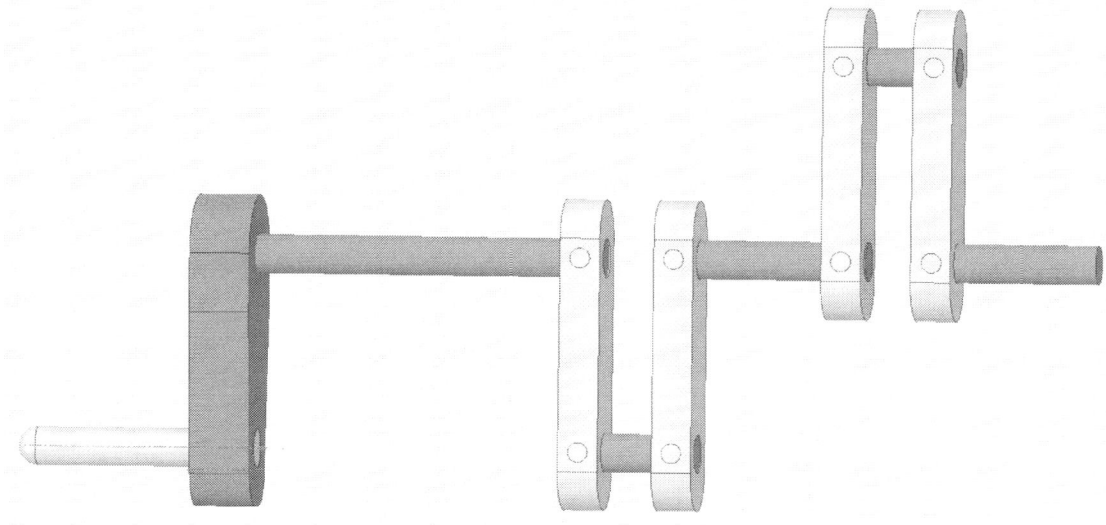

The crankshaft is not difficult to make but does require careful assembly. The goal is to keep the main shaft in perfect alignment. Perfect alignment requires careful alignment of the "Journals".

"Journal" – *The part of the crankshaft which transmits the torque*

We'll make the journals first and then insert the shaft to complete the crankshaft.

The journal sides are made from ¼" stock. The trick to making a crankshaft journal is to make both sides identical as possible. That is not too difficult when working with metal but wood offers a bit more of a challenge. An easy solution is to make both sides at the same time.

The dimensions for the basic journal sides are shown in the print below.

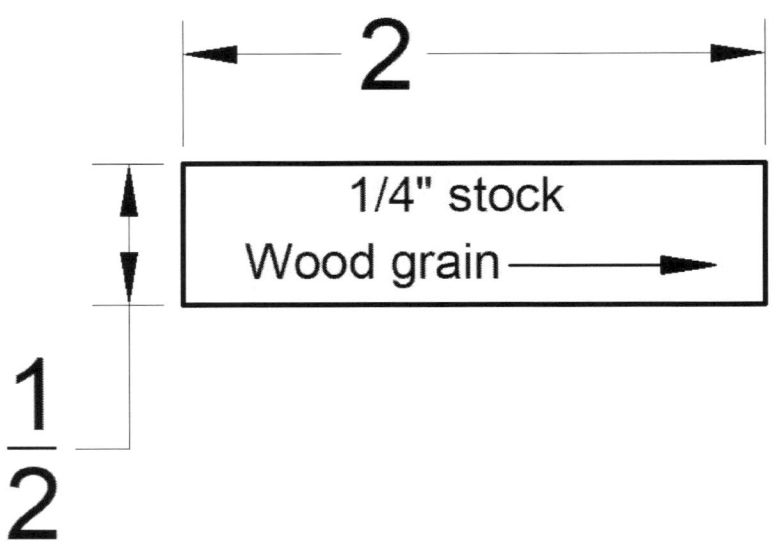

The journal sides are made from ¼" stock. I suggest using good quality wood here such as oak, maple, walnut, etc. It's good for cosmetics and will help prevent splitting when inserting the wood dowel.

Also make note of the grain on this part. The holes will be relatively close to the ends and may break off when you insert the shaft if the grain is sideways.

There are two journals so we need to make four sides. Do not sand the edges until we pair them up.

Each journal side will have two ¼" holes. Do NOT drill the holes yet!

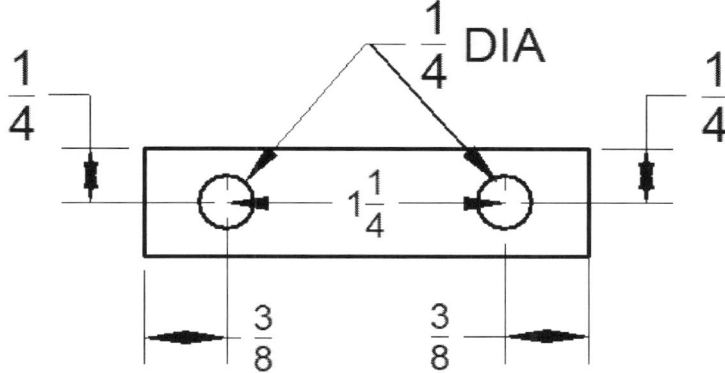

A little later we will round off the ends. Using a piece of ½" dowel for a guide, draw in the rounded ends.

Important! When drilling the holes, make sure the drill is exactly perpendicular (standing at right angle to the surface or 90°to the surface). Even if you use a drill press, a small sliver of wood under the journal will cause the drill to be slightly off from 90°.

Drilling a hole in wood at a precise point is very difficult. The most important dimension is the 1 ¼" between the holes. The distance between them is not as critical as making sure the distance between the holes on both sides is identical.

To make sure each distance between the holes is exactly the same on both sides of the pair, we can drill the holes in both pieces at the same time.

Mark the holes on all four journal sides. Drill the ¼" hole on one end only on all four pieces. Then stack two sides on top of each other. Insert a scrap ¼" dowel rod through the hole on one end through both pieces.

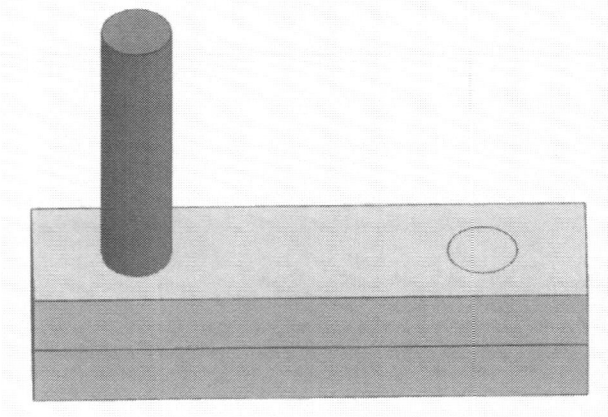

Clamp the two pieces and drill the other hole through both pieces. Do the same for the other journal pair.

Insert another scrap ¼" dowel rod into both pieces in the holes just drilled.

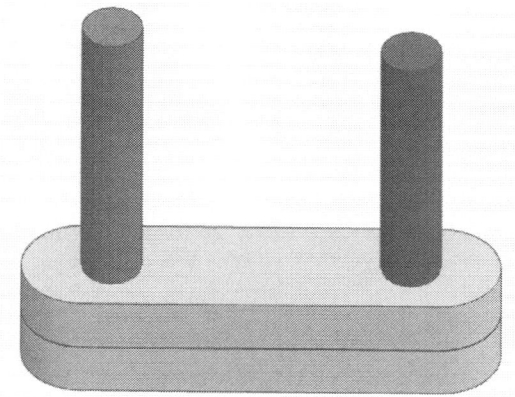

With both sides "pinned" together, round off both ends of the journal. Sand the sides to remove any saw marks and to insure both journal sides are the same size. You will find life more pleasant if you mark both sides of each pair with a small piece of masking tape to make sure the pair is assembled the same way they were sanded.

Now we are ready to assemble the crankshaft.

Locally here wood dowels are available either in Oak or Poplar. There is a significant difference between them.

Oak dowel:

1. Slightly bigger in diameter than Poplar

2. Will not change size with repeated use. That means if you insert the dowel in to a tight fit the wood will not compress.

3. More expensive

Poplar:

1. Slightly smaller in diameter than Oak

2. Will compress when inserted into a tight fit. That means it will be easier to remove if needed and it will be easier to insert the next time.

3. Less expensive than Oak

All wood dowels:

1. They may not be perfectly round

2. They are rarely perfectly straight

I would recommend using the poplar dowel version. It will be a little easier to slide the journals on to the dowel rod. Very little of the dowel rod in the crankshaft is visible so cosmetics are not an issue.

Allow extra length on all the crankshaft dowels as you make the crankshaft. The dowels can be easily cut to the exact length after the crank is finished and it makes assembly much easier.

The primary goal here is to make the total crankshaft perfectly straight. The crankshaft dimensions are shown below.

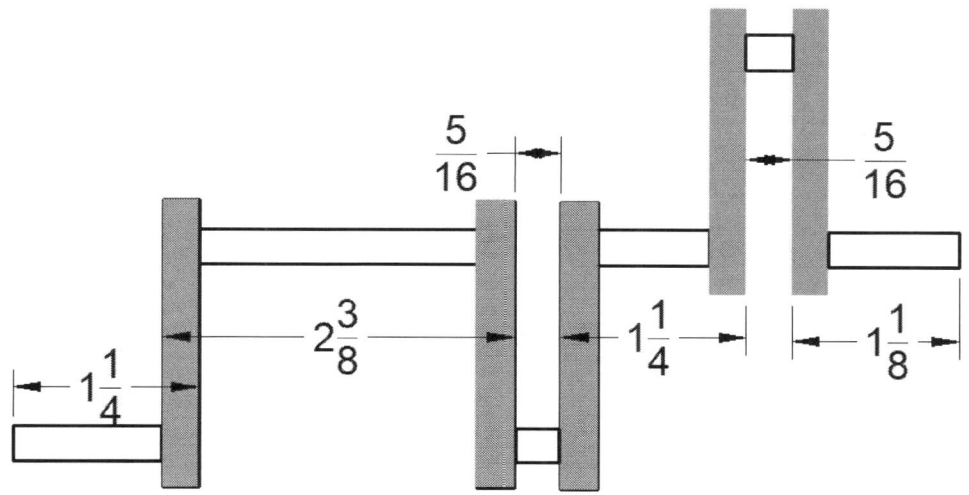

The dimensions given are actually an approximation. The dimensions are actually not that critical. The crankshaft journals are the most critical. The journals have a 5/16 spacing. The 5/16" spacing between the journal sides allows a little extra room for the 1/4" connecting rod to move without restriction inside the journal. The 5/16" spacing is probably the most critical dimension in the crankshaft, not because of the exact size but because of the need to make sure it is consistent the full length of the journal.

I strongly recommend you make a 5/16 wood alignment shim ~1" long and ~1/2" wide.

Make a connecting "pin" for each journal. The pin should be a ~1 ½" piece of 1/4" wood dowel. It will stick out both sides of the journal but will be easier to work with. It will be trimmed down to actual size after it is installed.

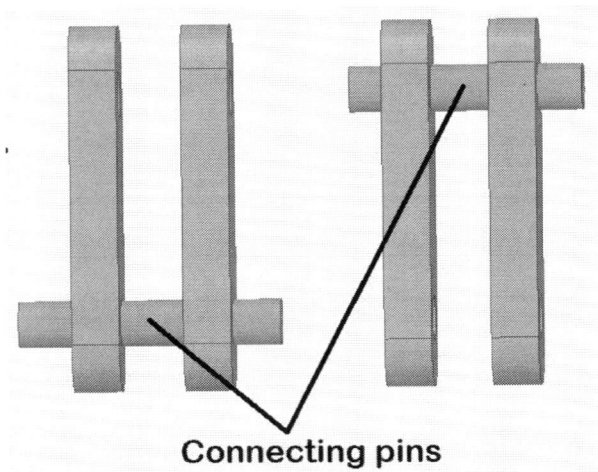

Connecting pins

Place your 5/16" wood shim between one pair of the journal sides. Insert the pin through the holes on one end of the journal. Check your shim to make sure there is an even 5/16" spacing between both sides of the journal.

Repeat the process for the other journal. The journals are now ready to be installed on the crankshaft.

Journal placement on the crankshaft should be close to these dimensions. The ¾" between the journals is the most important dimension.

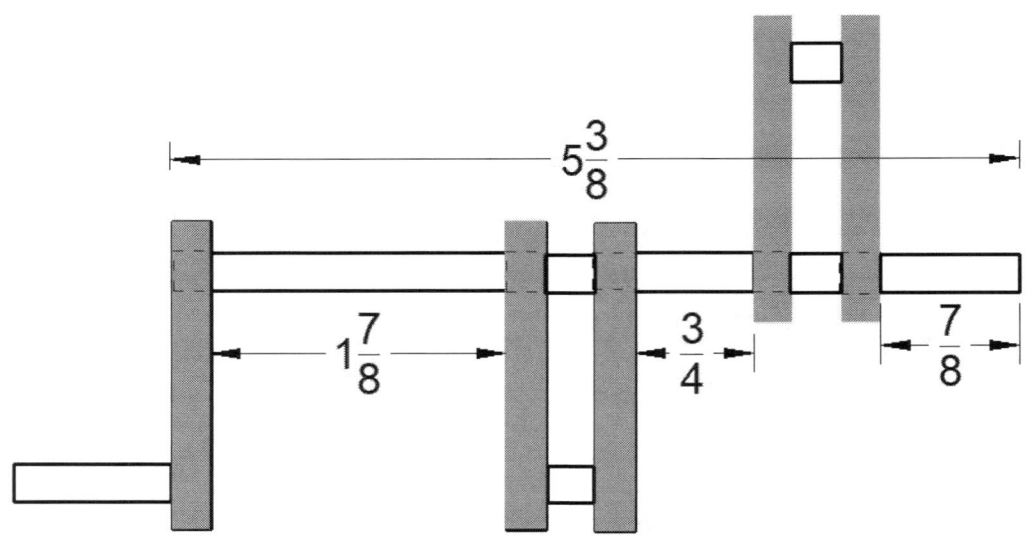

The finished crankshaft length should be about 5 3/8"
Start with a piece of ¼" dowel about 6" long.

Insert the main shaft into the unused holes on one of the journals. Make sure your shim is in place. The journal should be 7/8" from the end as shown above. Install the other journal on the other end of the shaft. Leave a 3/4" space between the journals as shown.

Lay the crankshaft on a flat surface. Make sure both journals are flat against the surface. Check the journal spacing with the shim one more time. Your crankshaft should now look like the photo below.

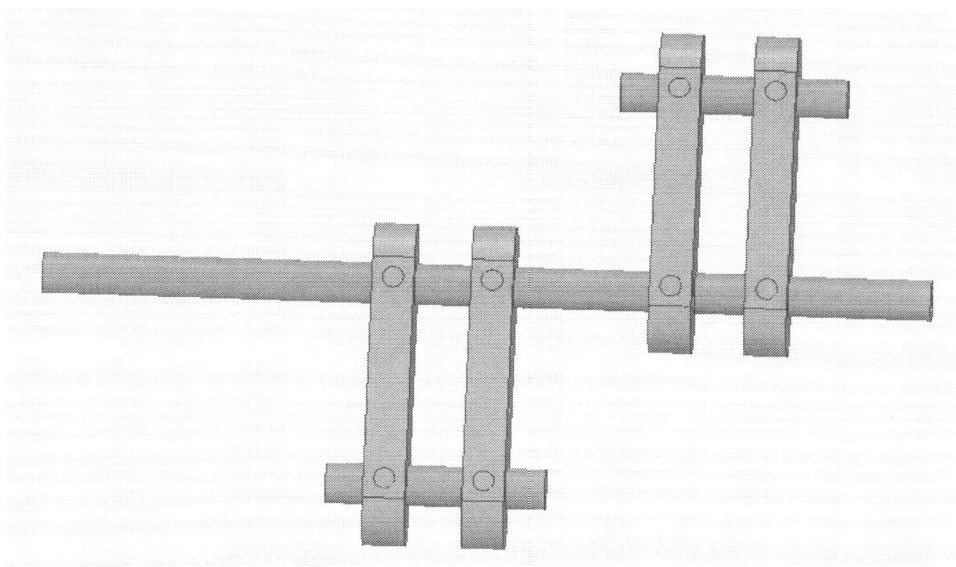

We will use "Lock pins" to pin the journals in place after you have positioned them on the main shaft in the appropriate positions. Mark a point centered on each journal where the shaft goes through and on the other end where the connecting pin goes through. Drill 1/8" holes all the way through the journal.

Cut pieces of 1/8" wood dowel about ¾" long for the lock pins. Gently tap the 1/8" lock pin in so it's flush on one side of the journal. After all the lock pins are in place, use a wire cutter to cut the excess length off of the lock pins. Sand the lock pins so they are flush with the journal sides.

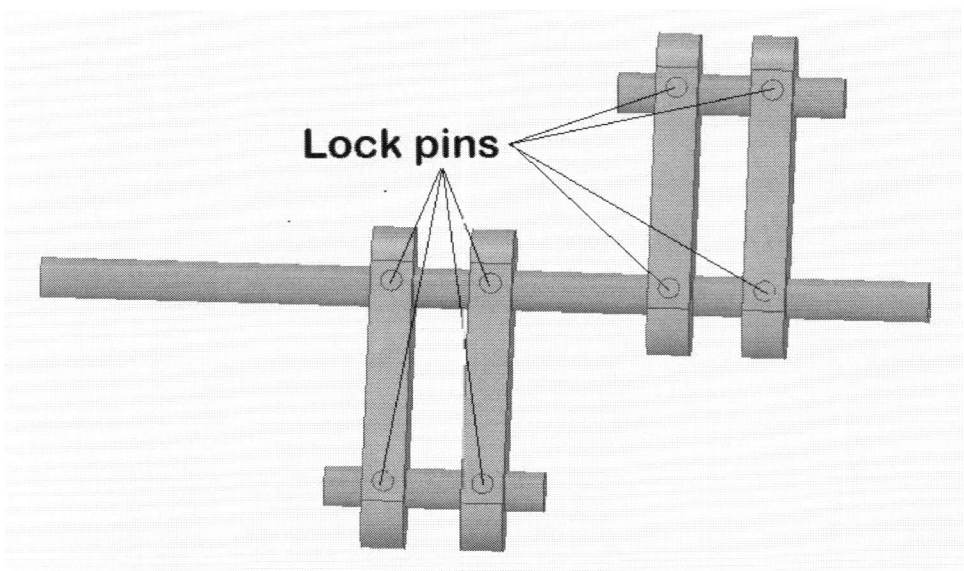

Now we can cut off the excess journal pin lengths. The journal pins should be cut flush with the side of the journals.

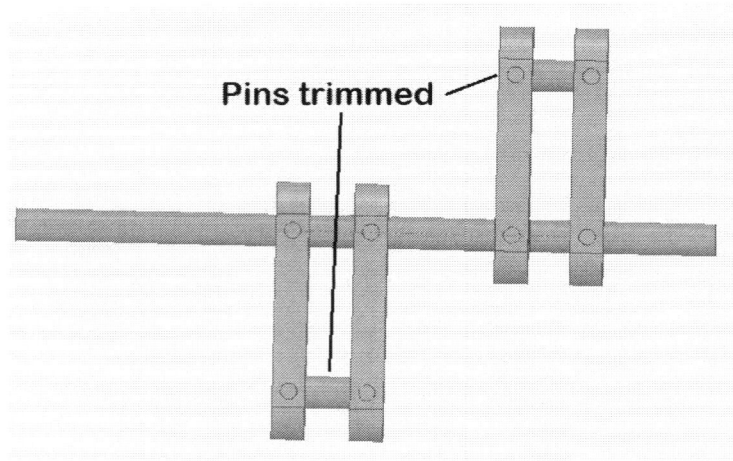

Now that we have all the pieces in place, cut out the two sections of the <u>main shaft</u> where it passes through the journals as shown below.

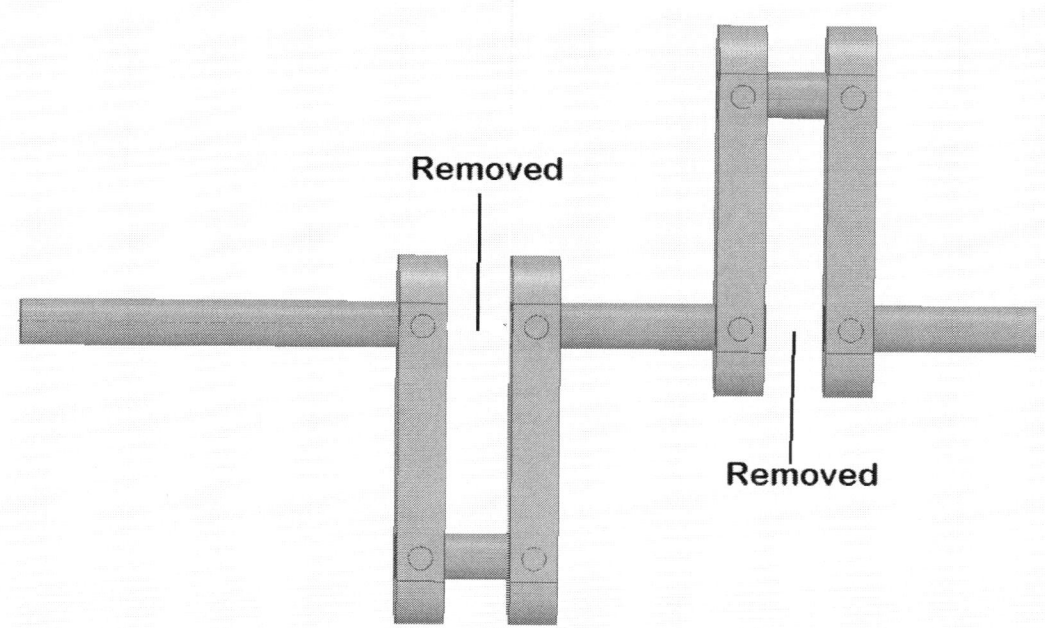

Now we can move on to the crankshaft supports.

There are three crankshaft supports, one on each end and one in the middle.

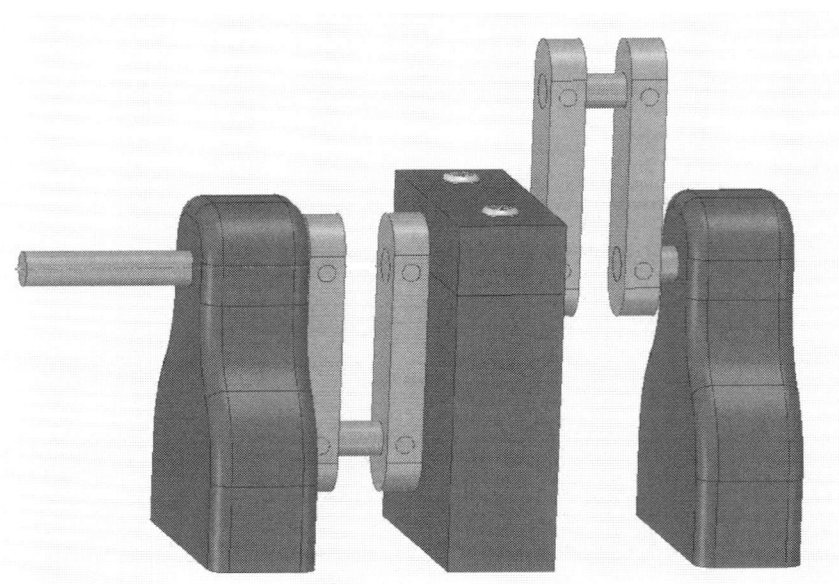

The dimensions for the end supports are given below

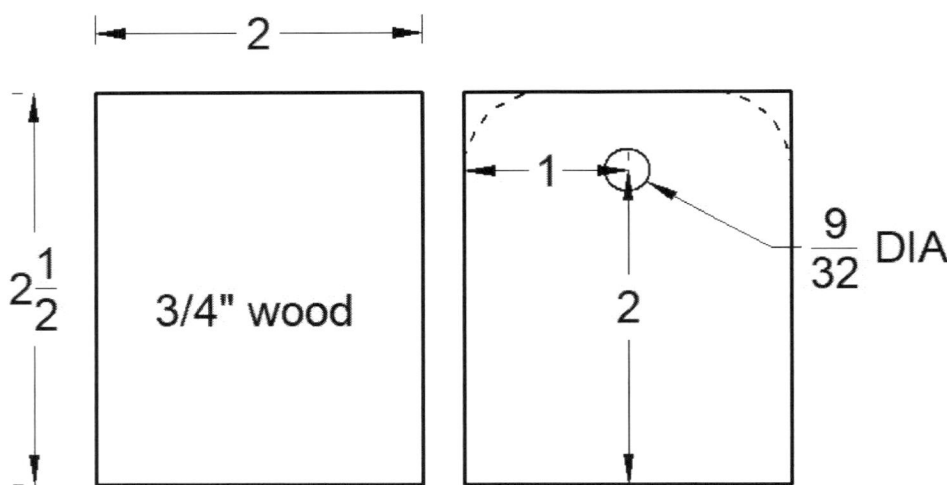

The dotted lines show suggested trim. Round the corners and sand all the edges except the bottom.

The middle support requires a little more work. You will find the need to remove the crankshaft numerous times as you build this project unless you have skills worthy of your own woodcraft TV show. It is not possible to insert the crankshaft into the middle support.

We will make a support with a removable top cap. The dimensions are given below.

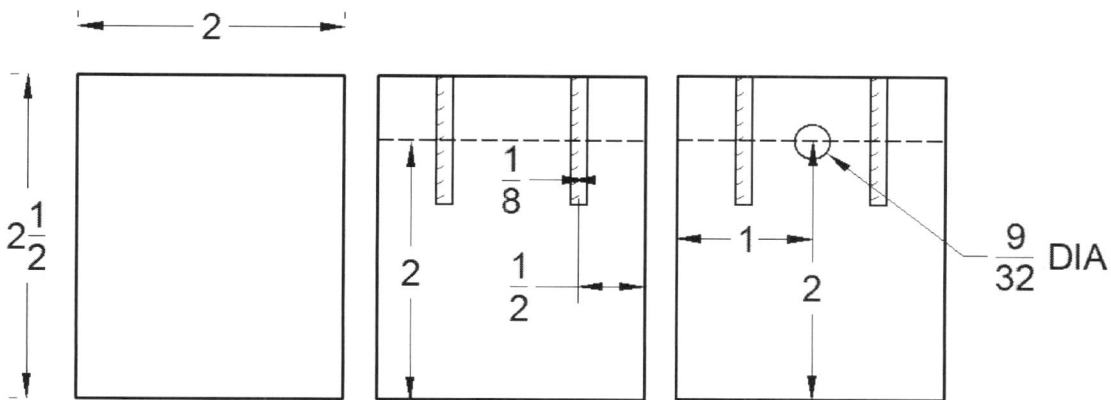

Cut the outside dimensions first (2 1/2" x 2"). Drill two 1/8" holes in the top, ~1/2 from the ends, centered. Mark a line 2" from the bottom as shown. Cut the top of the support along the line just drawn. Using two 6-32 x 1" pan head screws, attach the top. Now mark the center of the block, 2" from the bottom which should be on the exact cut you just made. Drill a 9/32" hole.

All of your supports should now be complete.

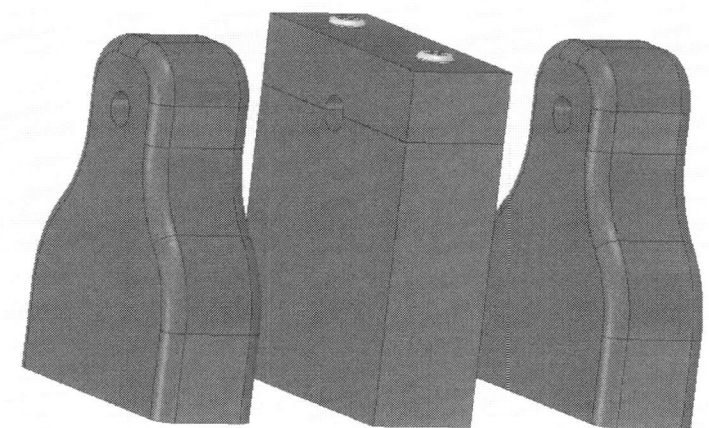

To test the supports, place all three supports somewhat close together with the holes lined up. Insert a piece of ¼" dowel into all three supports. Push down on all three supports to simulate being held down with screws. Turn the dowel. It should turn without much friction and with relative ease.

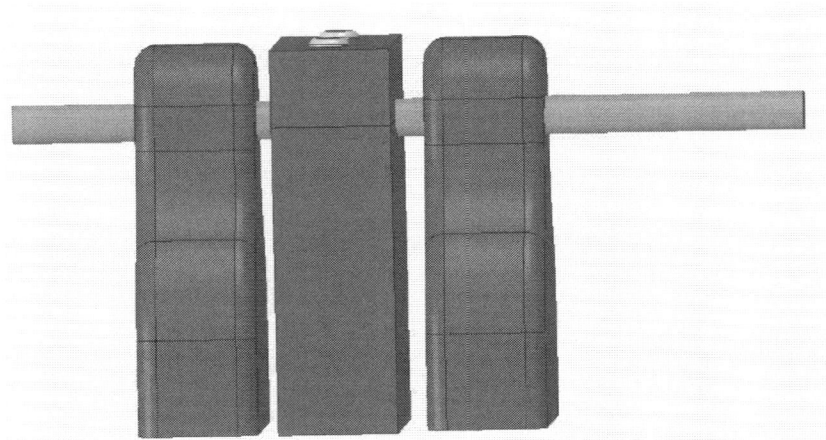

Although the dowel should turn easily, you may find that it does not. As stated before, wood dowels are not precision pieces! If the dowel does not turn easily, make the axle holes slightly bigger in all three supports until the dowel does turn easily.

Now replace the dowel with the crankshaft.

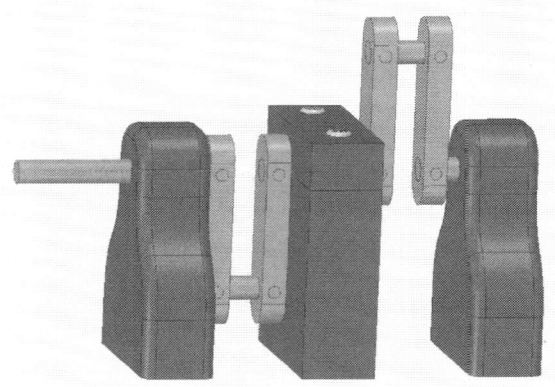

You will have to remove the cap on the middle support to mount the crankshaft. The crankshaft should turn with ease.

The crank handle is made from 3/8" wood. Cut the block as shown. Then cut the two holes. Round off the ends as shown with the dotted lines.

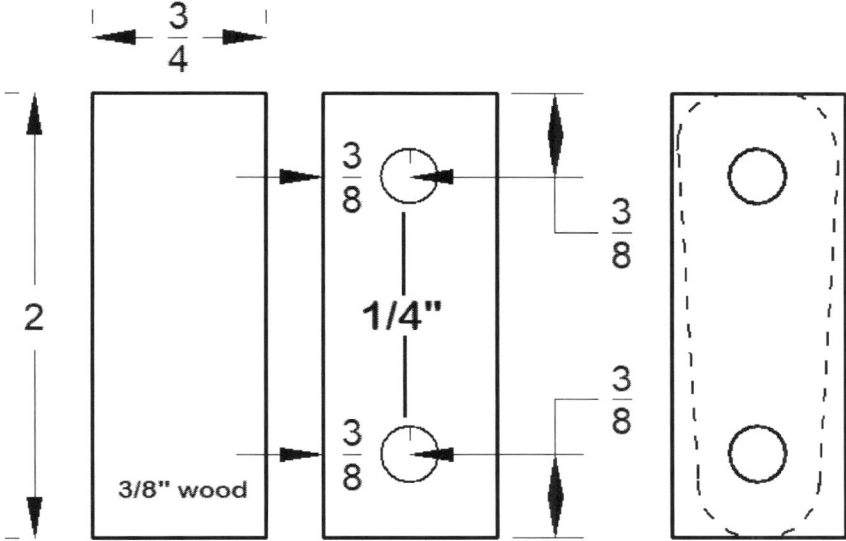

We need to add the crank handle. Cut a piece of ¼" dowel, 1 ½" long. Round one end. Glue the other end into the crank, flush with the back. Glue the crank onto the crankshaft.

The last two parts of the drive train are the connecting rods.

The connecting rods have to have a removable cap so they can be attached to the crankshaft journal pins.

This is what they should look like when complete.

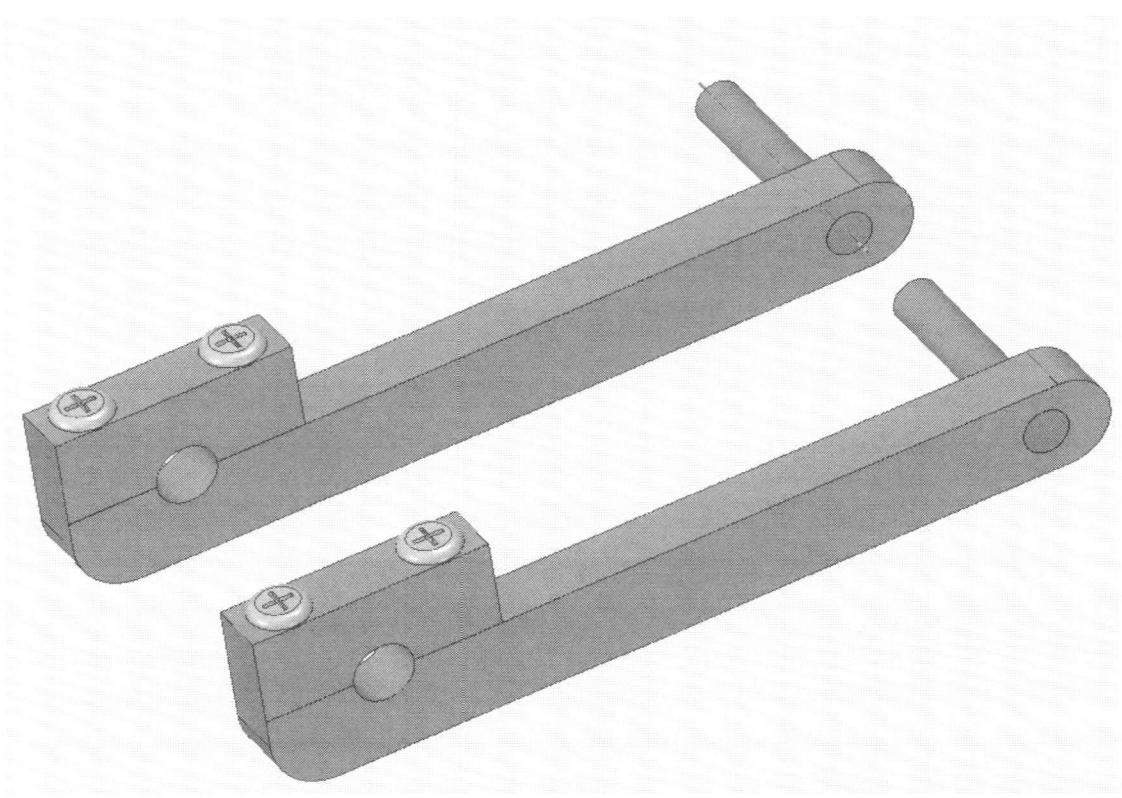

The connecting rods are made from ¼" stock. Before you begin making the connecting rods, insert the ¼" stock wood between the crankshaft journals to make sure it slides through easily.

Cut a blank for each connecting rod as shown below.

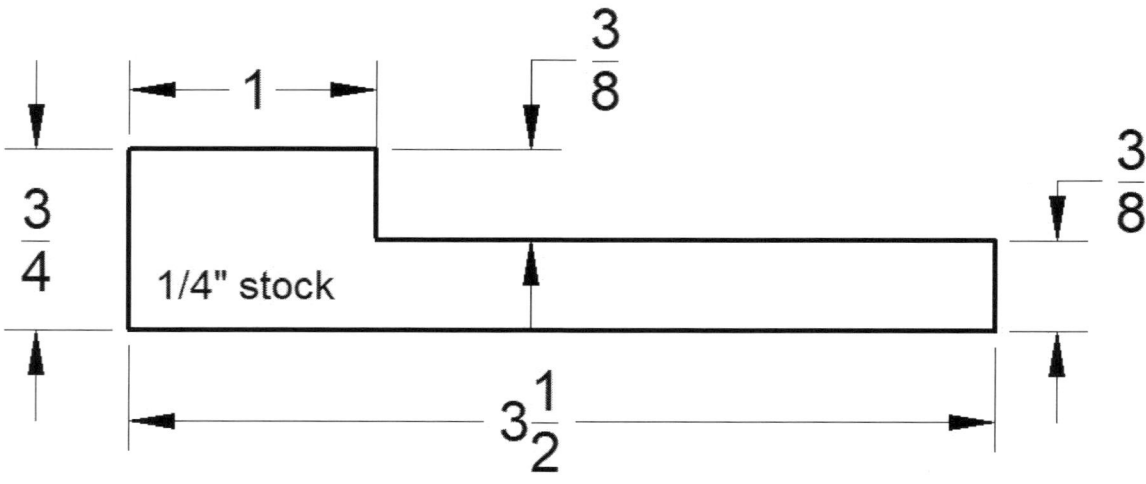

Drill two pilot holes for the screws on top for the mounting screws on the cap.

The pilot holes should be as close to the size of the screw as possible and still have some bite to them.

The pilot holes are essential because It is very easy to split the sides or the ends of the connecting rod when inserting the screws.

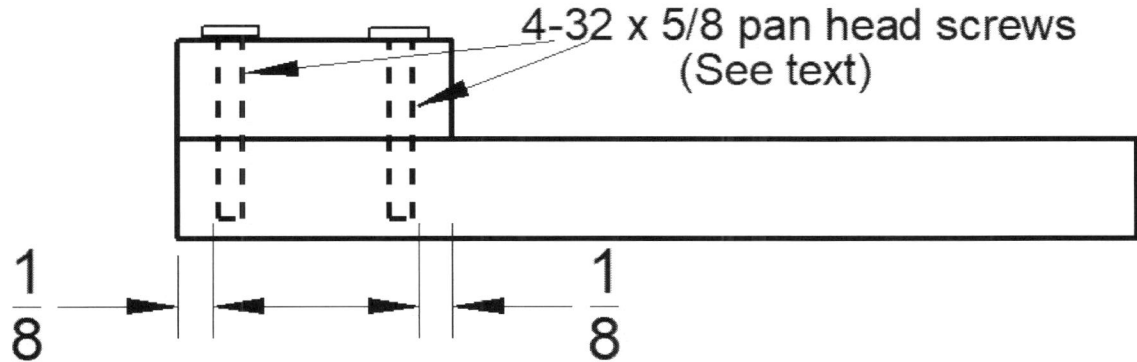

4-32 x 5/8 pan head screws (See text)

The wood is only ¼" thick so the screws have to be small. 4-32 x 5/8 Pan head would be ideal but they are hard to find.

I used 6-32 x 5/8 Pan Head and they work but you have to be a little more precise with the pilot holes. Try to space them ~1/8" from the ends of the cap as shown.

Insert the screws into the pilot holes to form the threads. Remove the screws. Then cut the cap. Re-attach the cap with the screws.

Drill a 9/32" hole 1/2" from the end and centered on the cut just made. Drill the 3/16" hole on the small end, centered, 3/8" from the end.

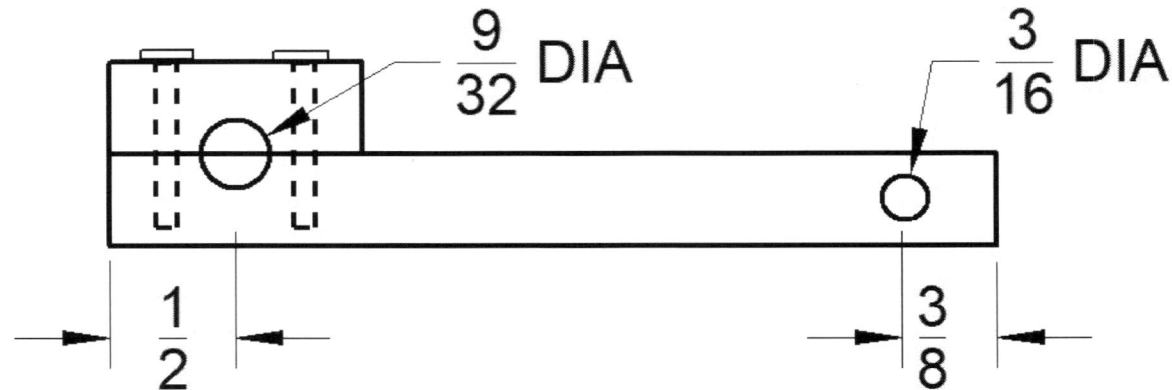

$\frac{9}{32}$ DIA $\qquad$ $\frac{3}{16}$ DIA

$\frac{1}{2}$ $\qquad$ $\frac{3}{8}$

The connecting rods can be sanded and the ends rounded off for a better finished look as shown below. The pins on the ends will be added later.

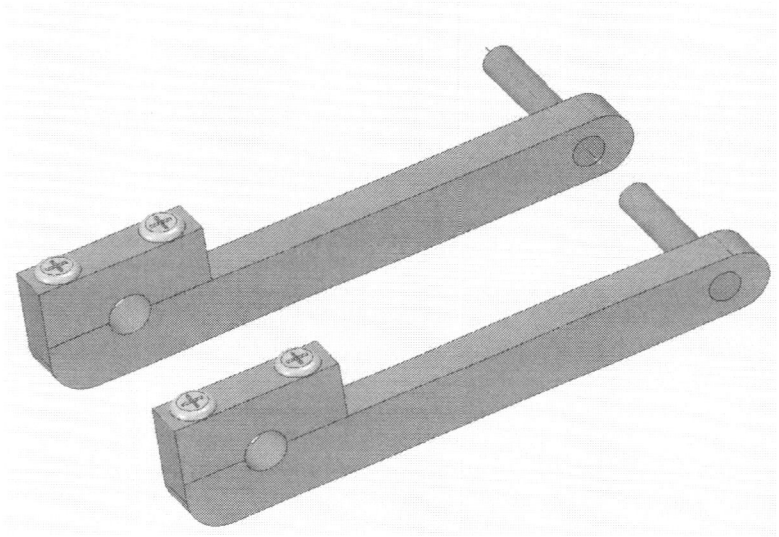

Install the connecting rods onto the crankshaft.

The drive train is now complete.

Treadmill

The treadmill "roller" is the most important part of the treadmill. This is the part that the action figure walks on.

Start with the basic block made from ½" wood. I used black walnut since the actual tread on a treadmill is usually black.

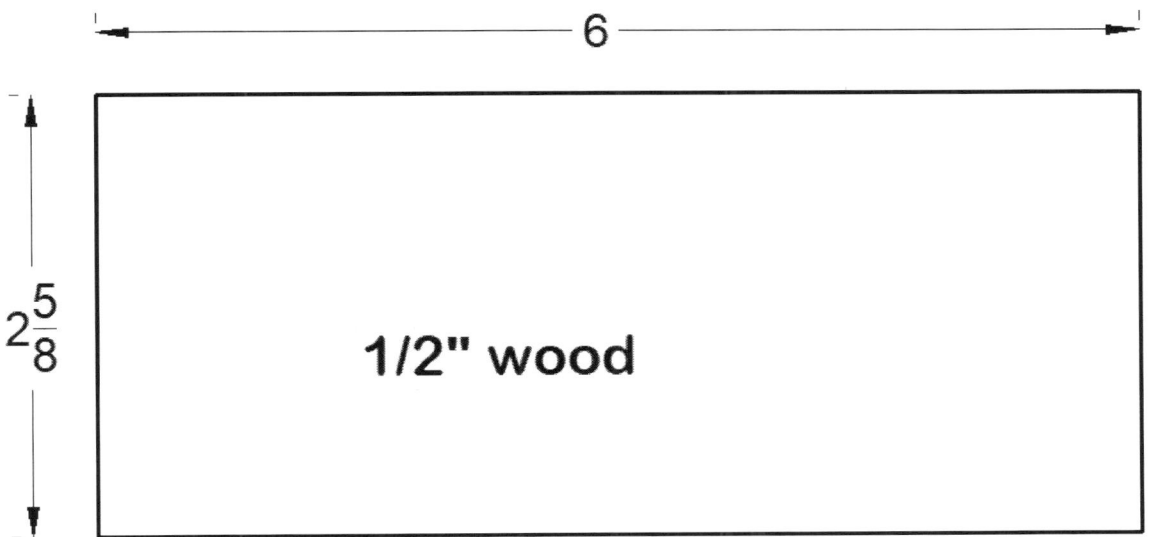

Drill a 3/8" hole on each end of the slots. Then draw the lines to connect them. Cut out the slots.

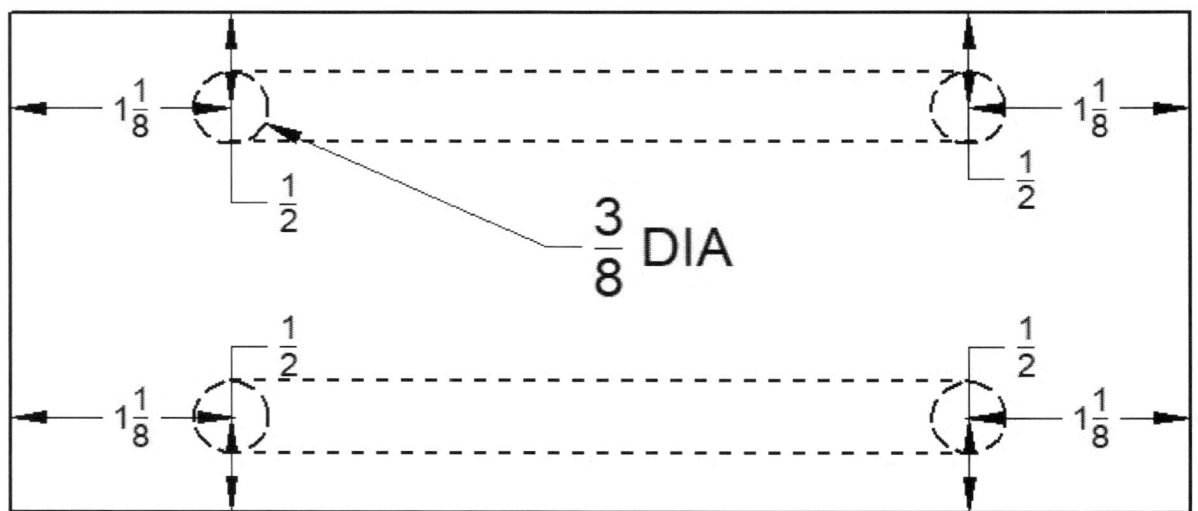

Make diagonal lines from corner to corner to find the exact center of the roller. Dill a 3/8" hole in the center.

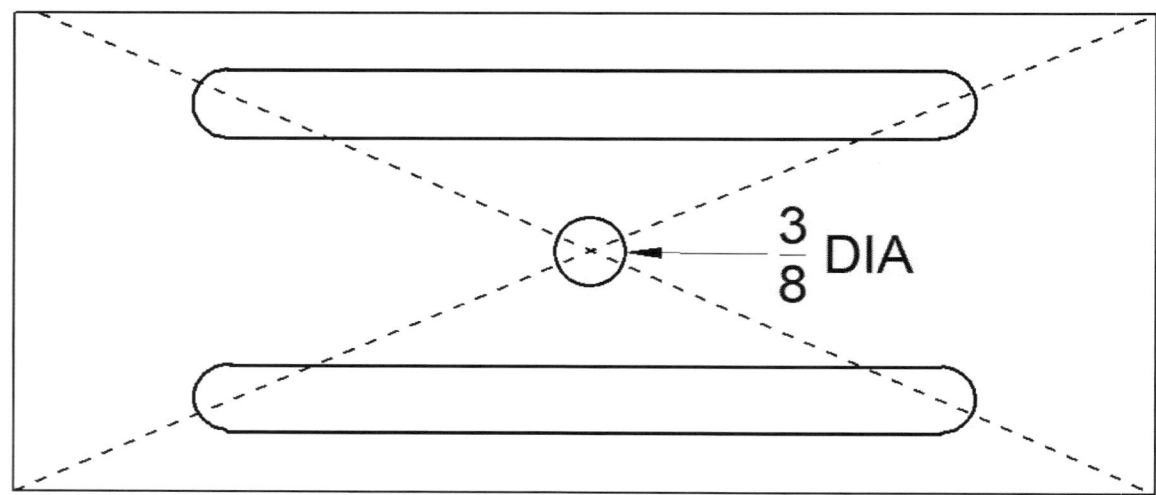

Round both ends of the roller.

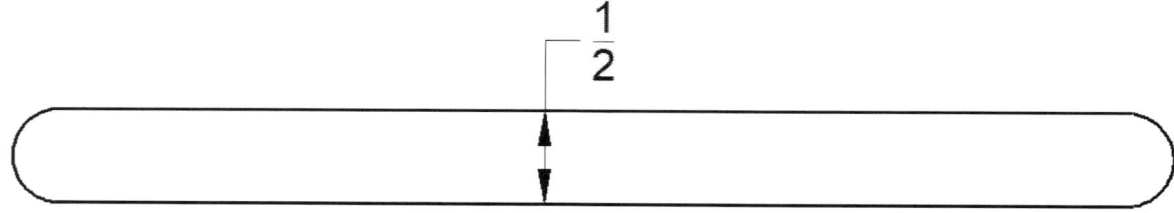

The treadmill frame is next.

The treadmill frame is made from ½" wood.

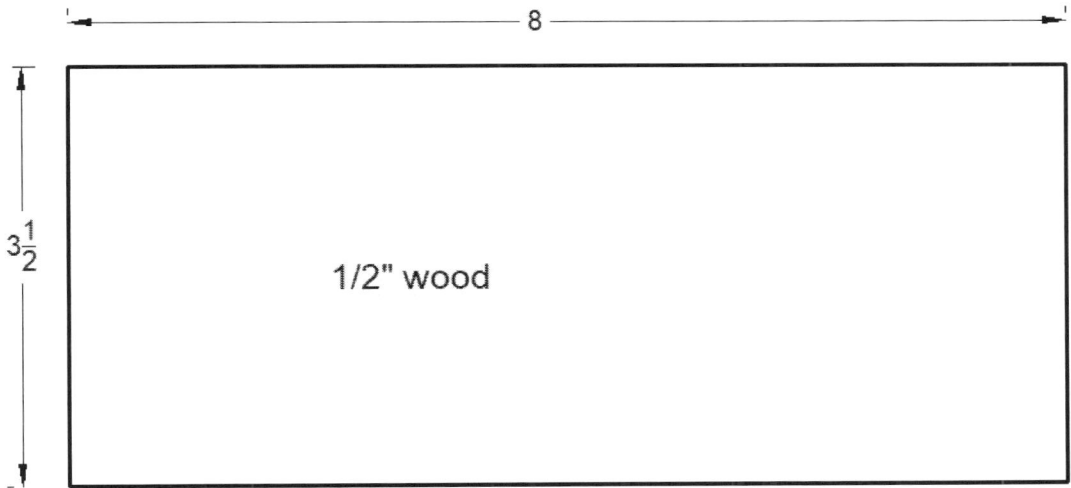

Cut the opening on the inside for the treadmill roller.

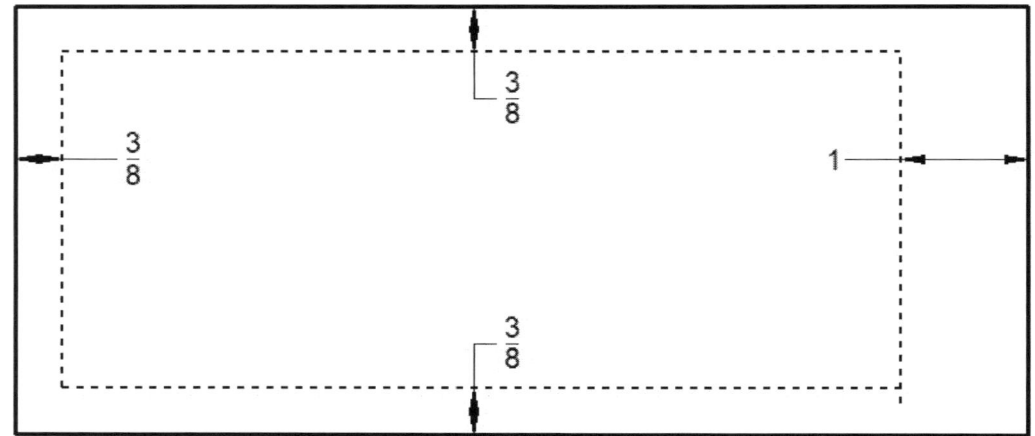

Drill the holes for the console posts.

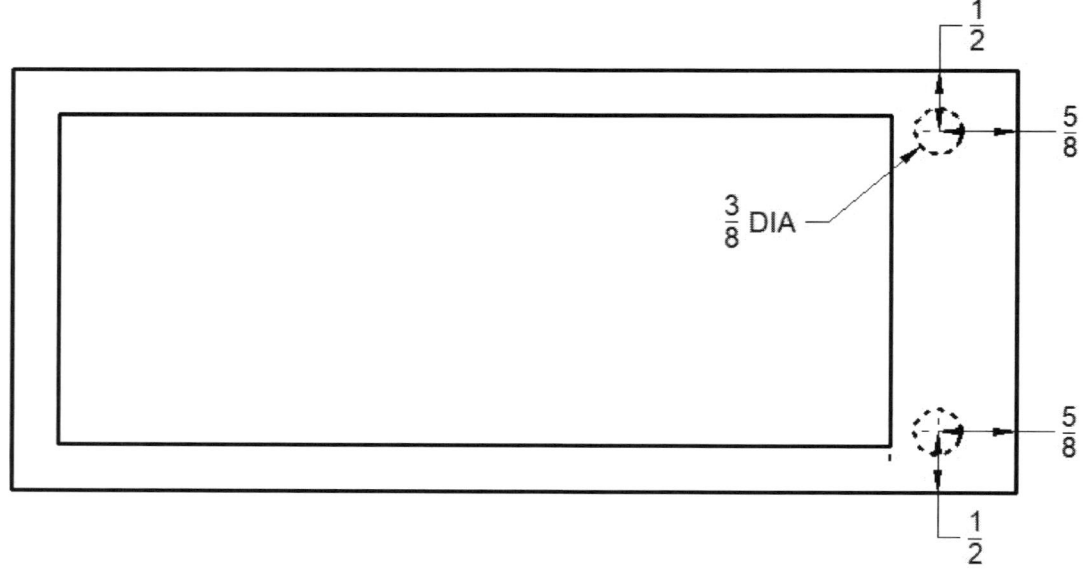

The treadmill console can be made in three steps.

Cut the basic block.

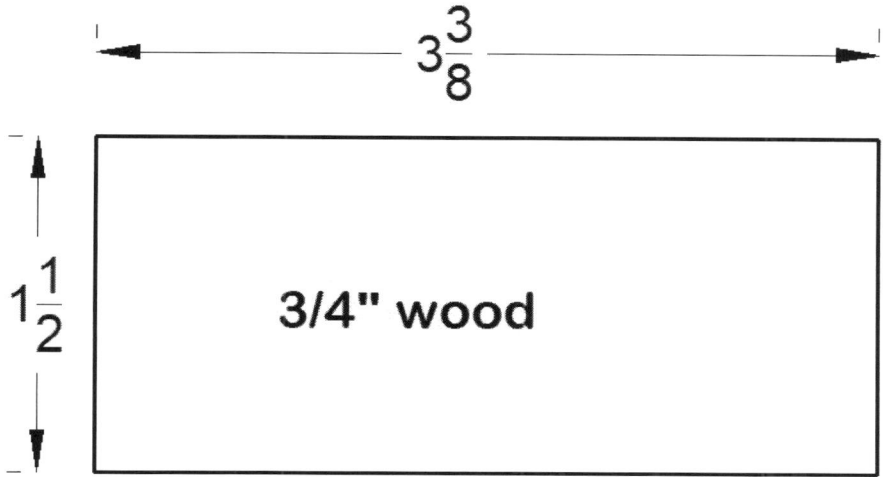

Add the mounting holes. Drill the holes ½" deep.

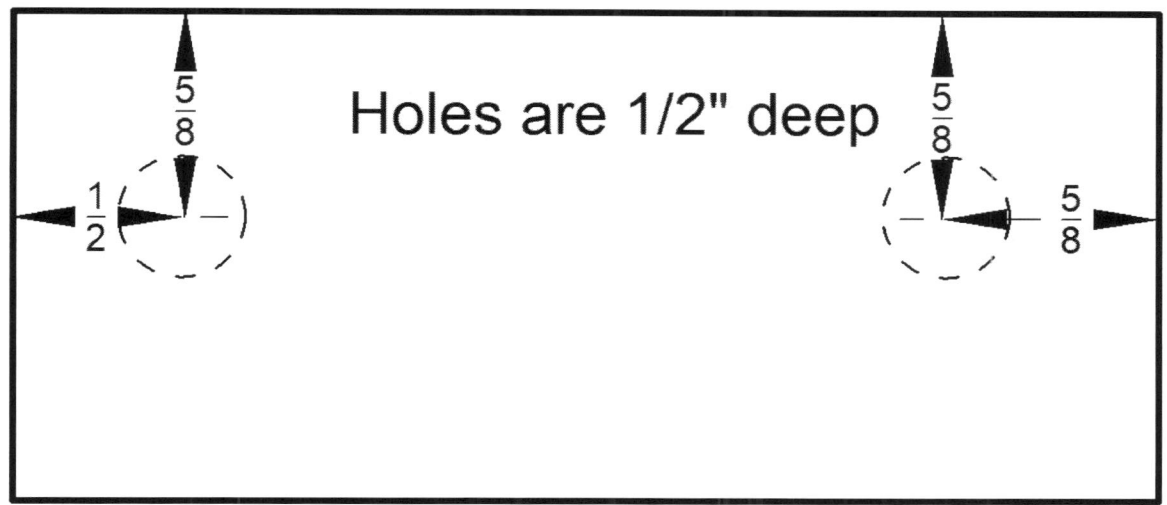

Add the holes on the back of the console for the handlebars. Then round the front corners.

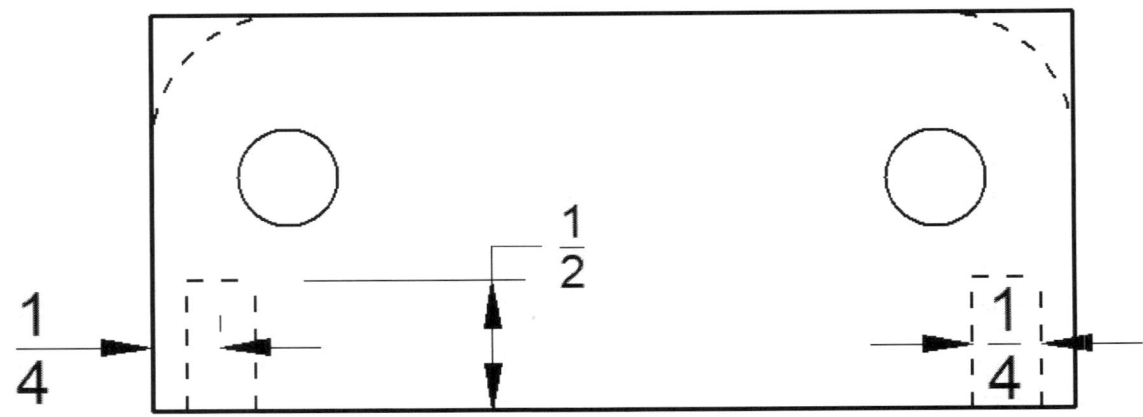

The console will be supported with two 3/8" dowels. The actual length will be set to match the hands of the action figure later. Cut two pieces of 3/8" dowel, each 4 ½" long to begin with. Temporarily mount the console to make sure the holes line up.

The hand rails are made from 3/16" dowel. Cut two pieces 2 ½" long. Round the tip on one end. Insert the other end into the console. Do not glue the hand rails yet.

Set the treadmill roller in the middle of the treadmill frame. There should be about 1/8" space on each end. Center it side to side.

Your treadmill is now complete. We will mount it a little later.

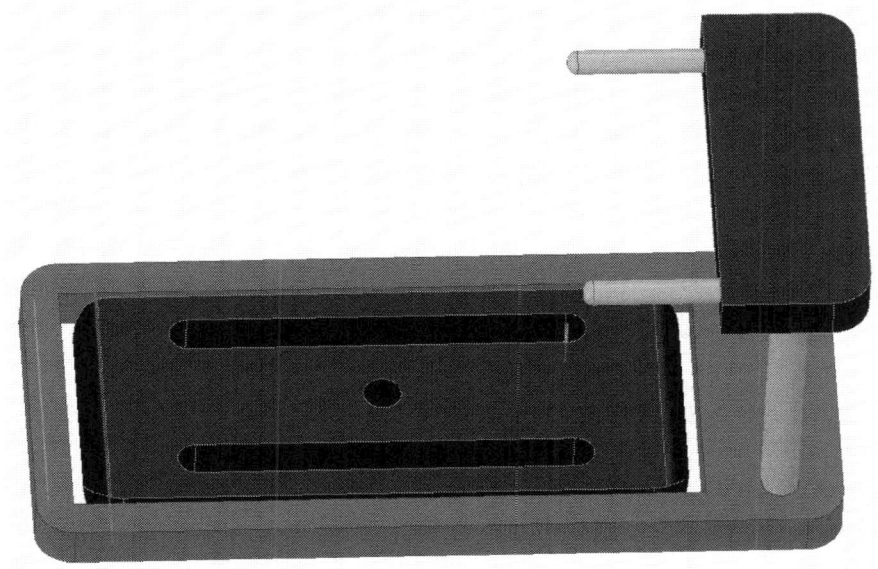

Action figure

We'll do the shoes first. Remember there are two shoes so make two of everything connected to the shoes.

There is a link attached to the bottom of each shoe which will hook up to the drivetrain connecting rods. Linking up the shoes with the drive train will also give us our first chance to see if all the mechanical parts are working correctly.

The shoes will have a connector link on top (ankle) and long connector link on the bottom.

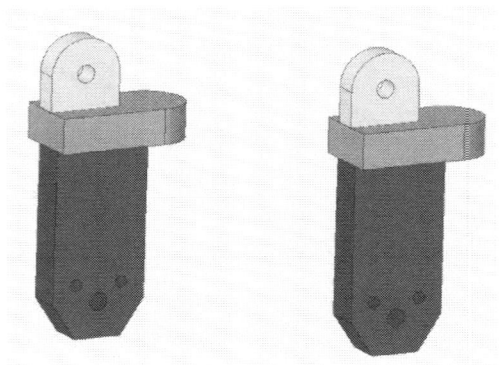

Start with the basic shoe.

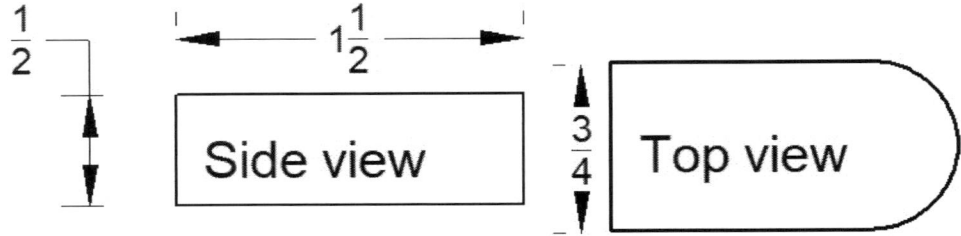

The ankle is next. The ankle is cut from ¼" wood.

Tip: A paint stir stick for 5-gallon pails is ~¼" thick and is usually FREE from most home improvement centers.

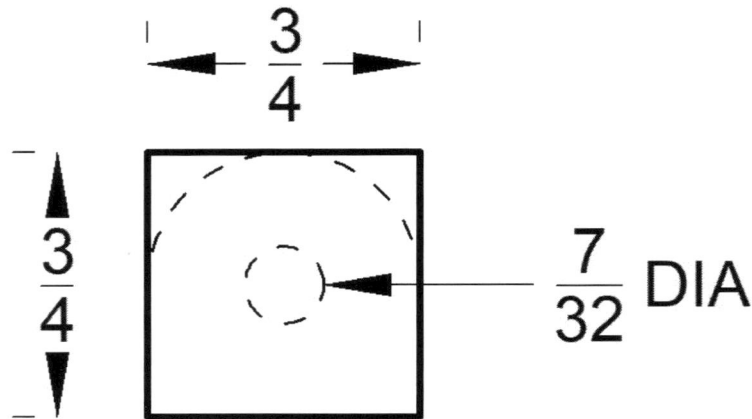

Round one end. Center the 7/32" hole. Glue the ankles to the back of each shoe, centered.

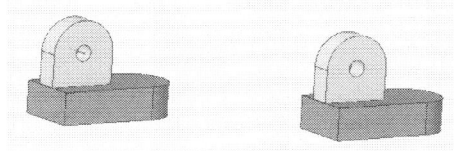

The bottom links are made from 3/8" wood.

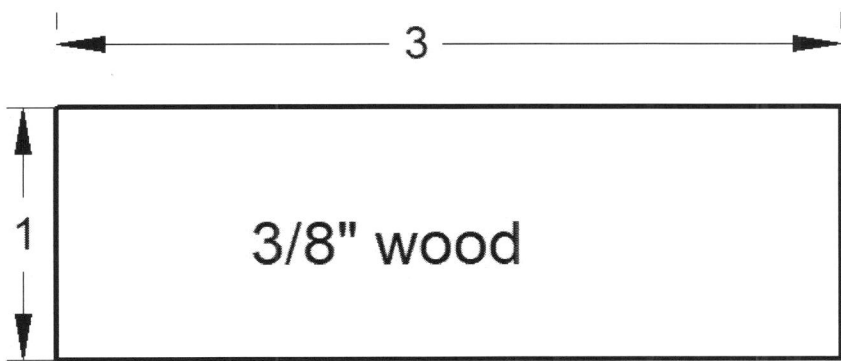

Cut the basic block. The length will be trimmed to actual size when it is installed.

Glue one end of the link to the bottom of the shoe. Center it, front to back and side to side.

Temporarily place the treadmill frame and treadmill roller into position on top of the main frame. Align the slots in the treadmill roller with the slots in the main frame.

Insert one shoe link into one slot. Make sure the bottom of the shoe itself is flat against the roller. Lift the connecting rod from the drive train and place it next to the shoe link. On the other side of the link, draw a line across the link ~1/8" down from where it exits the main frame.

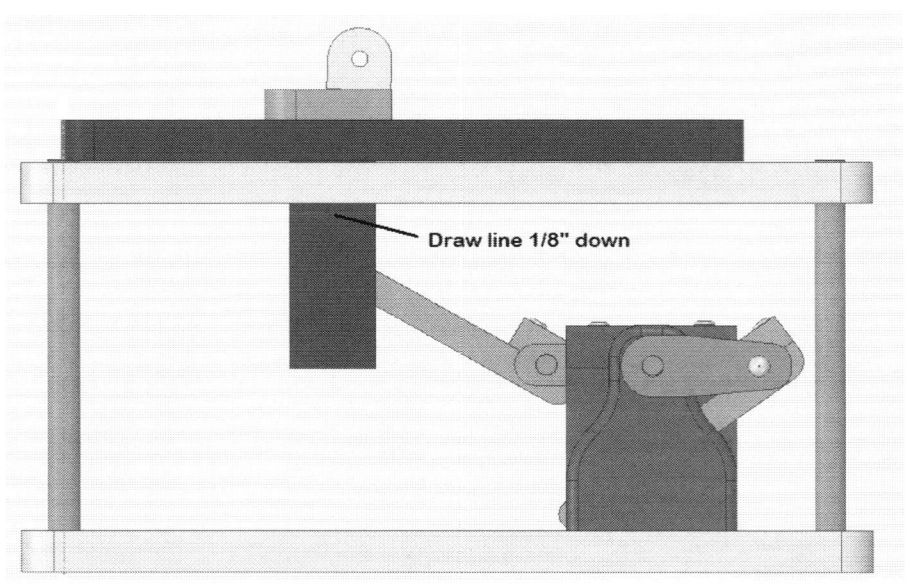

Draw line 1/8" down

The shoes by themselves will tilt front to back when hooked up to the drive train. To eliminate that we will add "Stabilizer bars".

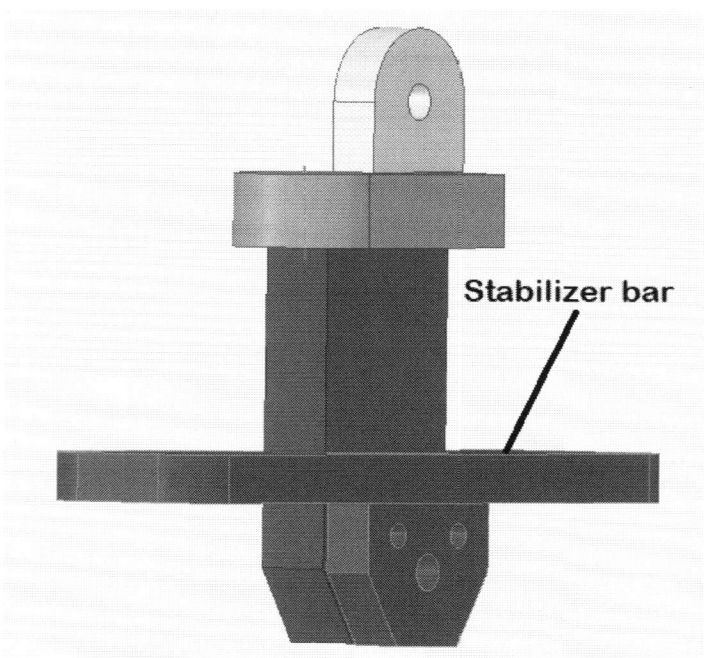

Stabilizer bar

The stabilizer bar is made from ¼" wood.

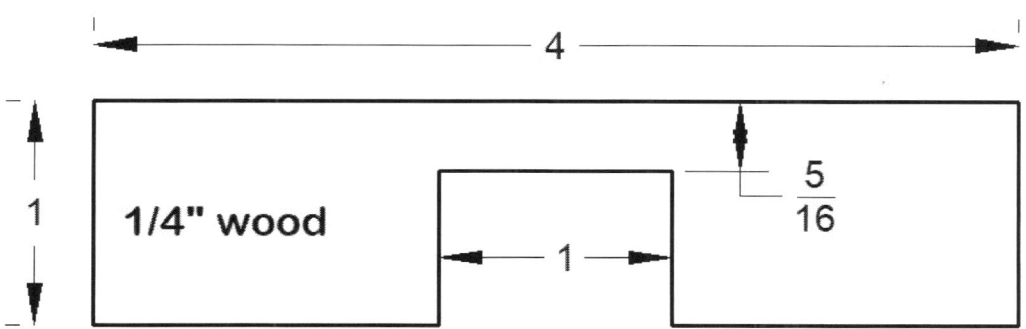

To mount the stabilizer, we need to make a support also made from ¼" wood.

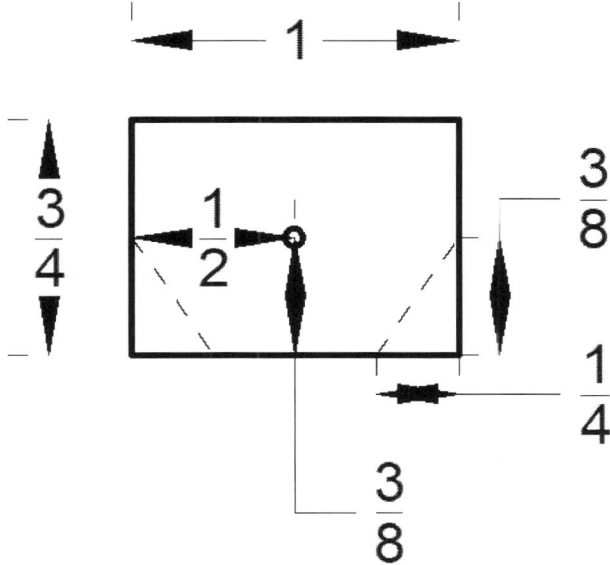

Trim the support shown by the dotted lines. Make a mark in the center as shown. The mark identifies the placement of a future hole for the connecting rod link.

Glue the support to the stabilizer bar. The support should be centered over the opening in the stabilizer bar and flush with the edge of the cut-out in the stabilizer bar.

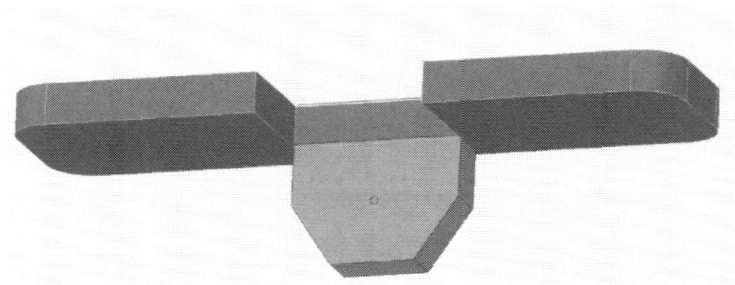

Note that the support will not be flush with the back of the stabilizer bar.

Place the stabilizer bar and support on the shoe link. The shoe link is placed into the cut-out in the stabilizer bar. See the illustration below. Align the top of the stabilizer bar to the line drawn on the shoe link.

With the stabilizer bar in place, drill a 7/32" hole through both the support and the shoe link. Drill two 1/8" holes through both the support and the shoe link. The holes should be above and equally spaced beside the existing hole in the support piece. Exact location is not critical.

Temporarily place scrap pieces of 1/8" dowel in the support and shoe link to make sure the holes line up.

Cut the length of the shoe link to match the bottom of the support. Make angle cuts on the shoe link to match the cuts on the support.

The shoes are now ready for the initial test.

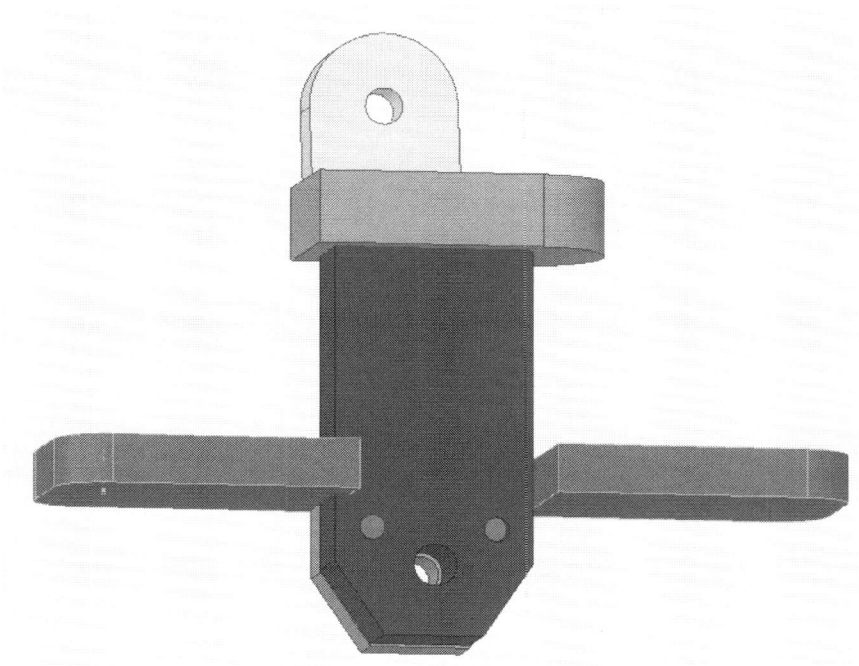

Remove the temporary 1/8" pins on the stabilizer bar support. Insert both shoe links into the treadmill roller slots.

Install the 1/8" stabilizer support pins. Cut them flush with the edge of the stabilizer support and the shoe link.

Slide both shoes back and forth on the treadmill roller. They should slide the full length of the slot without any restriction.

Temporarily insert a 1 1/8" long piece of 3/16" dowel through the hole in the bottom of the shoe link into the end of one of the connecting rods on the drive train.

Placement of the drive train will be primarily trial and error. The back of the crank supports should be ~1 ½" from the back of the bottom frame.

The right crank support should be ~1/16" from the edge of the bottom frame.

It will require an additional person to hold the drive train in place while you test it.

Turn the crankshaft. The shoe should go back and forth without restriction. You may have to hold the other connecting rod to keep it from interfering.

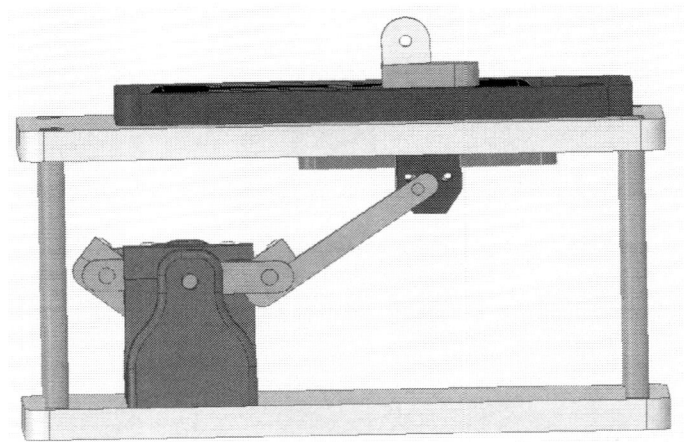

If the shoe does not slide back and forth with ease, make sure the chest is straight in line with the roller. You may have to rotate the chest slightly on the support pole. You may also have to re-position the power train. This actually is a precise setting so you may have to experiment with the settings. Once you find the correct setting, mark the location of the crank supports.

After you have tested out one shoe, temporarily remove the connecting rod link pin for that shoe. Now repeat the process for the other shoe.

After both shoes have been tested out, hook both shoes back up and give them one final test working together.

Permanently install the drive train. Glue all three crank supports in place. You could also mount them with screws from the bottom of the frame.

Make permanent 1/8" pins for both shoe links. Cut them flush with each side of the shoe link assembly.

Permanently install the two 1 1/8" long pieces of 3/16" dowel into the connecting rod. Insert one through each shoe link assembly and into the end of the connecting rod. It should be flush with the outside of the connecting rod. If it does not fit tight, glue it in place.

On the other end of the dowel, glue a small round thin piece of wood to lock the dowel in place.

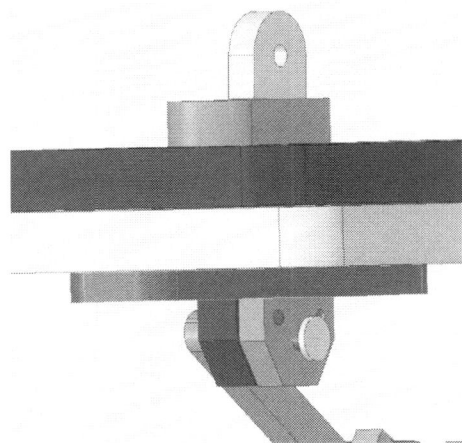

At this point you should be able to turn the crank and watch both shoes move back and forth without restriction. It should be easy enough to turn the crank with one finger.

Now we can finish the body parts. The legs will be next. The shoe is shown in the image below only to help put things in perspective.

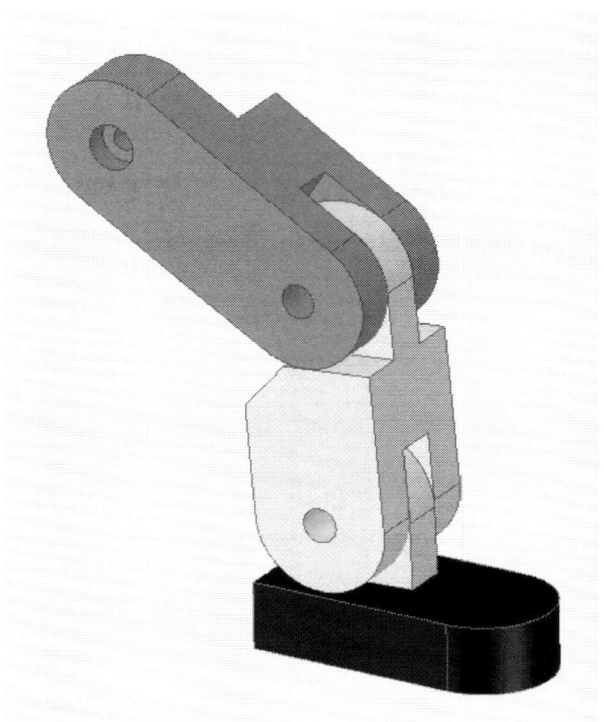

The lower part of the leg will connect to the ankle. Cut the basic block. Then drill the two holes, each centered side to side.

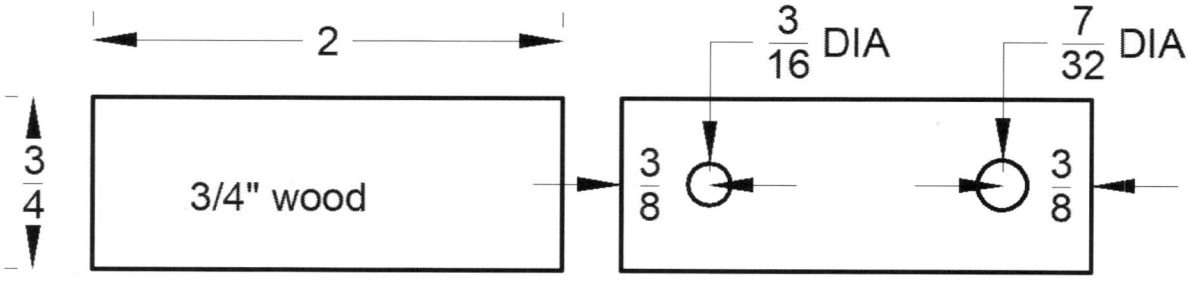

Trim both ends and then round off both ends.

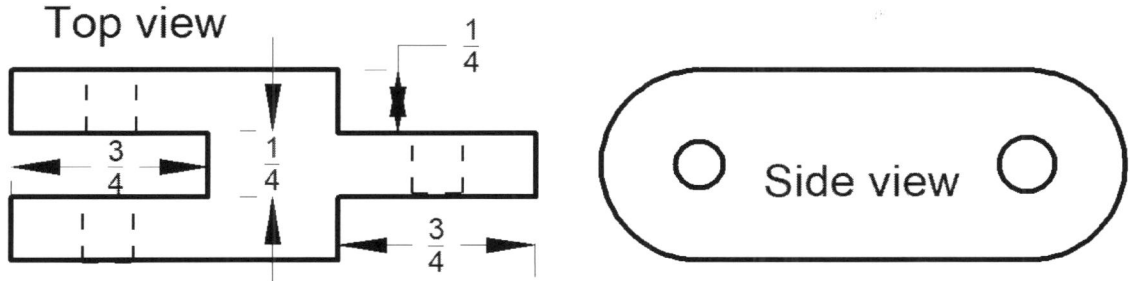

Using a scrap piece of 3/16" dowel, connect the lower leg to the ankle. Rotate the leg. The leg should be able to rotate a full 180°. If not, find where it is binding and cut or sand as needed.

The upper leg will complete the moving parts for the legs. Drill the 1/8" hole all the way through. The ¼" hole is a countersink to hide the head of the mounting screw. Countersink the hole about 1/8" deep depending on the size of the head of the mounting screw that you use to attach the leg to the body.

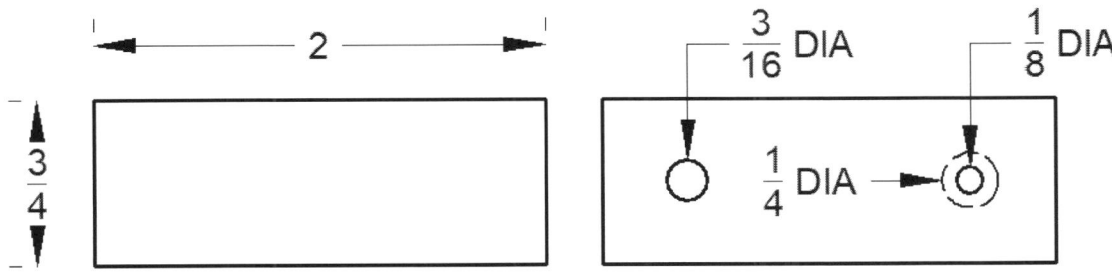

Trim the upper leg as shown. Round off both ends.

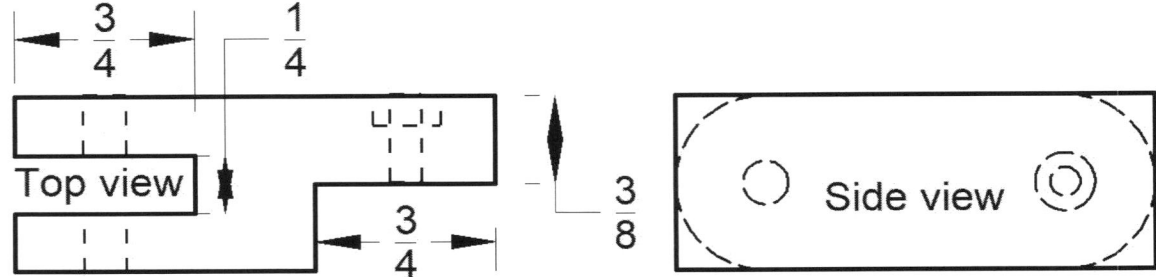

Using a scrap piece of 3/16" dowel, connect the upper and lower leg pieces. The pieces should rotate 180°without any problems.

The body is next.

The chest is 1 ¼" thick. You could start with a piece of common 2 x 4 and trim it down to 1 ¼" thick.

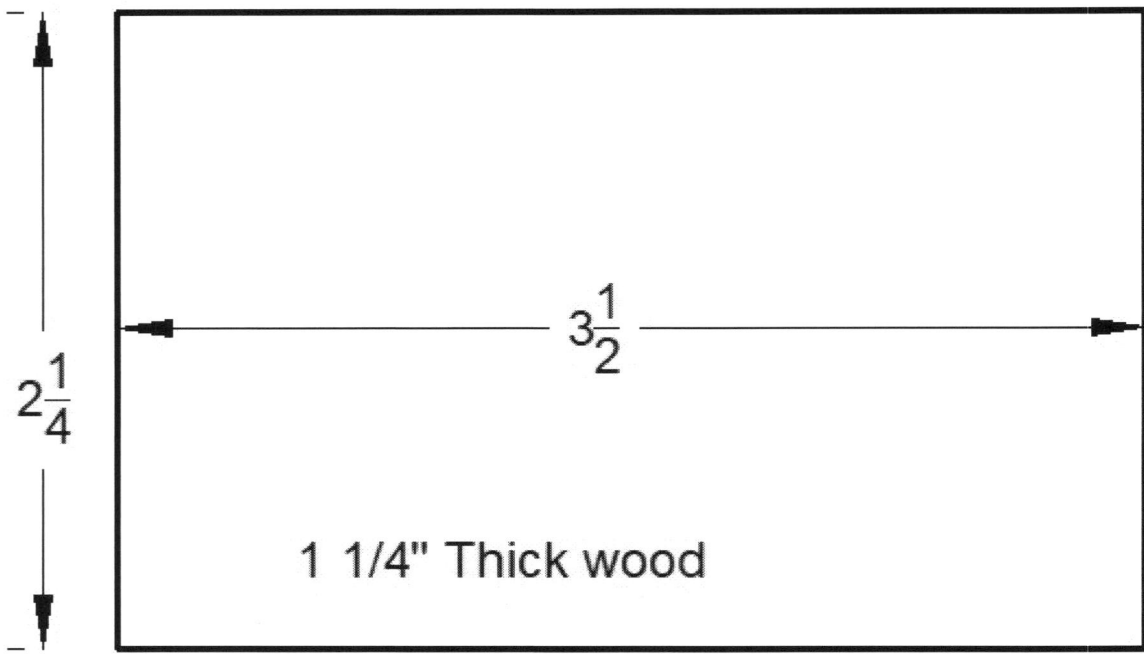

I will refer to the bottom end from now on as the "Hinge" because the legs will pivot from here.

Drill a ¾" hole on one end of the block, centered, 5/8" deep. On the other end cut the outside edges for the hinge.

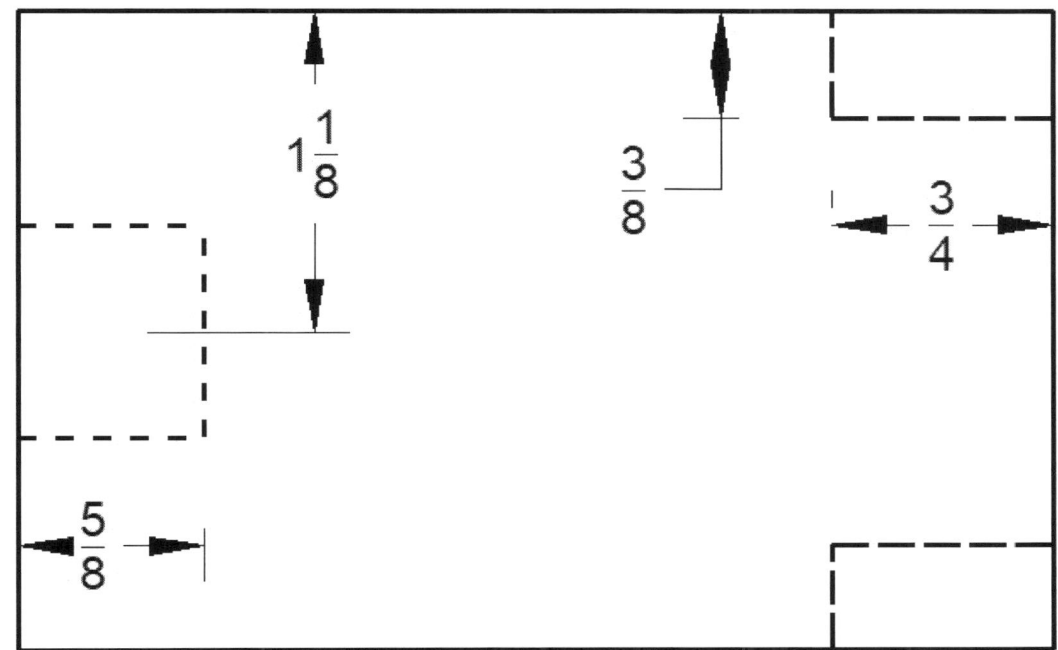

Make the trim cuts.

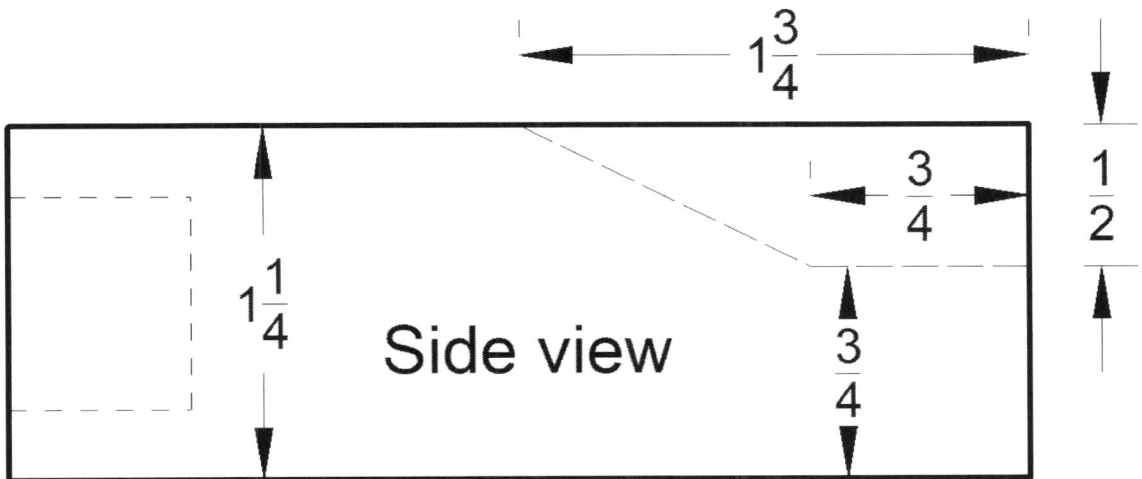

Drill a 3/8" hole ¾" deep, centered, on the hinge end of the chest.

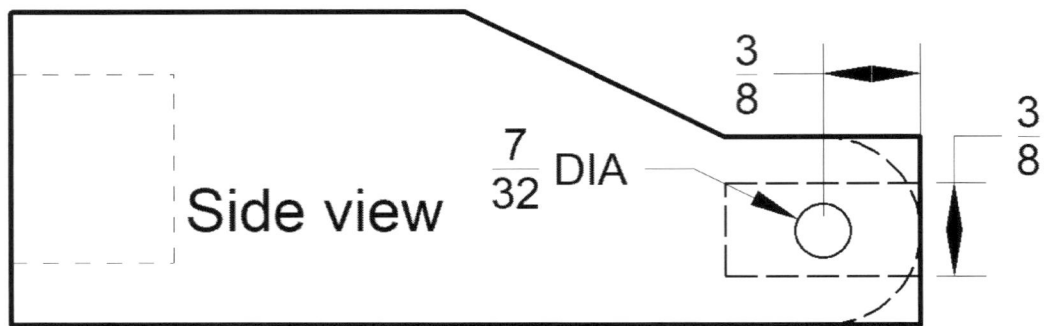

Side view — $\frac{7}{32}$ DIA, $\frac{3}{8}$, $\frac{3}{8}$

Drill a 7/32" hole all the way through the hinge. Round the bottom of the hinge. Round off all the edges except the sides on the hinge.

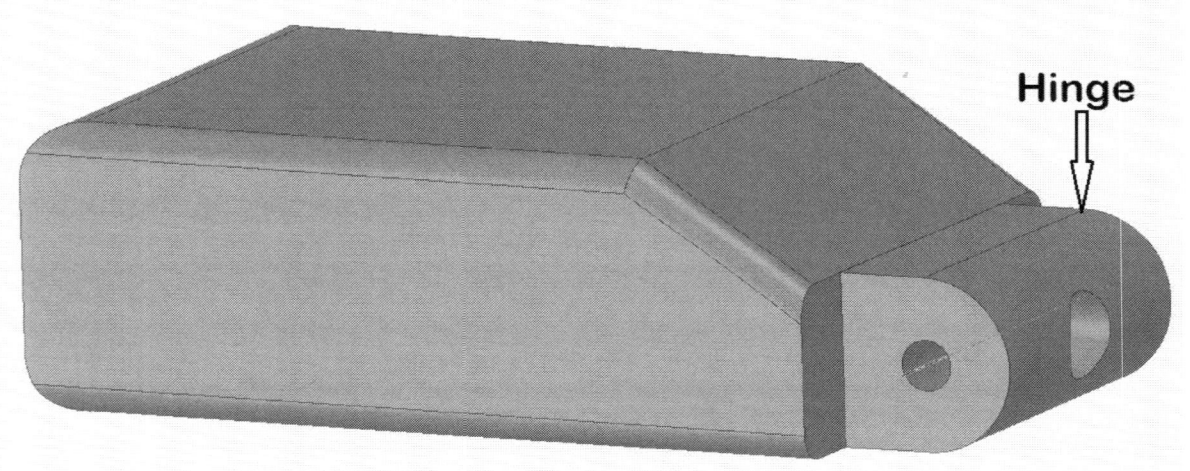

Hinge

We will use a piece of 3/8" dowel for the body support pole. Cut a piece 3 5/8" long. Insert and glue one end into the center hole on the treadmill roller. Make it flush with the bottom.

Temporarily mount the body onto the support pole. There should be 2 1/4" between the bottom of the hinge and the treadmill roller.

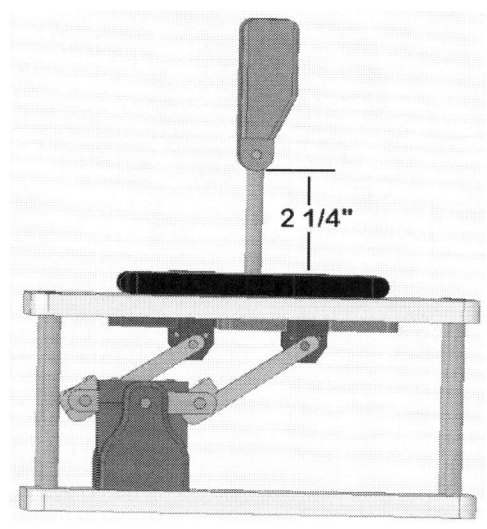

2 1/4"

Remove the chest from the support pole. Hold one upper leg against the side of the body hinge. It should be centered on the hinge and ~ 1/16" from the bottom of the chest. Mark the location of the screw hole on the side of the chest hinge. Using a 1/8" drill bit, drill a pilot hole ~3/4" deep in the chest hinge at the mark. Using a 6-32 pan head screw 1" long, attach the upper leg to the chest hinge. The screwhead should be recessed flush with the side of the leg and still be loose enough to allow the leg to swing freely. Do the same with the other leg. Make sure both legs can rotate easily

Using extralong pieces of scrap 3/16" dowel, connect the lower legs to the upper legs.

Hold the chest in the air and wiggle it to make the legs move. Both parts of the legs should move easily. If there is any restriction on the leg movement it can easily be fixed with sanding or cutting away the parts that rub.

Cut the knee pins to length which should be ¾", flush on both sides of the knee. You should be able to get by without having to glue any of the body pins which makes any maintenance a lot easier.

With the legs still attached, set the chest back on the chest mount pole. Maintain the 2 1/4" clearance between the bottom of the chest hinge and the roller. Make sure the chest is aimed straight to the front. Glue the chest to the support pole.

Attach the lower legs to the ankles with 3/16" dowel. Turn the crank. You should now be able to see the normal treadmill action with both legs. Trim the ankle pins to length which should be ¾".

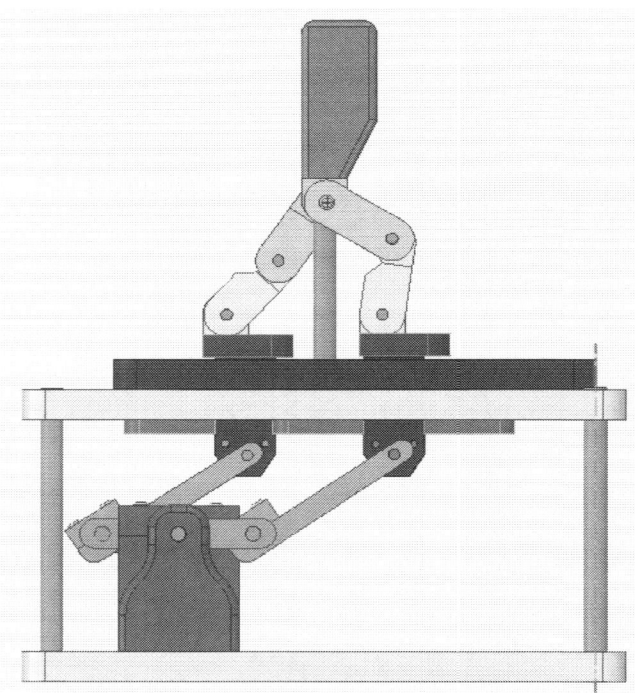

The arms are made from ¾" wood.

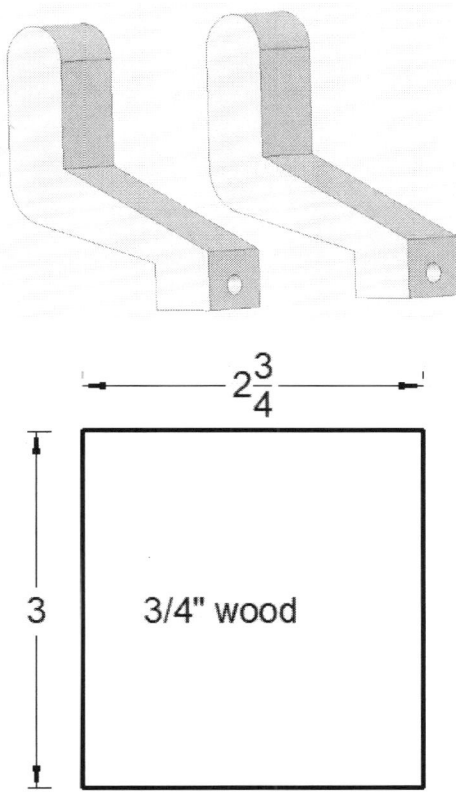

Stand the basic block up on end and make the 7/32" hole for the handrail. Center the hole ¼" from the bottom.

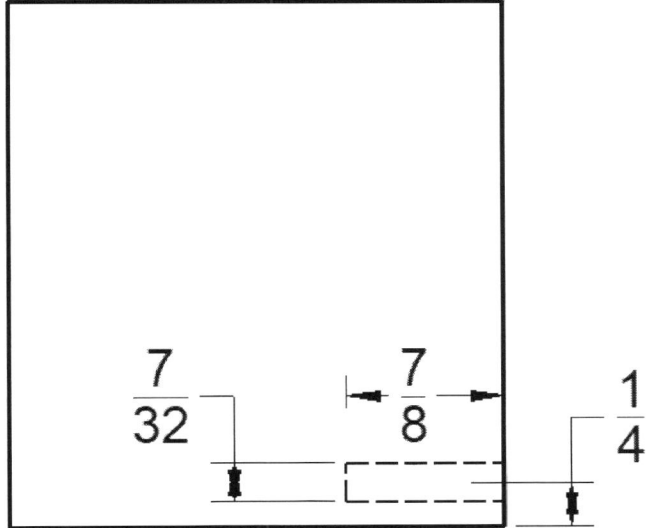

Cut the arm from the block. Round off the corners as shown with the dotted lines.

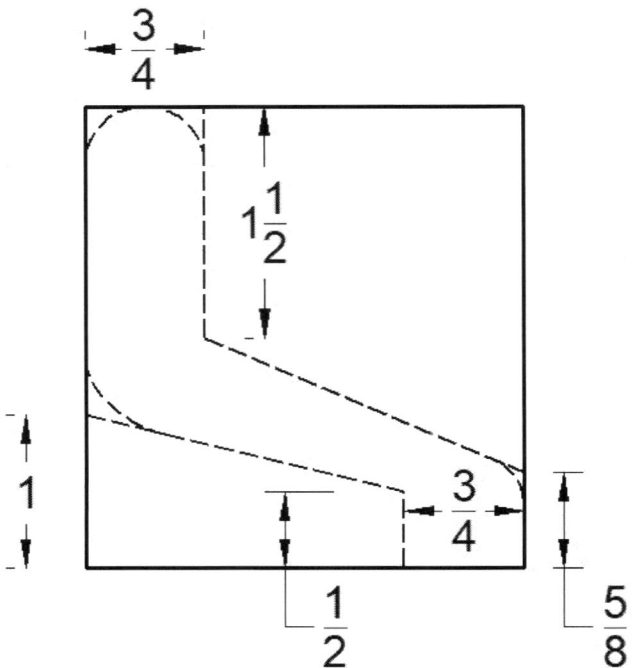

Attaching the arms to the chest involves setting the correct height of the treadmill console also.

Hold or clamp one arm in the middle of the side of the chest with the top of the arm level with the top of the chest. The upper arm should be straight up and down and parallel with the back and front of the chest.

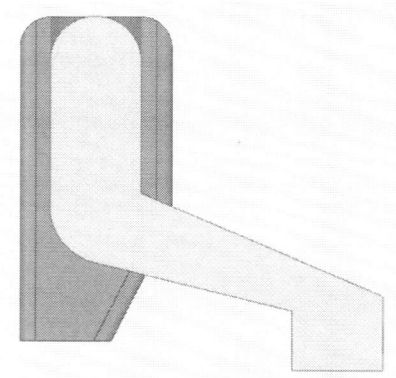

Place the other arm into position also. Insert both handrails from the treadmill console into the hands. The handrails should be parallel with the roller.

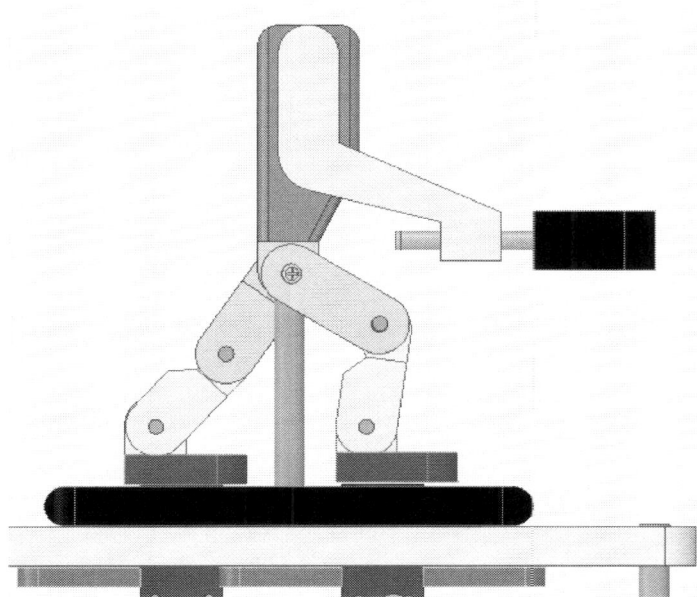

Glue both arms into position.

The console posts are 3/8" dowel. The posts should be inserted 3/8" into the bottom of the console. The other end of the post should be inserted ½" into the treadmill frame. Measure the distance between the console and the roller. The distance between plus the 3/8" on the top and the ½" on the bottom equals the total length of the console post.

Mount the console on the posts. Insert the hand rails from behind the hands into the console. If all looks good, glue the treadmill posts and hand rails in place.

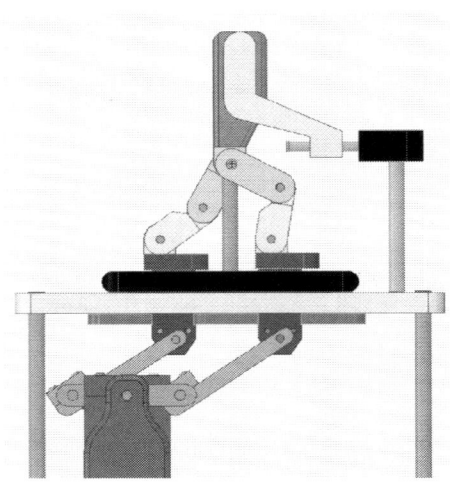

Just one more thing to add to finish the project and that is the head. Instructions for the head are found on page 177.

Install the neck and head on the chest. You may prefer to not glue the head in place to allow changing the position of the head or even changing to another head design.

Your project is now complete!

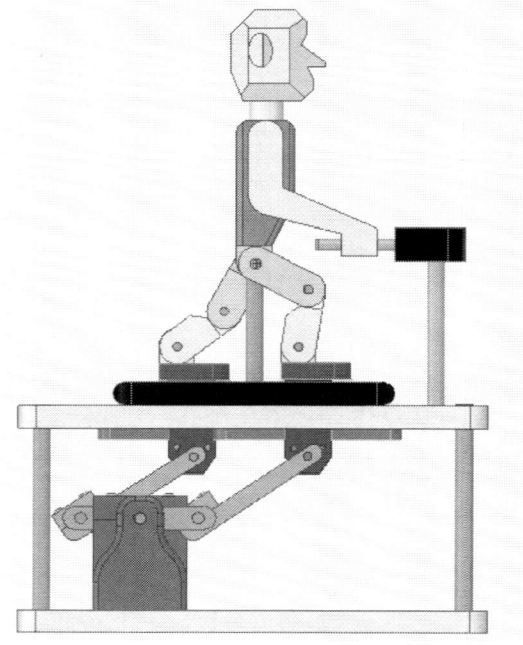

Sit Up Guy

The sit-up guy action figure has only one moving part but offers some new challenges. There are three main parts to this project, The action figure, the drive train, and the main frame. Let's start with the action figure.

Action figure

The chest is the primary moving part so we'll do that first.

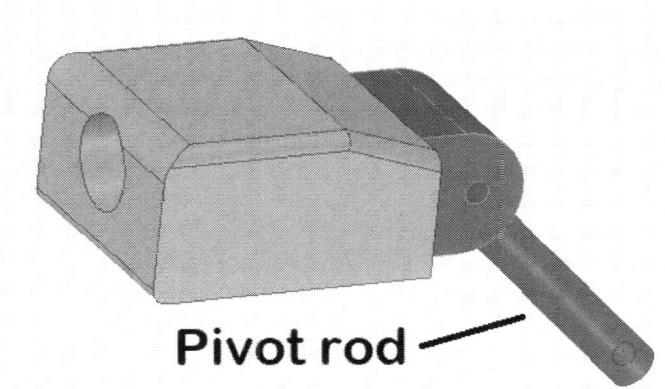

Pivot rod

Refer to the image above as needed while we make the various cuts and holes.

Start with a block 3" x 2" x 1 ¼". A standard 2 x 4 is a good source for this piece. Trim it down to 1 ¼" thick.

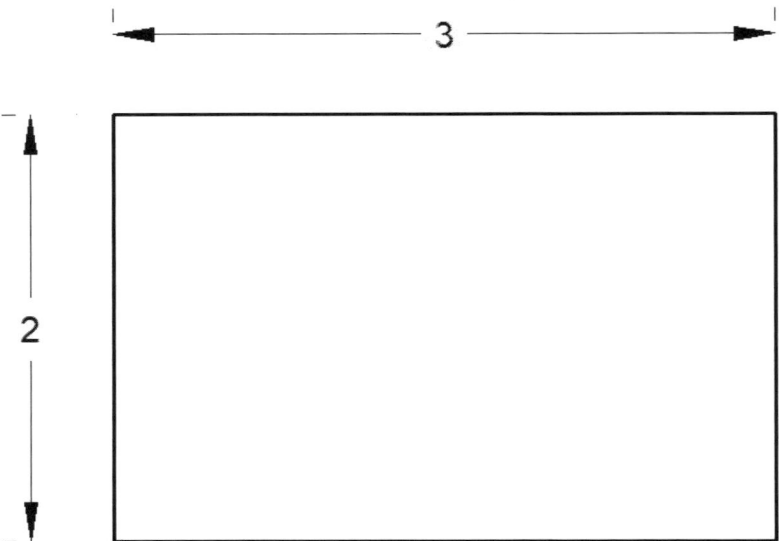

On one end drill the hole for the neck piece. Note that the neck is slightly closer to the front of the chest. That is to allow the hands to fit behind the head.

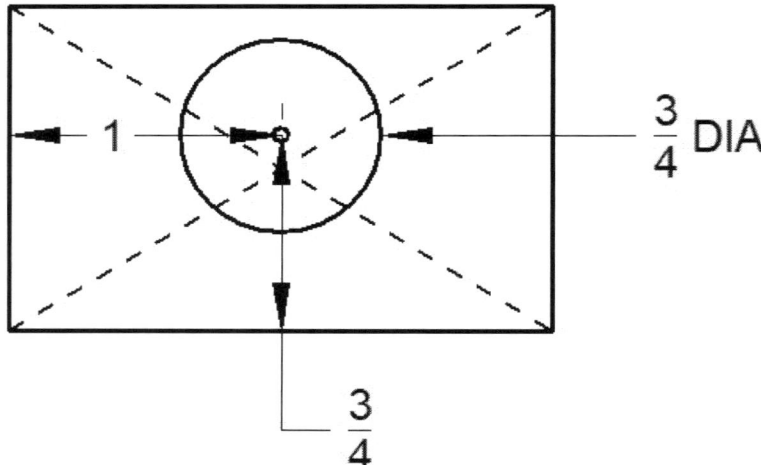

An easy way to locate the position for the neck hole is to draw two diagonal lines as shown above with the dotted lines. That will give you the exact center. Then move the center up 1/8".

The neck hole should be 5/8" deep.

On the bottom end of the chest there will be a pivot rod. The drive train will pull on the pivot rod to rotate the chest ~90° The pivot rod is mounted at a 45° angle. To help drill the pivot rod mounting hole at an angle, we will make a small flat surface at 45°.

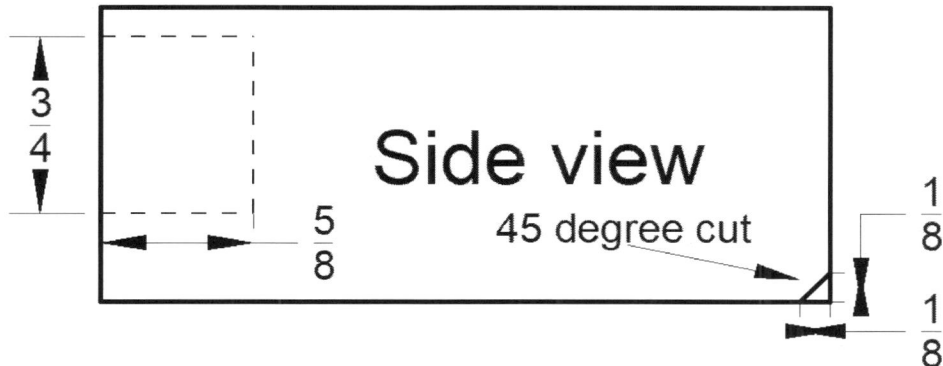

The pivot rod hole is 3/8" diameter and centered. Drill the hole ~5/8" deep.

We need to add a few more cuts to continue shaping the chest.

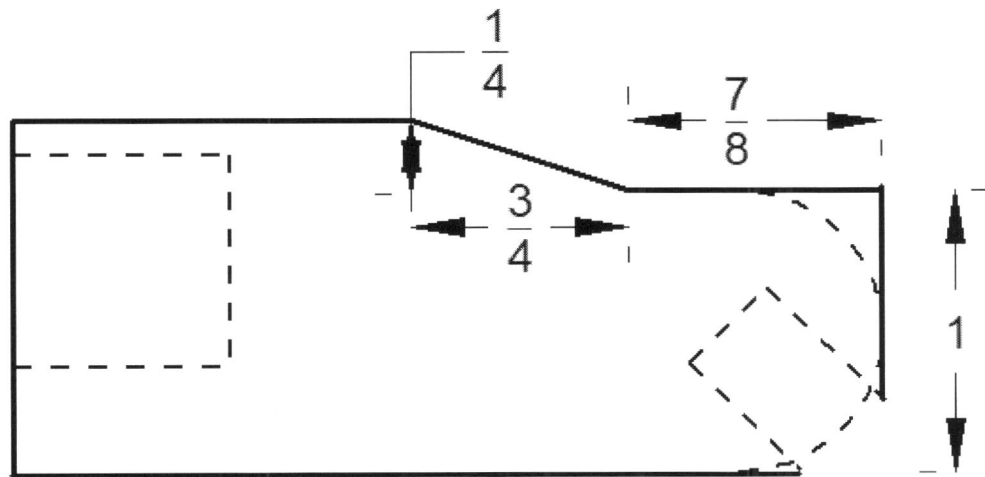

Round the pivot end of the chest as shown above with the dotted lines.

The pivot end has a hole to connect the legs. You can either drill the hole all the way through or ~5/8" deep on both sides. Note that the hole will intersect with the pivot rod hole.

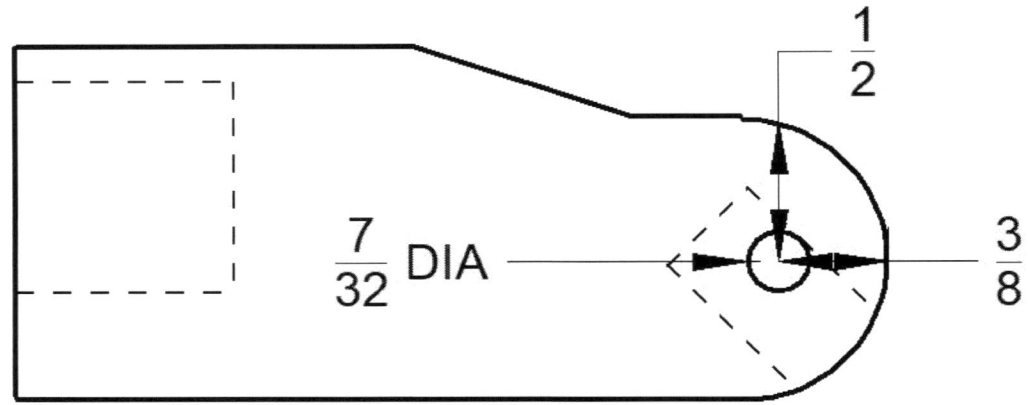

To finish the chest, we need to trim 3/8" off both sides of the pivot point.

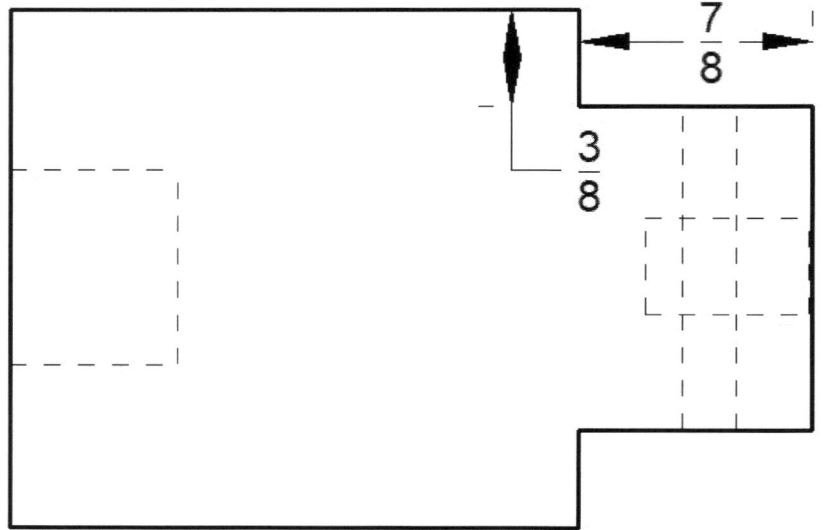

The pivot rod is a piece of 3/8" dowel. The actual length will be determined during final assembly. Start with a length of ~3". Drill a 7/32" hole, centered, ¼" from one end.

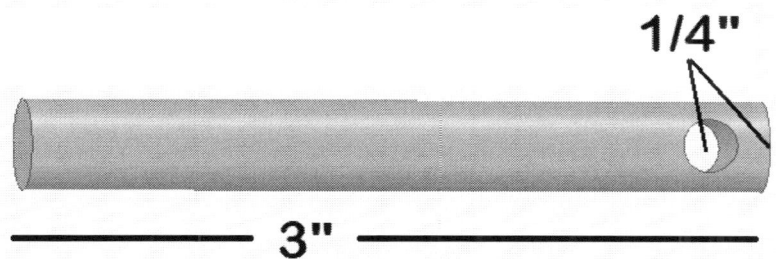

Insert the pivot rod into the chest. Do NOT glue it in place.

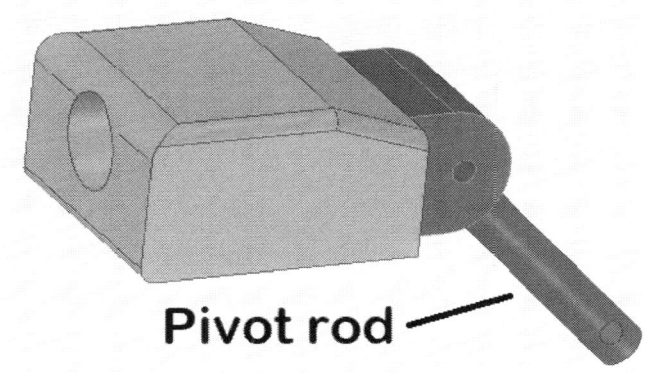

The Chest is now complete.

The legs are next. Remember that you need to make two legs.

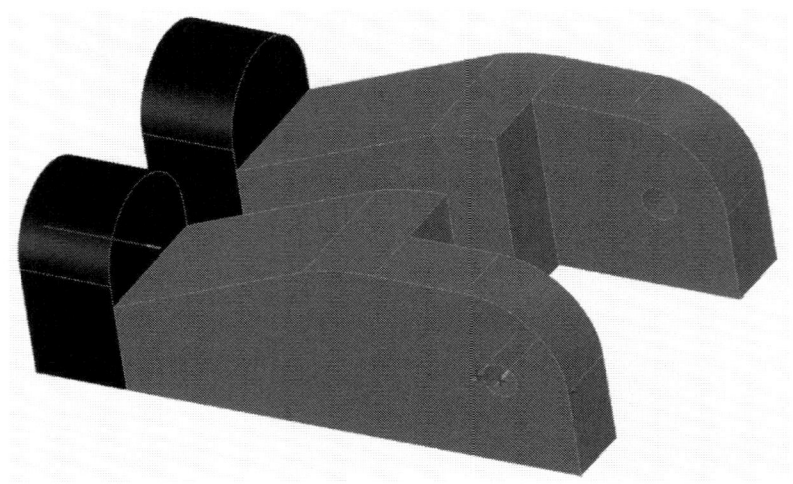

Cut the starting basic block from a piece of ¾″.

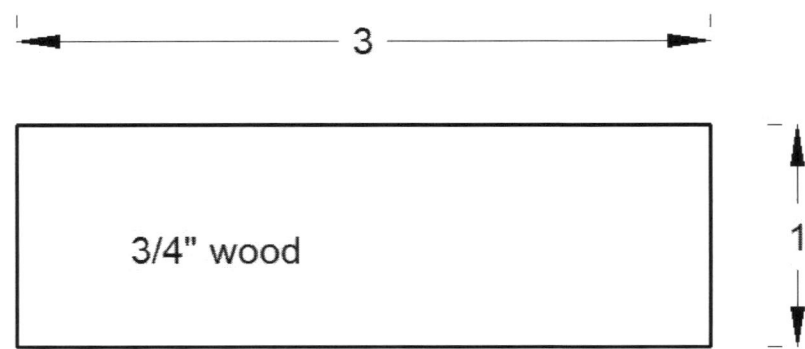

Drill the pivot hole.

Looking at the top, remove the area to attach the leg. Cut the opposite side for the other leg.

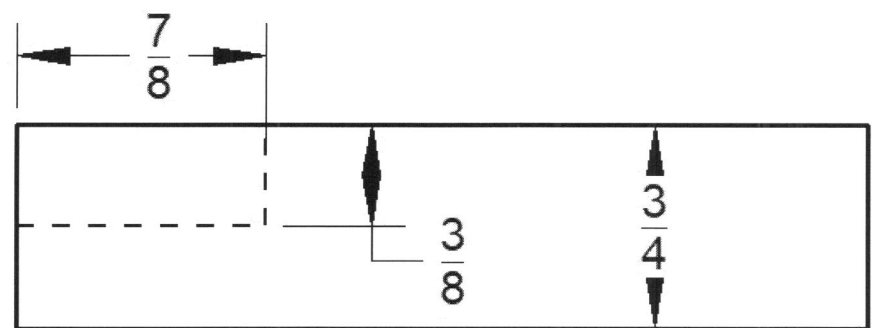

Make the cuts for the shoe and round the other end.

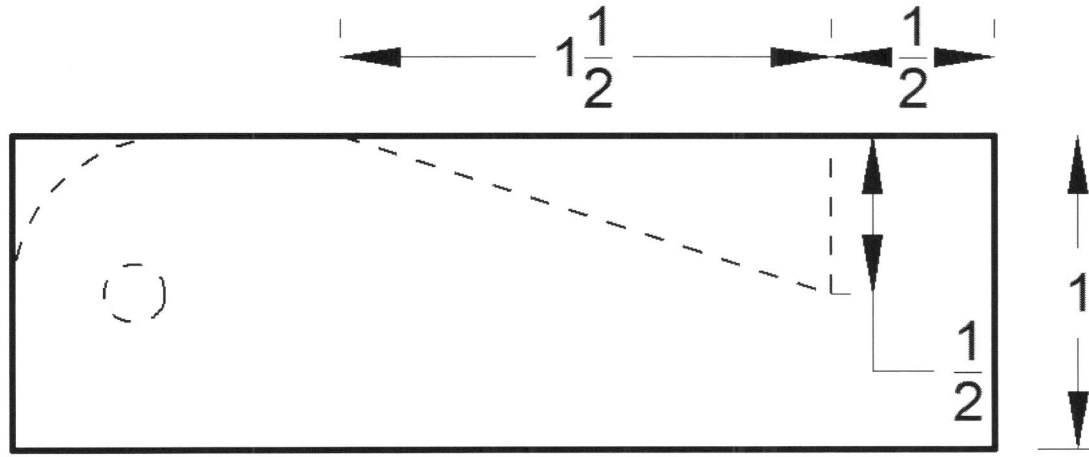

Temporarily insert a piece of 3/16" dowel into the leg hole. There should be ~1/2" of the dowel to insert into the chest pivot hole. Attach the leg by inserting the dowel into the pivot hole on the chest. Rotate the chest 90° so the chest is straight up. You may have to sand some edges to get the chest to rotate without binding.

Do the same with the other leg. Hold both legs flat on the surface and rotate the chest 90°.

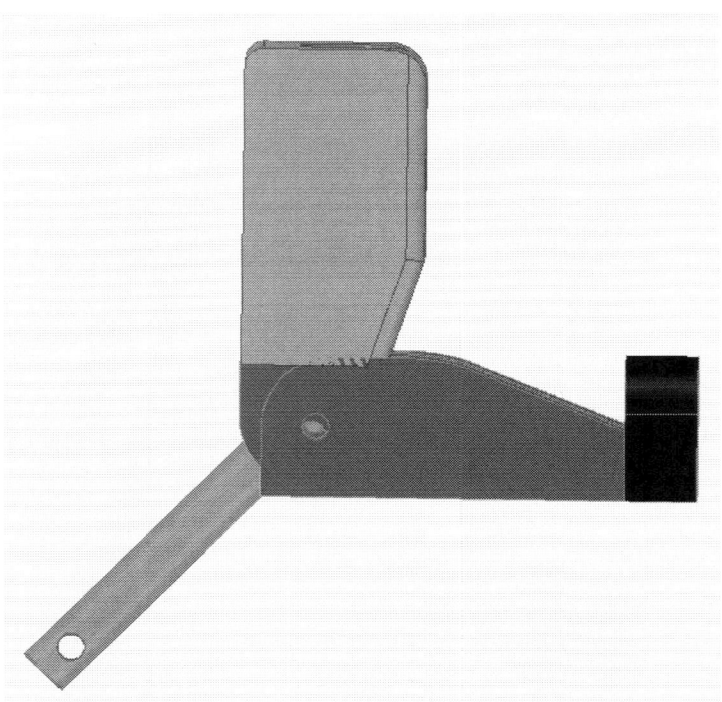

Remove the pivot rod.

The arms are next. There are two pieces to each arm.

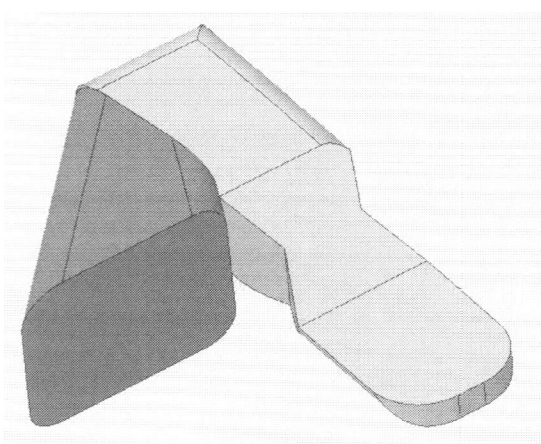

We'll start with the upper arm. The starting basic block is cut from ¾" wood.

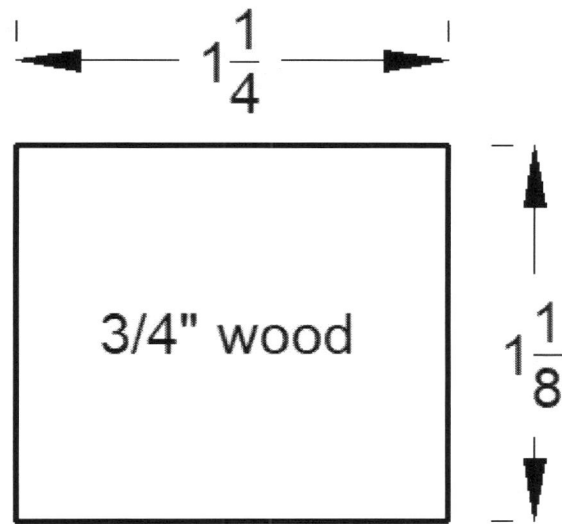

You will need two of these for the two arms. However, from this point on the location of the cuts will not be the same. The cuts shown are for the right arm.

The upper arm narrows down from ¾" where it attaches to the chest, to ½" at the elbow. Stand the block on end and make the cut as shown. The left arm will have the cut on the opposite side.

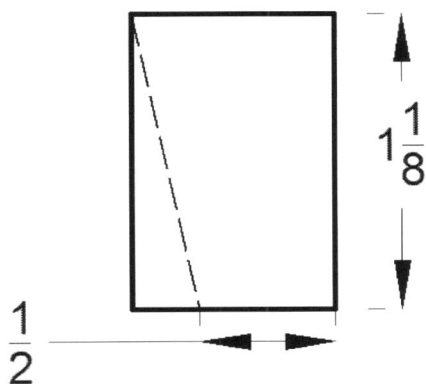

Lay the block flat. Draw a diagonal line as shown. The line will be from the opposite corner for the left arm. Cut along the diagonal line.

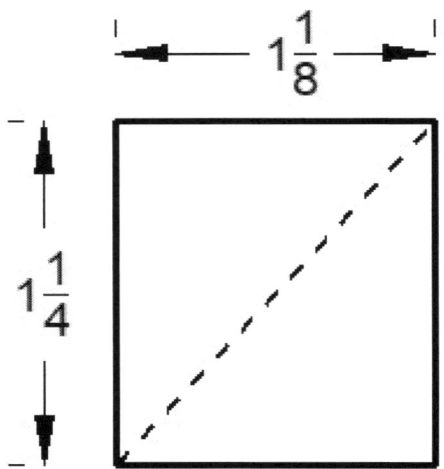

Draw a small diagonal line as shown to help separate the upper arm from the lower arm. The line will be on the opposite side for the left arm.

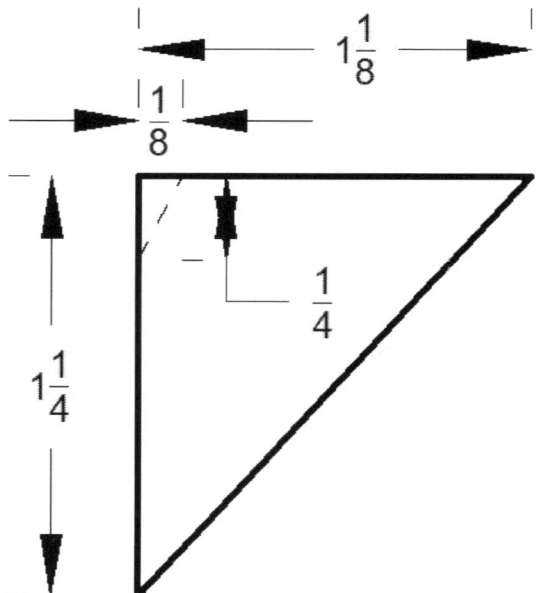

Glue the upper arms in place. Note the placement of the small angle cuts. Sand all the edges of the upper arms except the surface to attach the lower arms. You can also sand and round all the remaining edges on the chest.

This would be a good time to paint the chest and arms if desired. The pivot area on the bottom of the chest I consider to be part of the legs so it is a different color.

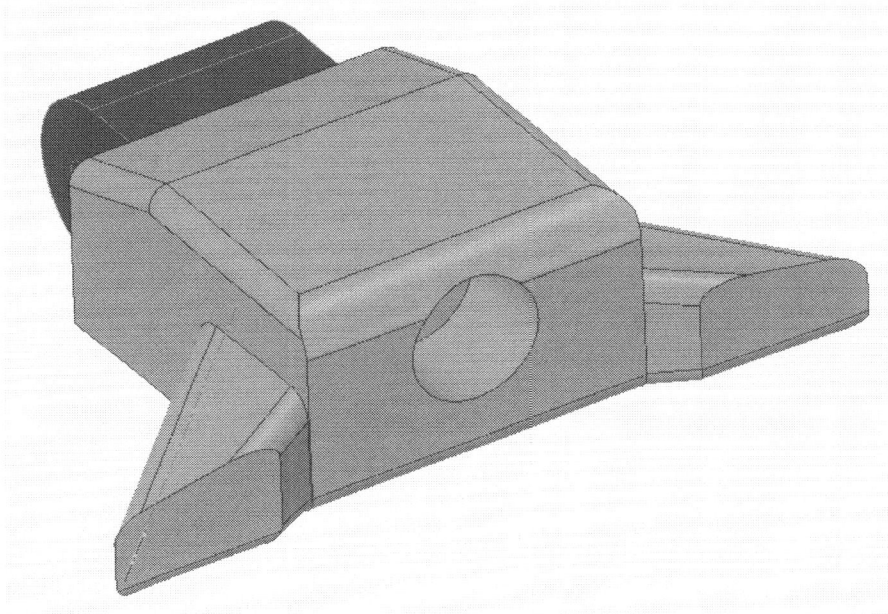

The lower arms are cut the same for both sides.

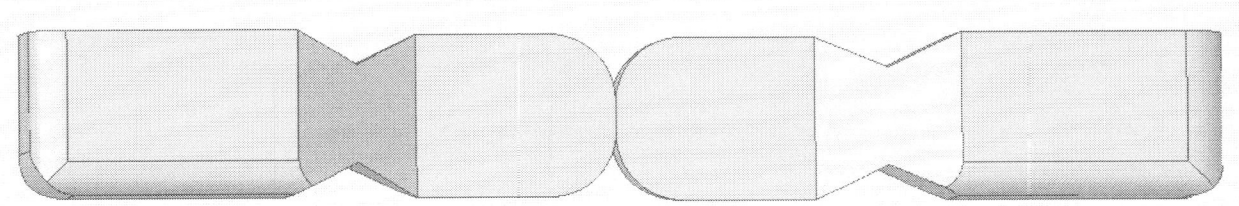

Start with a basic block of ¾" wood. Cut it down to ½" thick.

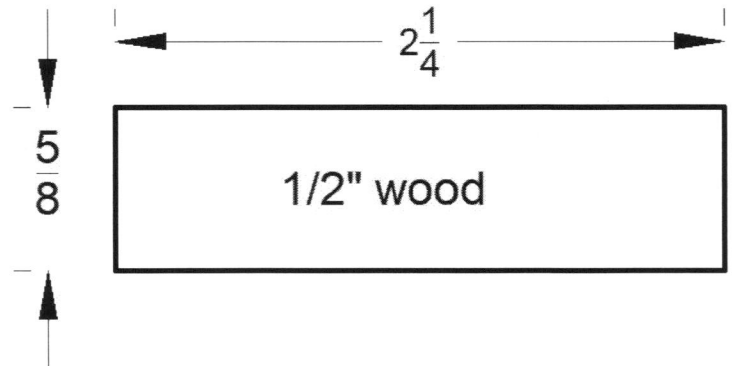

Begin to shape the arm with cuts from the side.

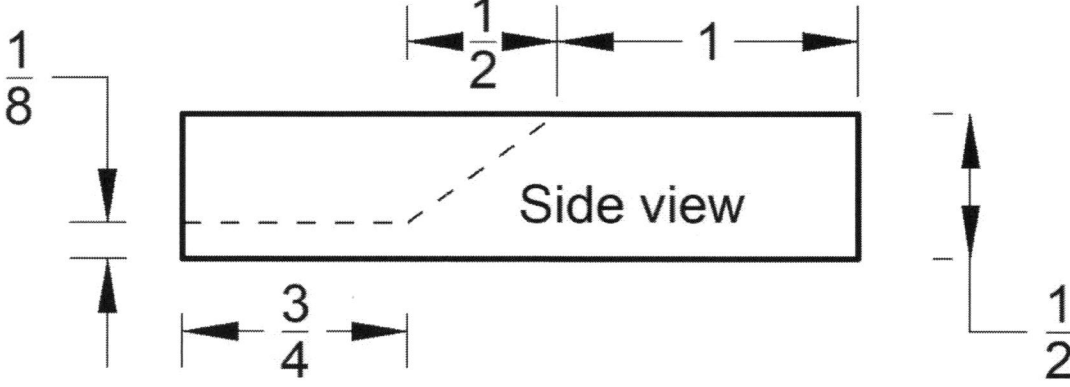

Add a few small cuts to identify the hand portion. Sand all the edges except the surface to attach to the upper arms.

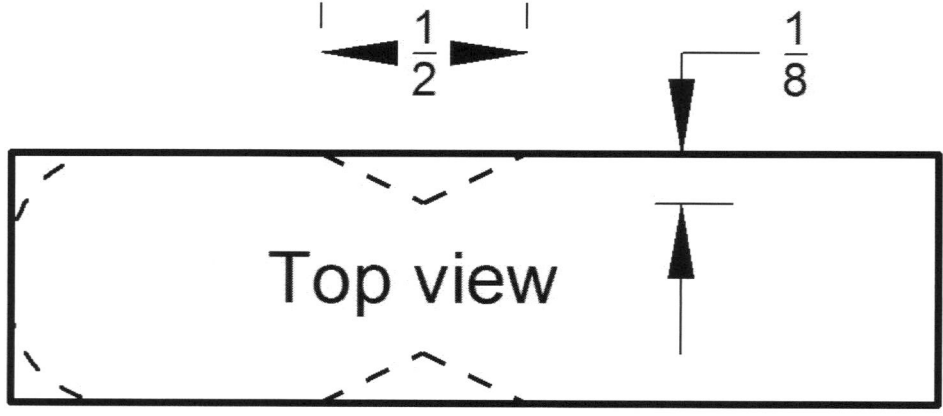

Glue the arms in place.

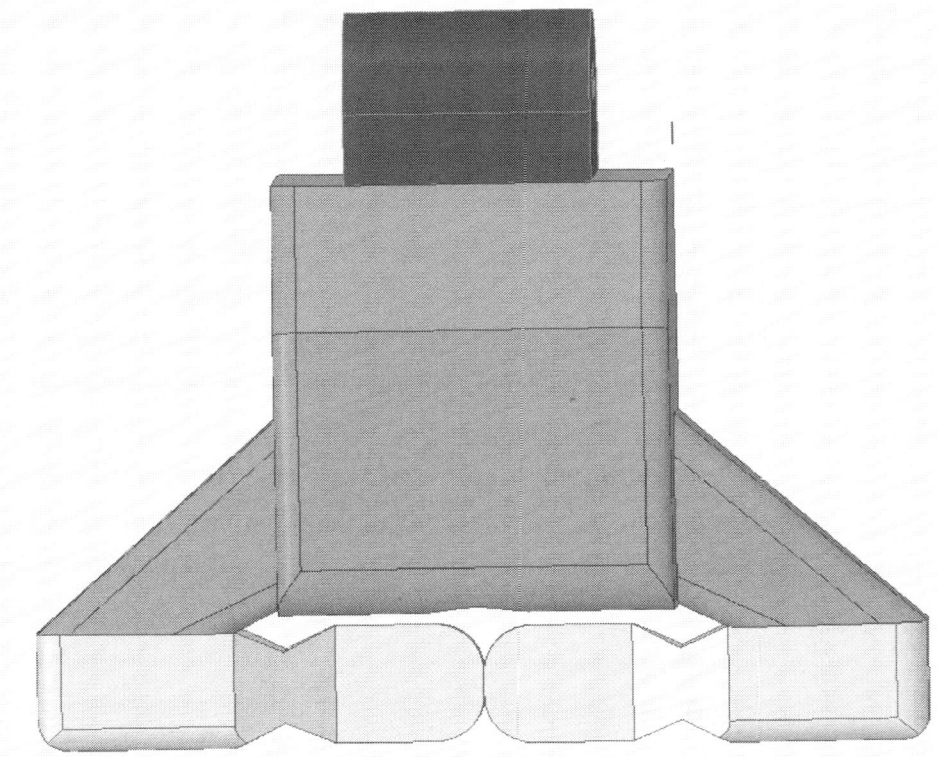

Sand all remaining edges on the arms, especially the elbows and edges where the upper arm attaches to the lower arm.

The instructions on how to make the head are on page 177. However, the head will have to be slightly modified to fit the hands behind the head. Replace the drawing on page 181 with the one below. Note the additional space behind the lower back of the head.

The space required for the hands also depends on how long you make the neck. The longer the neck the more room you will have for the hands. Start with a piece of ¾" dowel, 1 ½" long for the neck.

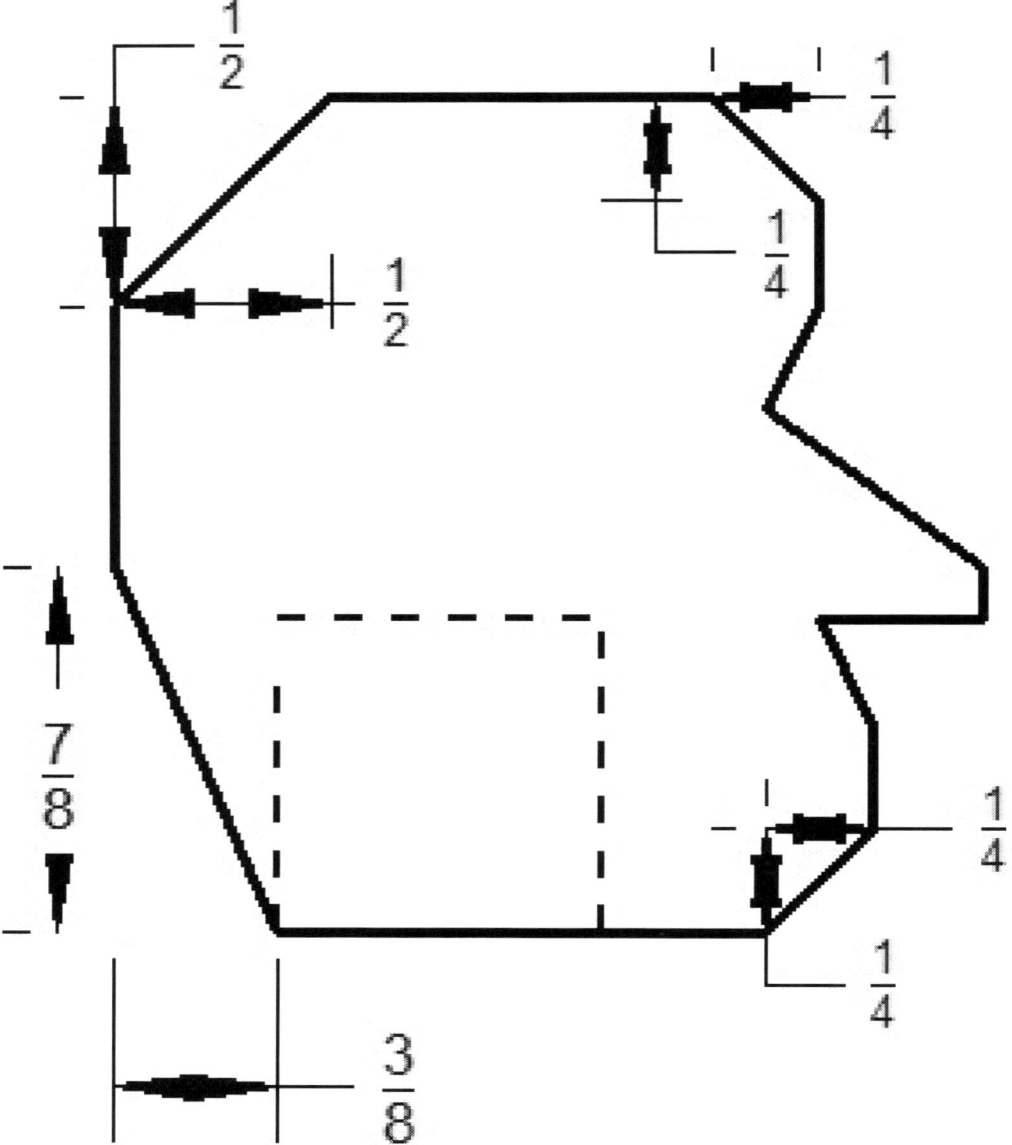

Insert the neck into the head. Insert the neck into the chest. If the head and neck appear to fit normally, glue them in place.

The action figure is now complete.

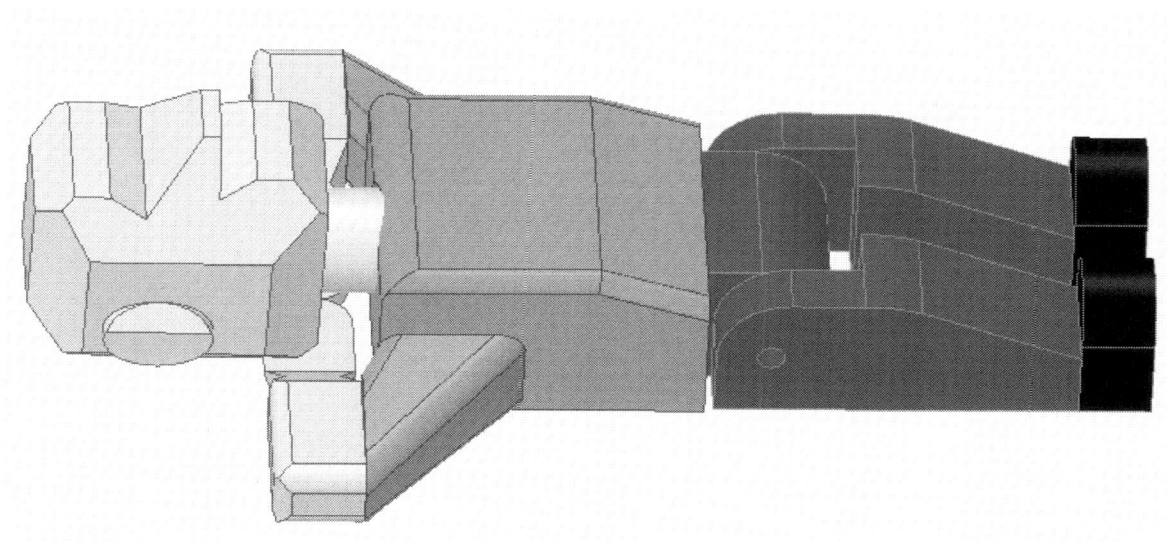

Main frame

The top and bottom frame pieces are the same size. Drill 3/8" holes in each corner, 5/8" from each side. Round the corners.

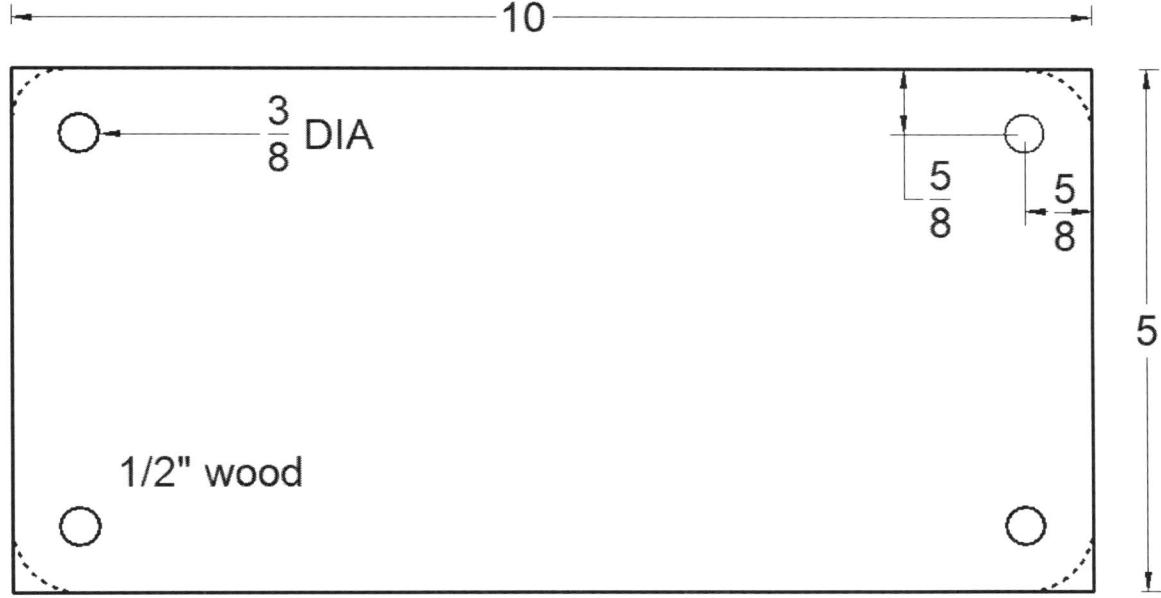

Slightly sand all the edges.

The top frame requires a slot to access the action figure.

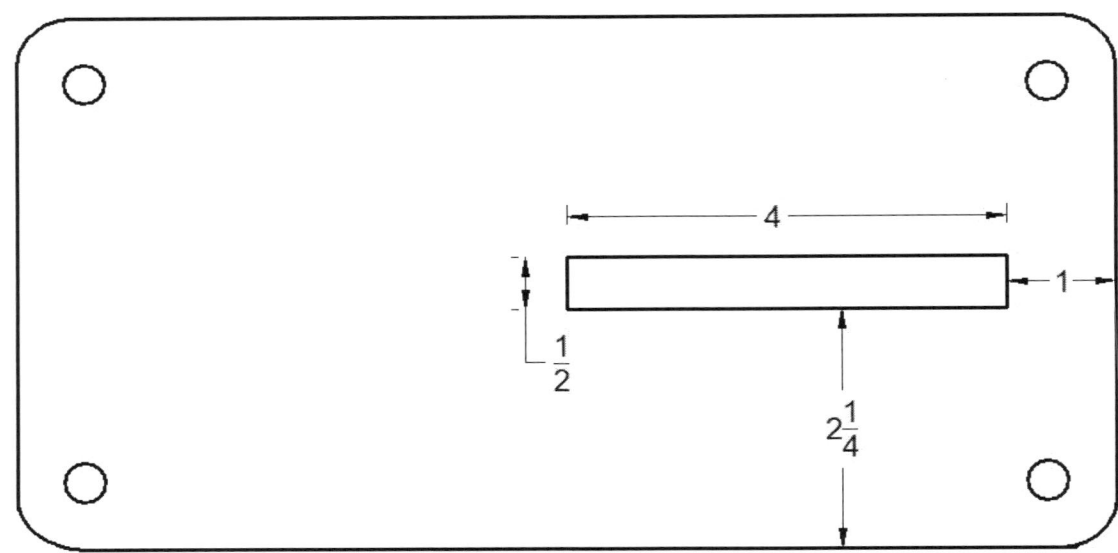

Cut four pieces of 3/8" dowel, each 5" long for the corner posts Temporarily mount the top frame onto the bottom frame piece to make sure the corner posts all line up. Glue the dowel pieces into the top frame piece only.

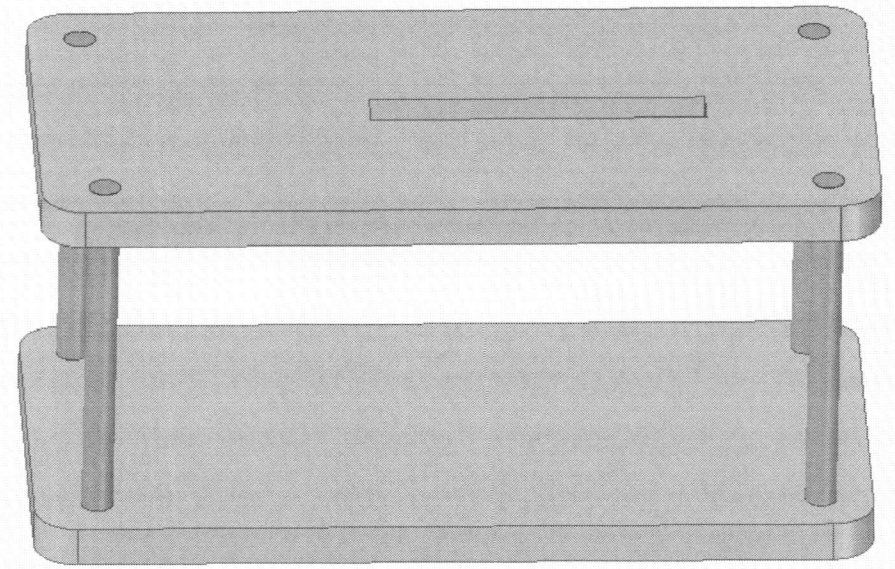

Now we can glue the body to the frame. Temporarily insert the pivot rod into the chest. The bottom of the shoes should be 1" from the end of the top frame.

The legs should be centered over the slot in the top frame. Be sure to only glue the legs to the frame.

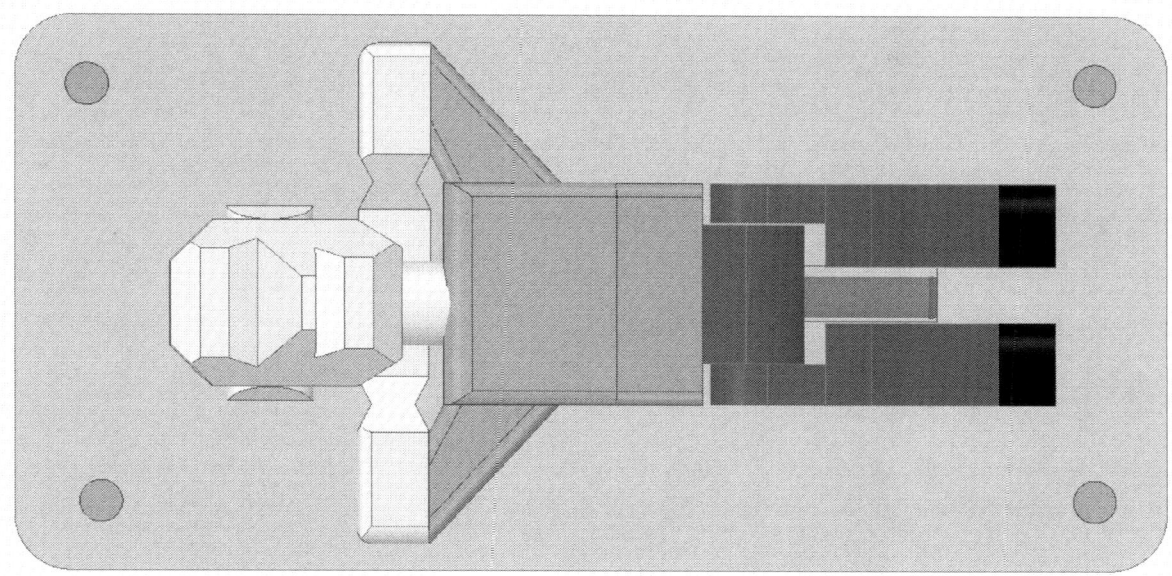

Rotate the upper body to insure free movement.

Drive Train

The main part of the drive train is the disc. Use 3/8" or ½" wood for the disc.

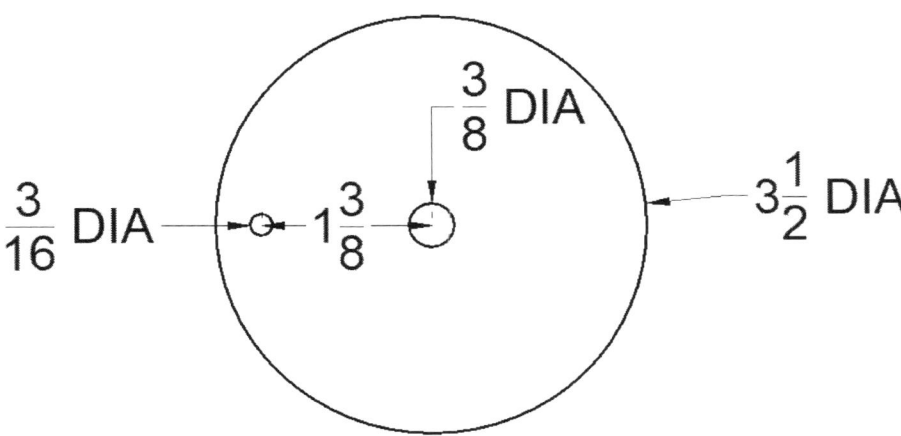

Drill the center 3/8" hole for the axle and the 3/16" hole 1 3/8" from the center for the link pin. Lightly sand the outside edges.

Insert and glue a 1 ¼" piece of 3/16" dowel in the link pin hole. It should be flush with one side.

To hold the link in place on the link pin we will add a small cap. The cap is a 3/8" piece of 3/8" dowel. Drill a 3/16" hole, ¼" deep, on one end. Round off the other end. Temporarily install the cap.

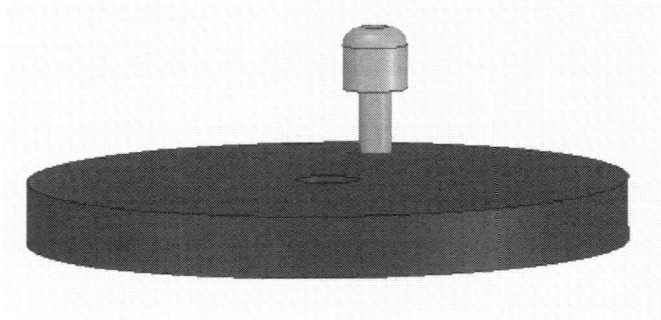

To support the disc, we'll make a mount from a piece of 2 x 4. The mount is 1 ½" x 1 ½" x 3".

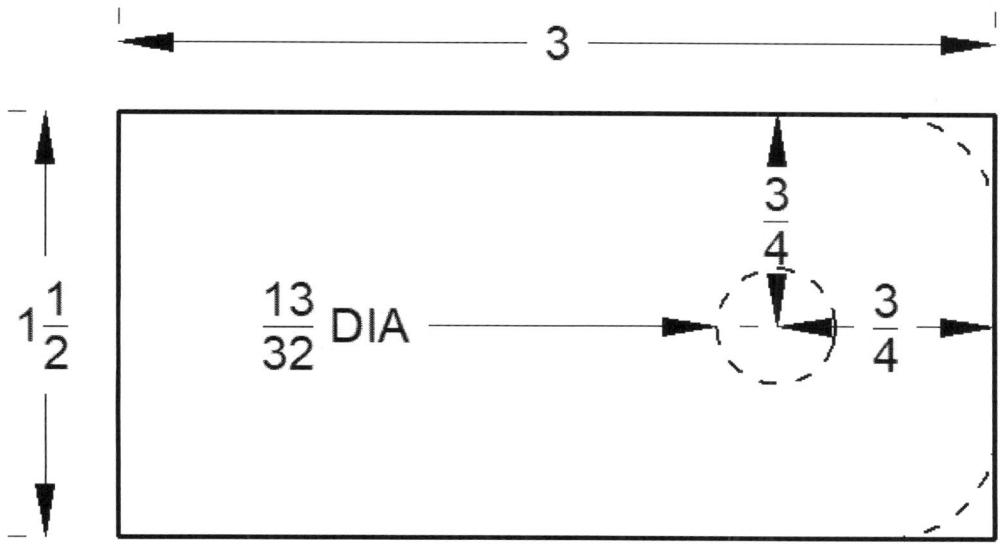

Round off the top edges.

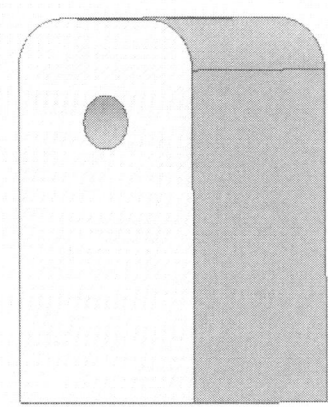

The drive axle is a 3 ½" piece of 3/8" dowel. To lock the axle in place on the mount we will make a pin from a piece of 1/8" dowel. Temporarily insert the axle into the disc. It should be flush with the surface of the disc. Slide the mount onto the axle. Allow ~1/16" between the mount and the disc.

On the other side of the disc mount, make a mark on the axle 1/8" from the side of the disc mount. Drill a 1/8" hole in the center of the axle on the mark on the axle.

Remove the axle from the mount. Permanently glue the axle into the disc. Insert the disk into the mount. Make a pin from a piece of 1/8" dowel ~1" long. Slightly round each end of the pin. Insert and center the pin into the hole in the axle. The axle pin will probably fit tight enough without glue. Spin the disc to make sure it spins easily.

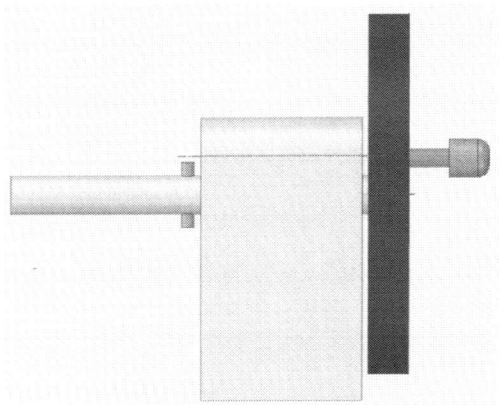

The crank handle can be any scrap piece of wood ¼", 3/8", or even ½".

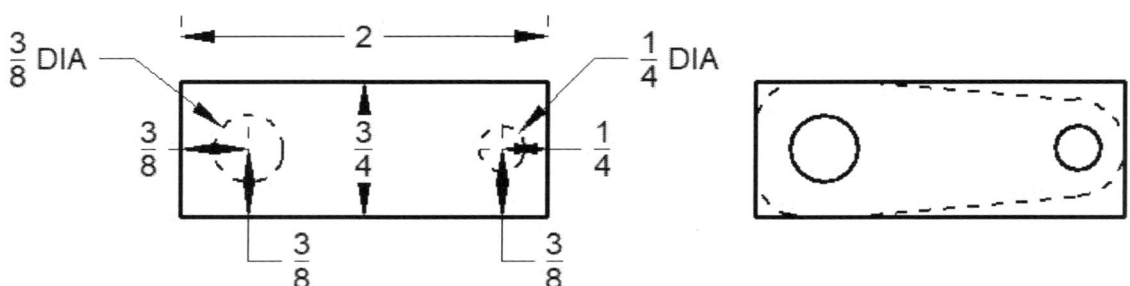

Trim the crank as shown with the dotted lines.

The crank handle is a piece of ¼" dowel, 1 ½" long. Round one end and glue the other end into the crank, flush with the side of the crank.

The primary part of the drive train is now complete.

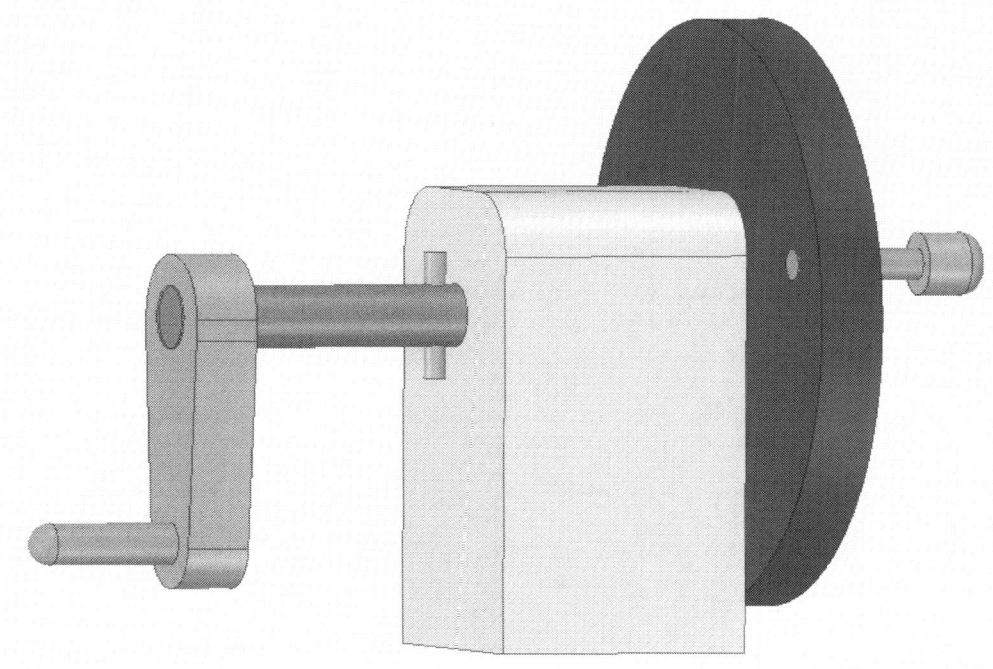

The last piece we have to make for this project is the drive train link.

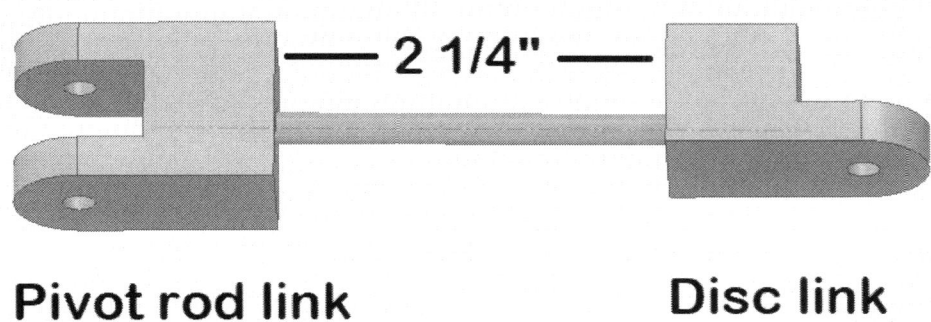

Pivot rod link   **Disc link**

The disc link is made from ¾" wood. Cut the basic block. Stand the block on end and drill a 3/16" hole, ½" deep, centered, on one end.

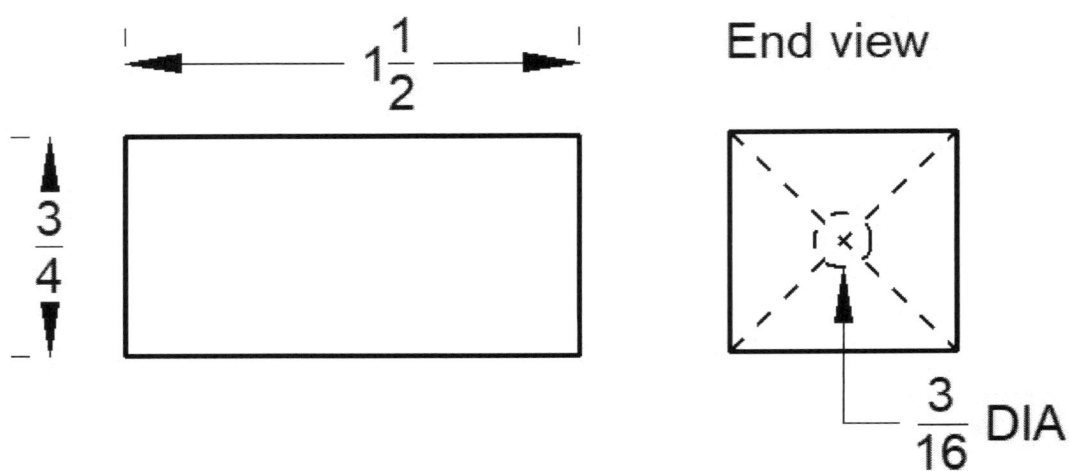

End view

$1\frac{1}{2}$

$\frac{3}{4}$

$\frac{3}{16}$ DIA

Lay the block on its side and drill a 7/32" hole as shown. Round the end. Make the final trim cut from the top.

Side view   Top view

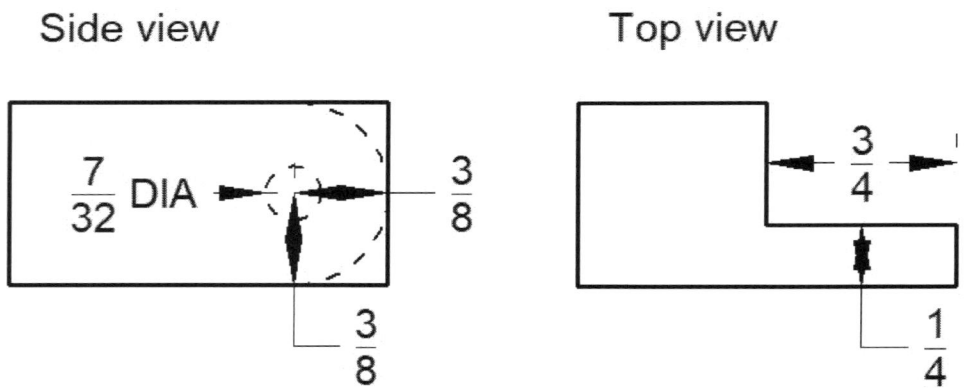

$\frac{7}{32}$ DIA $\frac{3}{8}$ $\frac{3}{4}$

$\frac{3}{8}$ $\frac{1}{4}$

The pivot rod link starts with a piece of ¾" wood.

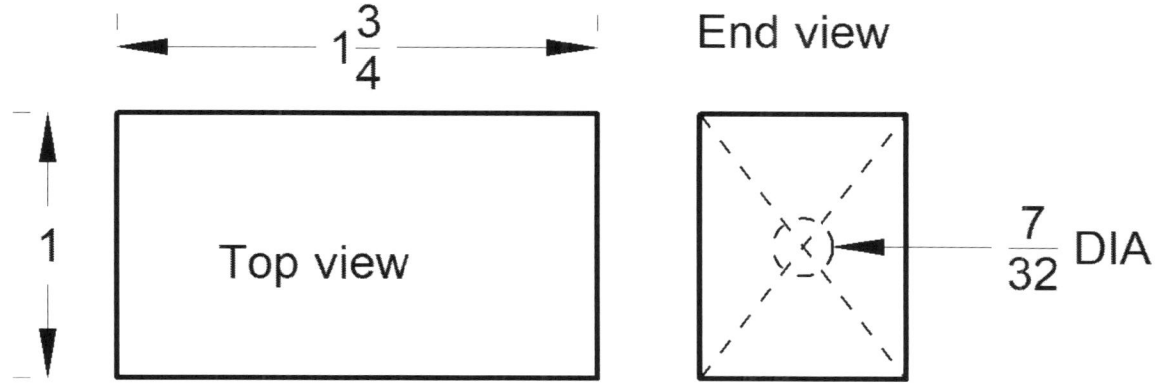

End view

Lay the block on its side and drill a 7/32" hole as shown. Round the end. Make the final trim cut from the top.

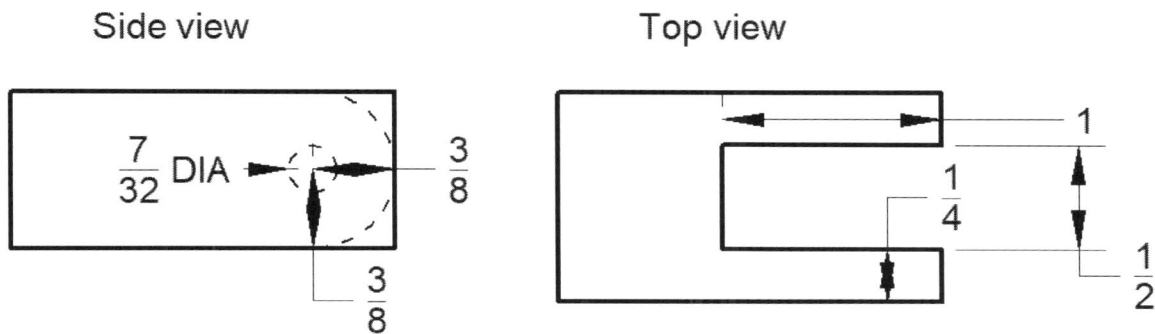

The link rod is a 3 ¼" piece of 3/16" dowel. Insert the dowel into the ends of both links as shown. Lay both links on a flat surface. There should be 2 ¼" between the link pieces.

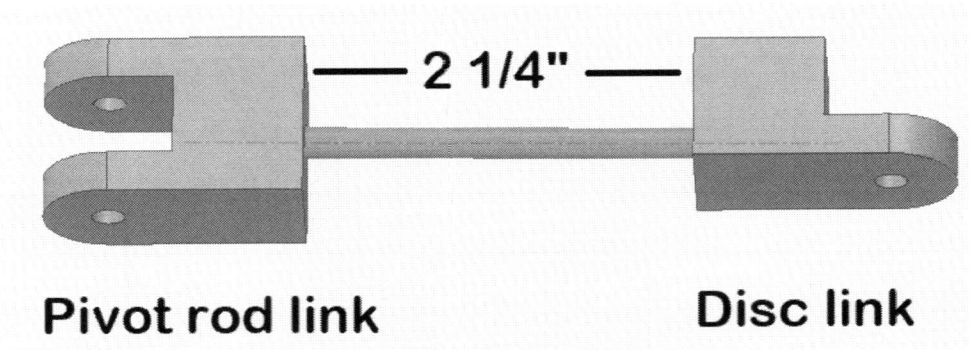

Pivot rod link   **Disc link**

Final assembly

Now we get to put it all together. The top frame and action figure should already be glued in place.

It will take some experimenting to get the action figure movement correct. The ideal movement would be to go from perfectly flat to 90°upright

The range of motion is controlled by two elements. One, The length of the pivot rod and two, the location of the drive train.

The length of the pivot rod will determine the amount of rotation. Once the amount of rotation is determined, the position of the drive train will determine where the motion will happen. For an extreme example, if the amount of rotation was only 20°, the position of the drivetrain would determine if the rotation happens from a flat position, near the straight up position, or somewhere in between.

Temporarily assemble all the drive train components. Make a small pencil mark at the insertion point of the pivot rod into the chest.

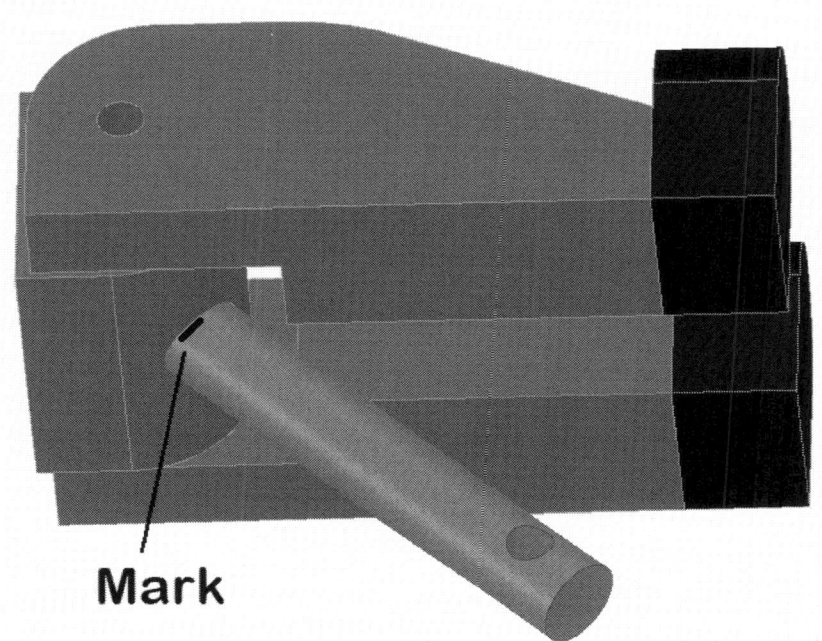

Mark

Position the disc mount so the drive link lines up with the pivot rod. Move the disc mount as far away from the pivot rod as you can without lifting the chest. Now while holding the disc mount, turn the crank. If you are lucky the chest will rotate near 90°.

If the rotation attempts to rotate the chest beyond sitting straight up, move the disc mount away until the chest is straight up. Continue turning the crank. If the rotation attempts to go beyond the chest lying flat, you have excessive rotation. To reduce the rotation amount, pull the pivot rod out the of the chest ~1/8", make another mark, and try the sequence again.

Reposition the disc mount each time you modify the pivot rod length. Once you have the rotation correct, shorten the length of the pivot rod by the amount between the marks. Fully insert the pivot rod into the chest again and re-test.

Once you find the correct range of motion, glue the pivot rod into the chest. Then glue the disc mount in place.

Your project is now complete!

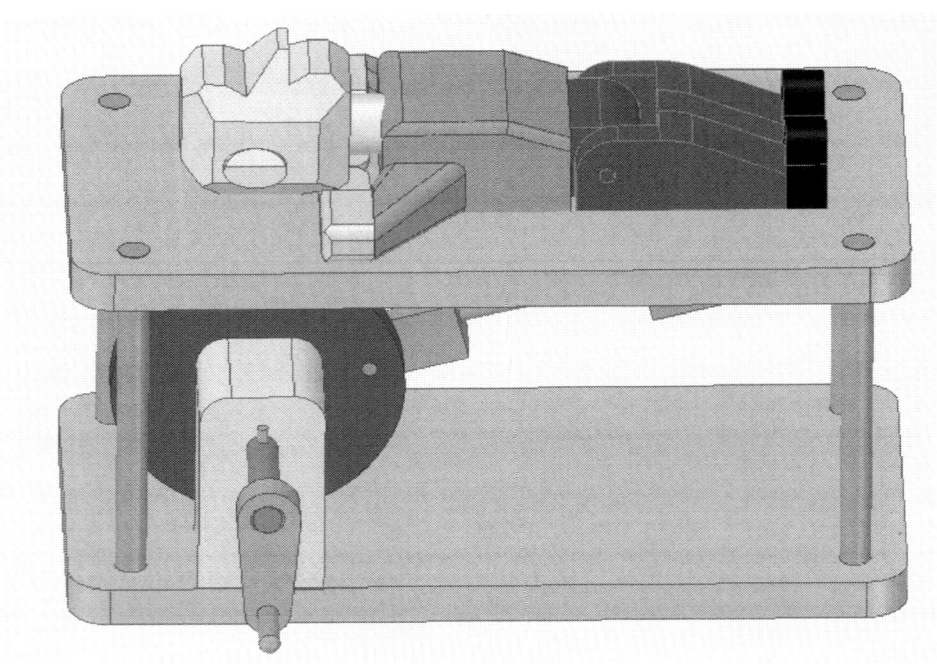

Action figure Head

*****

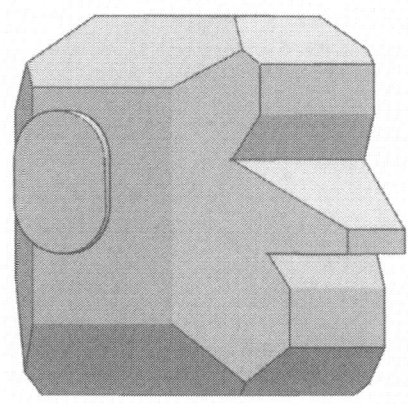

This head is used in all of the projects in this book.

The head starts with a 2" x 2" x 1 1/2" block. A piece of 2 x 4 is a good source for this.

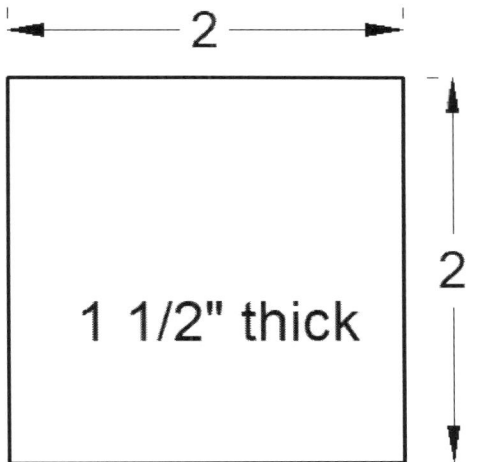

Drill the hole for the neck. The neck hole should be 5/8" deep.

Note: You can change the depth and diameter of the holes in the head and body to accommodate any size neck you prefer.

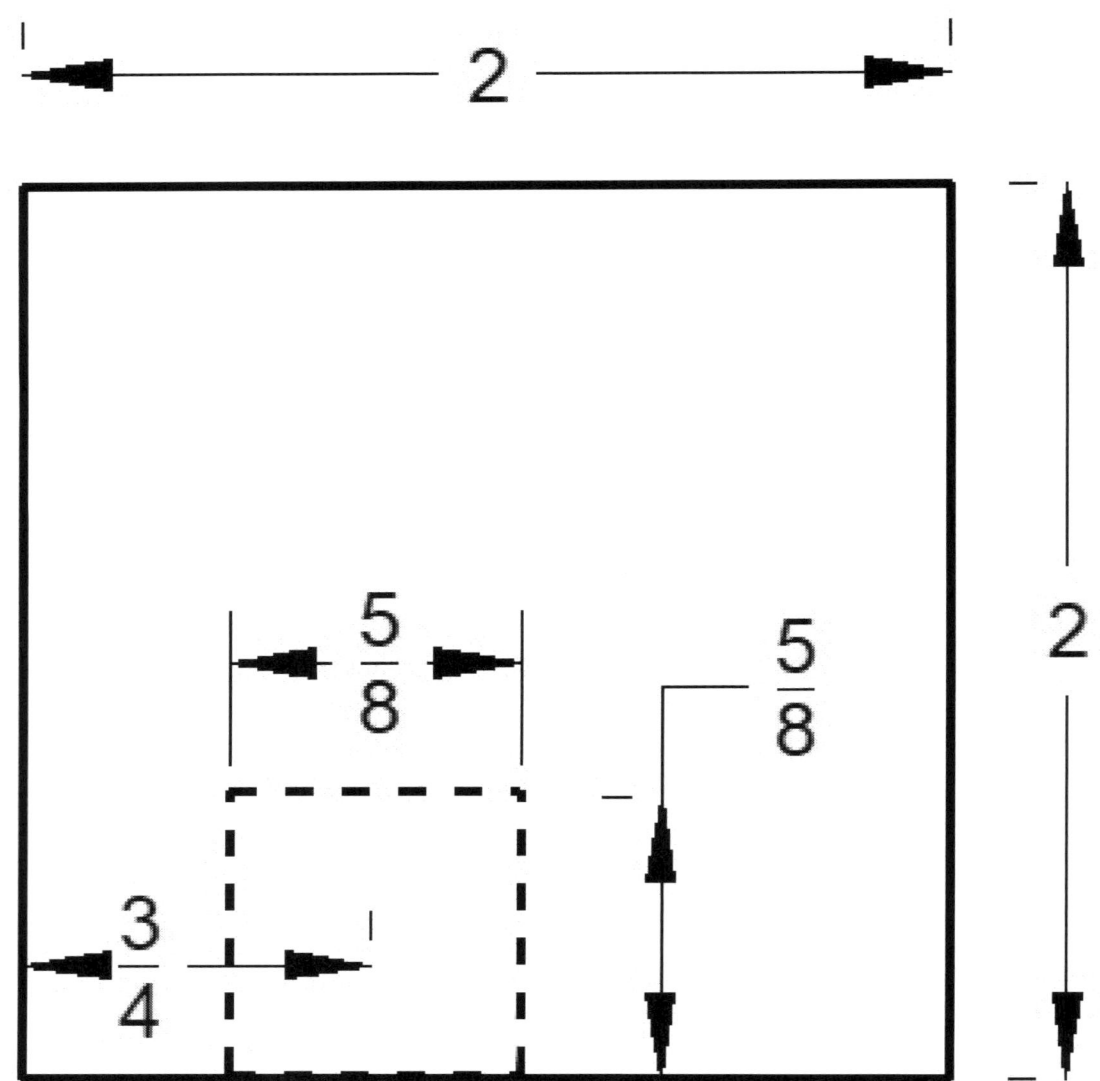

Now we can draw all the lines to define the head. Do not make any cuts until all the lines are drawn.

The first lines will rough outline the nose.

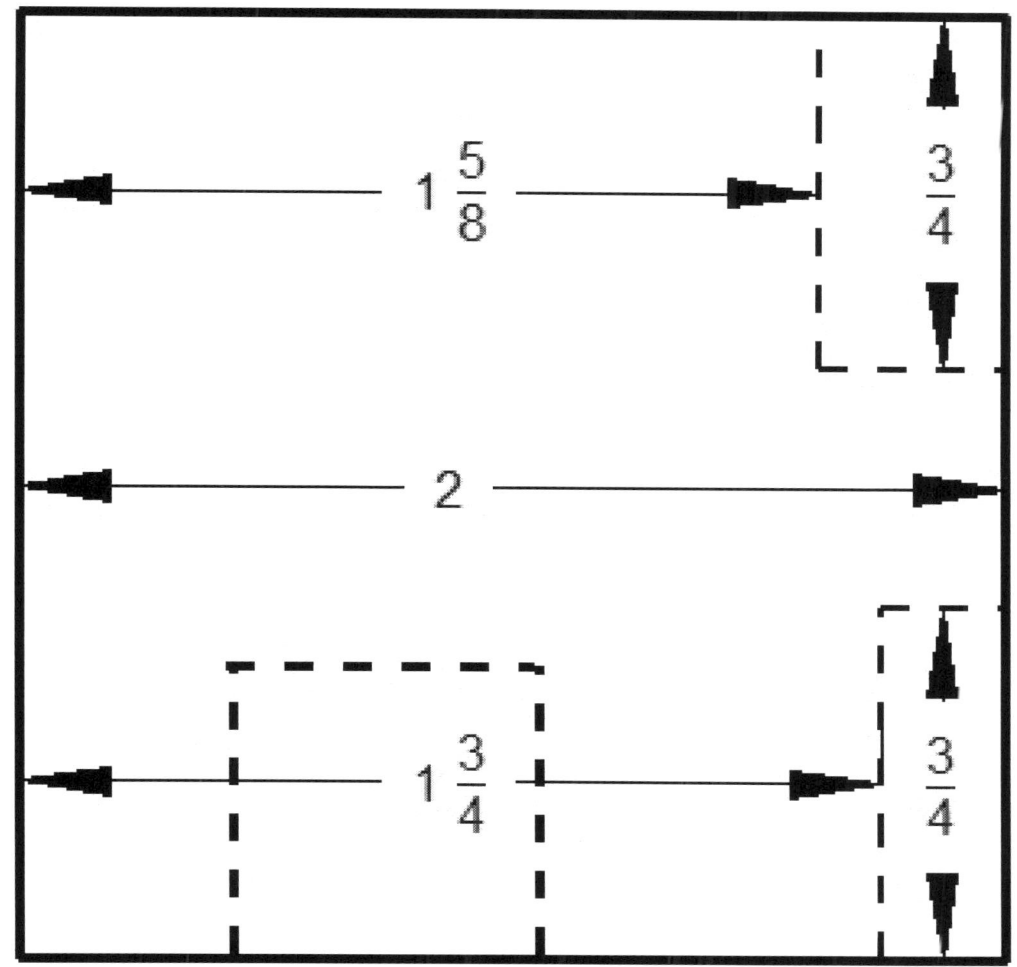

Now draw in the detail facial features

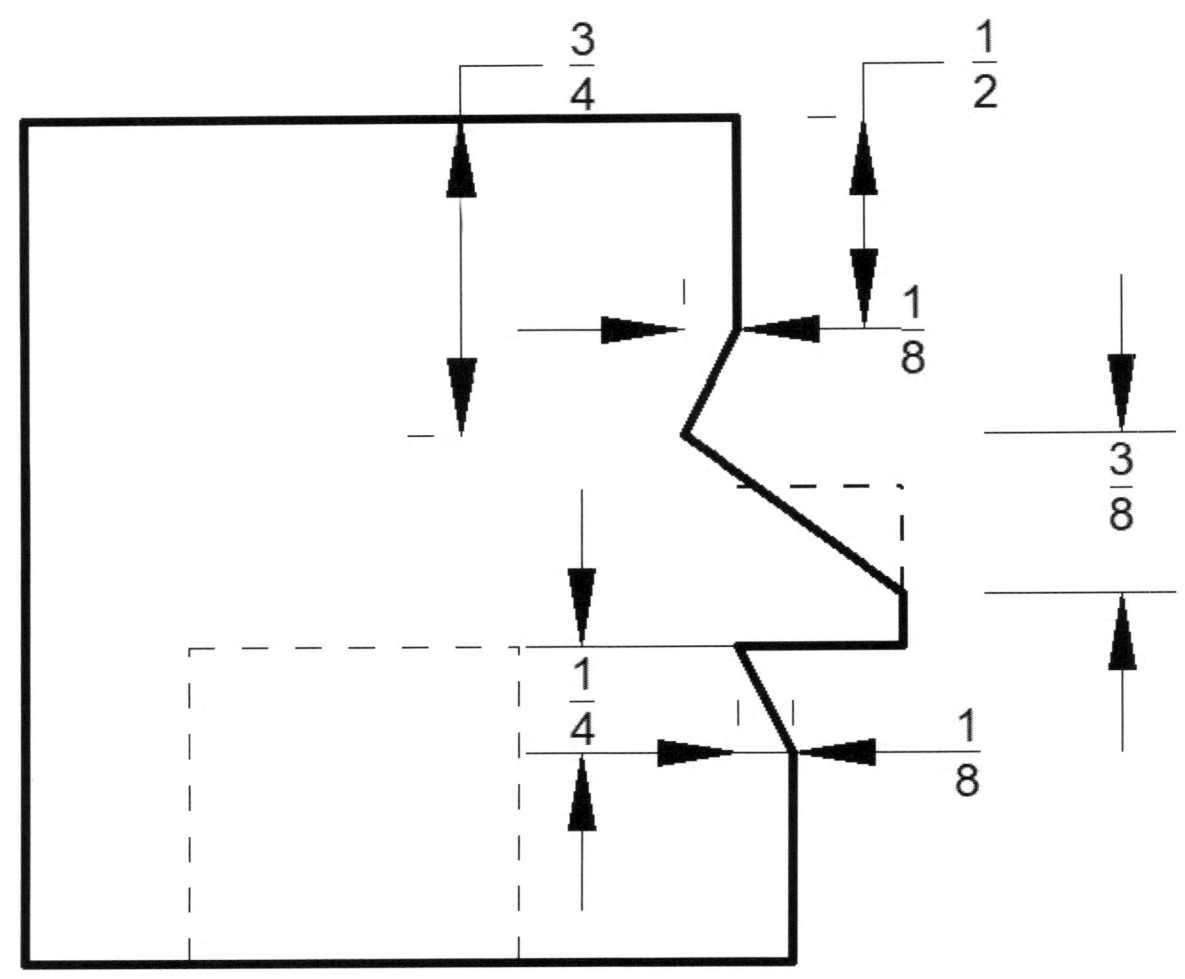

Trim the side of the head.

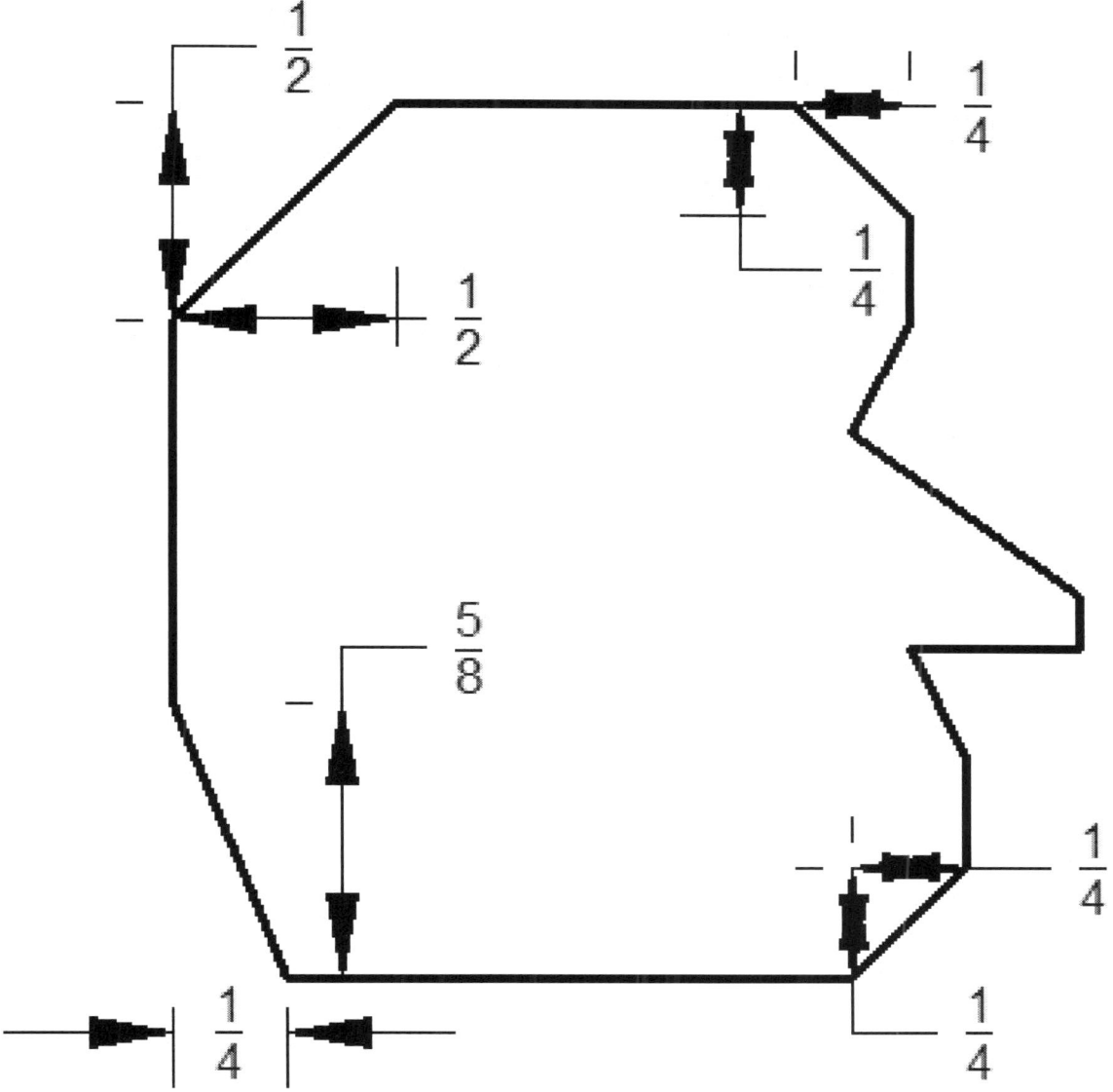

With a view of the head from the top, draw the lines to shape the head.

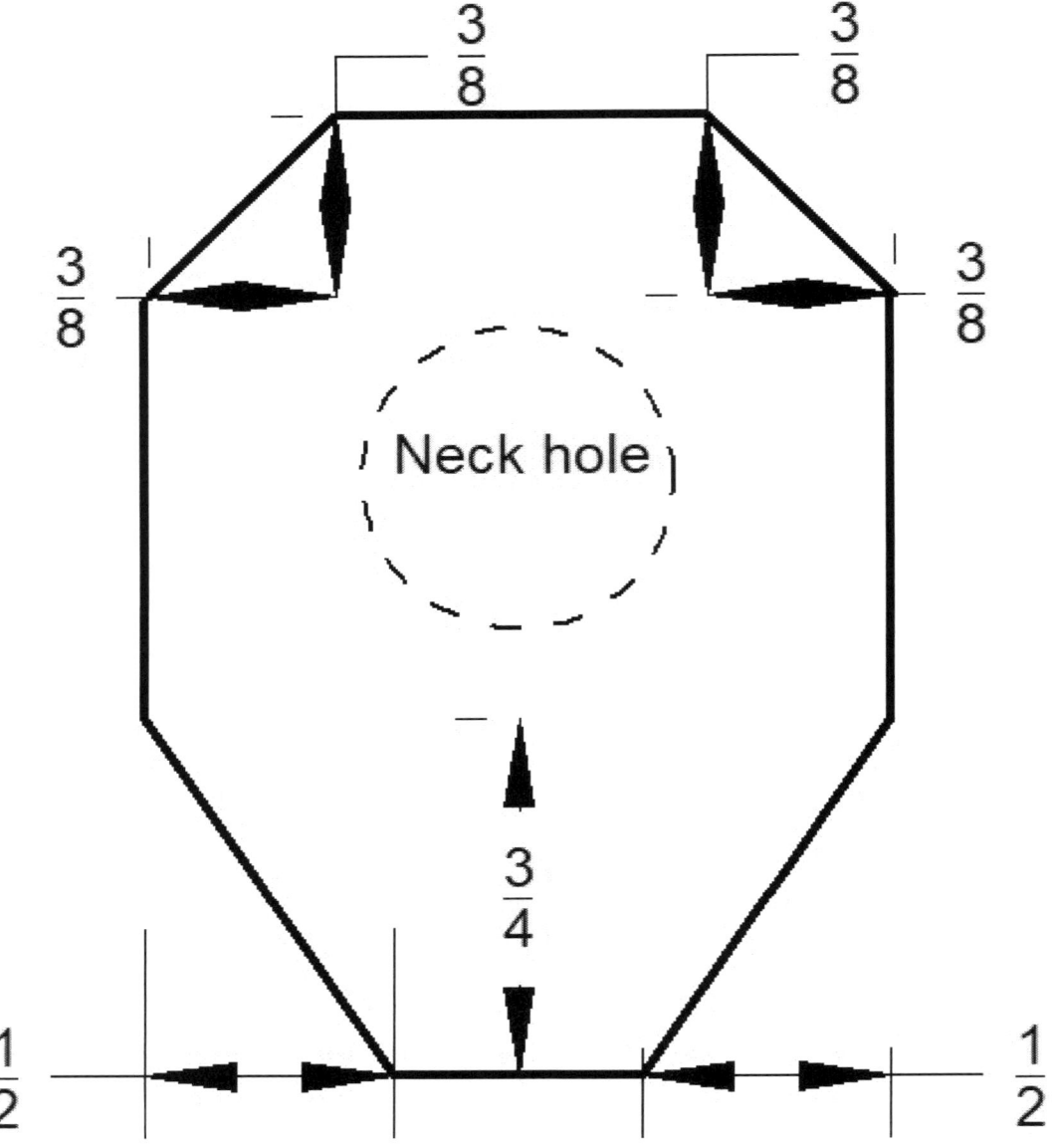

Looking at the head from the back, draw the lines to finish defining the head.

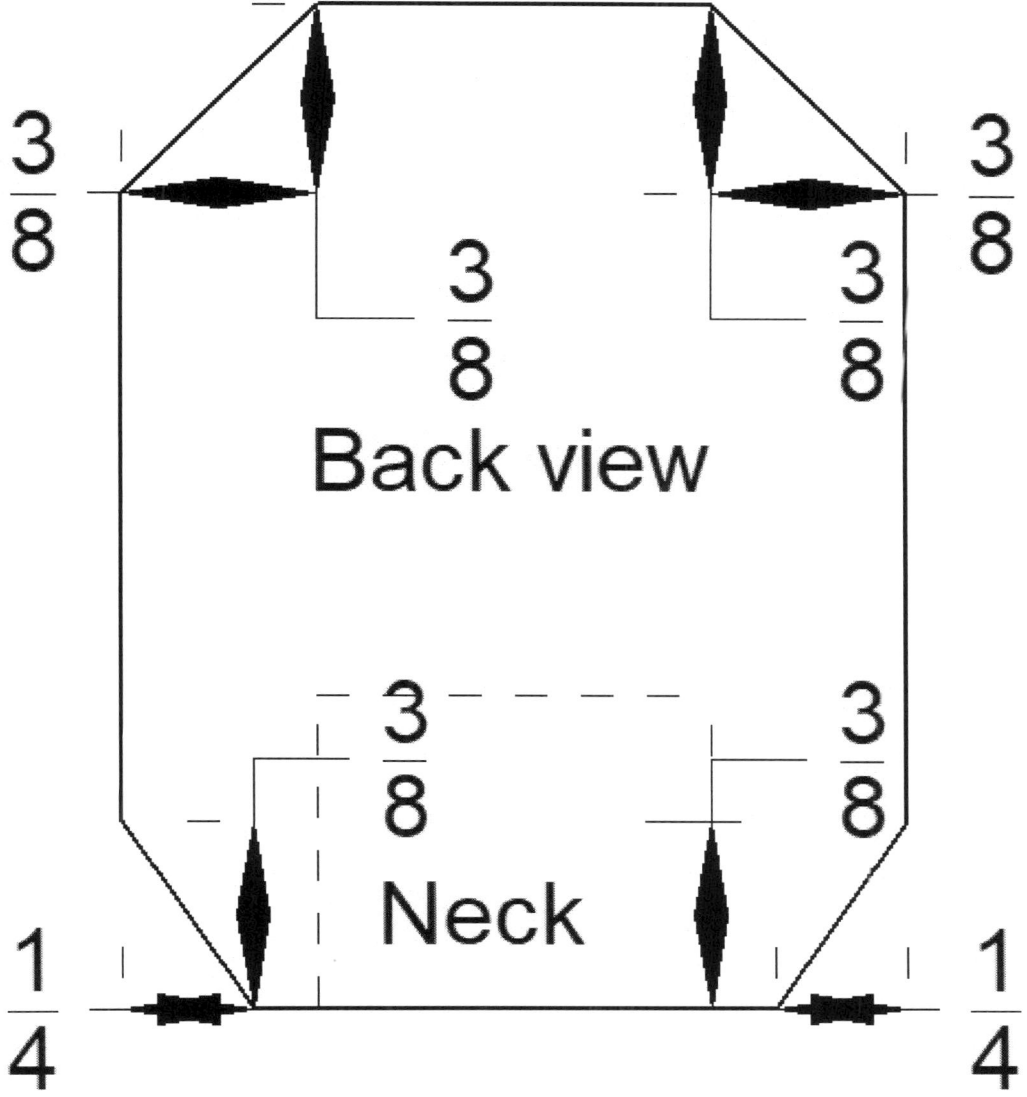

Back view

Neck

$\frac{3}{8}$ $\frac{3}{8}$ $\frac{3}{8}$ $\frac{3}{8}$ $\frac{3}{8}$ $\frac{3}{8}$ $\frac{1}{4}$ $\frac{1}{4}$

Now it is time to make the cuts. Make the cuts on the top of the head first. Do NOT cut all the way to the end of the line! Stop all the cuts ~1/8" from the end. Otherwise you will lose all the marks for the facial features.

Do the same thing with the cuts from the back. Again, stop all the cuts ~1/8" from the end.

Make all the cuts from the side. Make these cuts all the way through. Go back to the top and back and finish making the cuts.

You can also add some ears to give it a more realistic look.

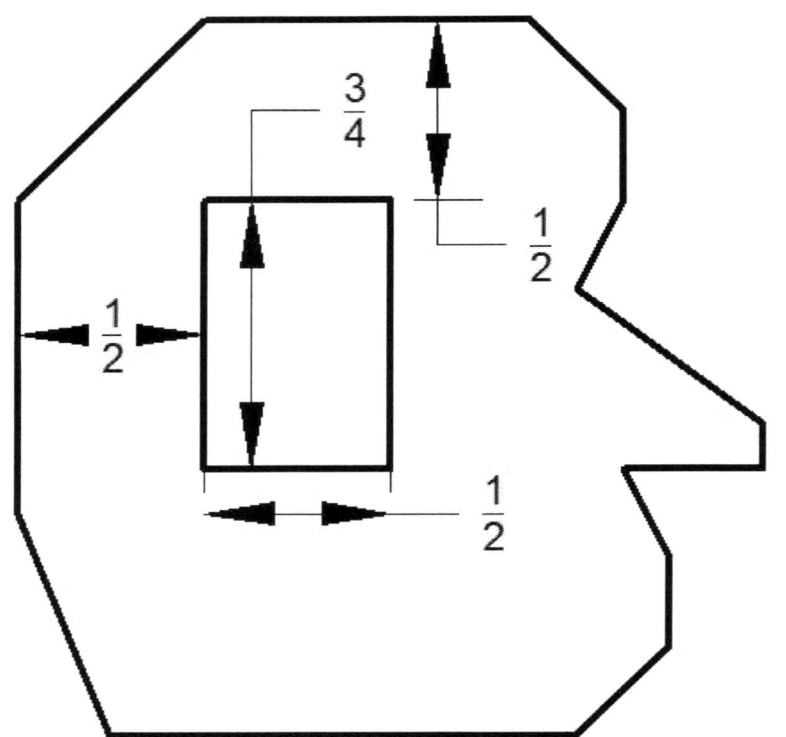

Use ~1/8" wood for the ears. You could use a Popsicle stick, paint stir stick, or cut them from wood that better matches the head.

Sand the front of the ear so the ear blends into the head. Then just glue them in place.

Sand all of the edges of the head to give it the final touch.

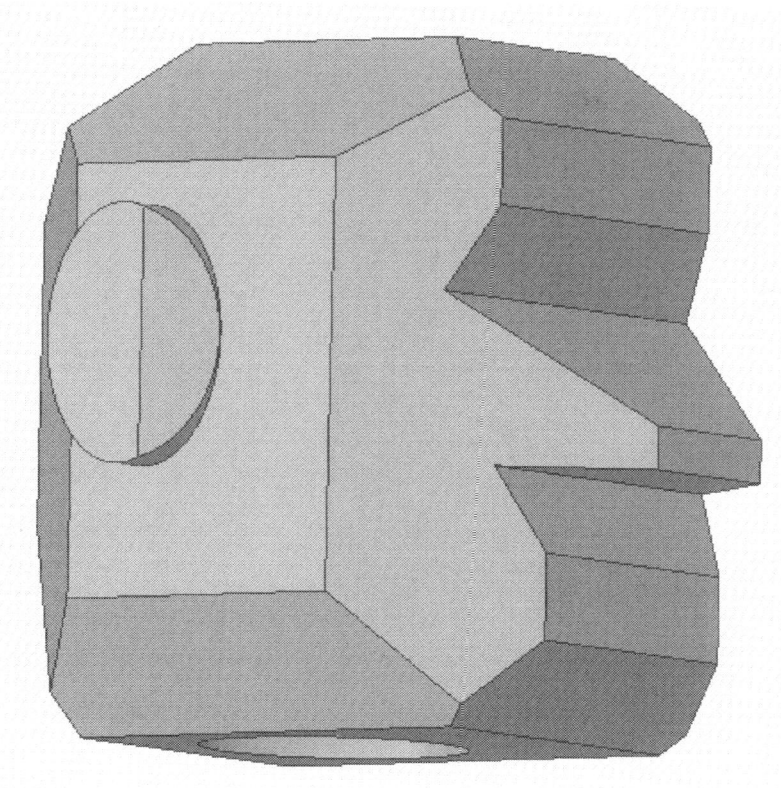

Printed in Great Britain
by Amazon

34660464R00104